THE RENAISSANCE UTOPIA

*This book is dedicated with love and gratitude to
my mother, Kathy Williams
and
my father, Tom Houston*

The Renaissance Utopia
Dialogue, Travel and the Ideal Society

CHLOË HOUSTON
University of Reading, UK

ASHGATE

© Chloë Houston 2014

All rights reserved. No part of this publication may be reproduced, stored in a retrieval system or transmitted in any form or by any means, electronic, mechanical, photocopying, recording or otherwise without the prior permission of the publisher.

Chloë Houston has asserted her right under the Copyright, Designs and Patents Act, 1988, to be identified as the author of this work.

Published by
Ashgate Publishing Limited
Wey Court East
Union Road
Farnham
Surrey, GU9 7PT
England

Ashgate Publishing Company
110 Cherry Street
Suite 3-1
Burlington
VT 05401-3818
USA

www.ashgate.com

British Library Cataloguing in Publication Data
A catalogue record for this book is available from the British Library

The Library of Congress has cataloged the printed edition as follows:
Houston, Chloë, author.
 The Renaissance Utopia : Dialogue, Travel and the Ideal Society / by Chloë Houston.
   pages cm
 Includes bibliographical references and index.
 ISBN 978-1-4724-2503-4 (hardcover : alk. paper)—ISBN 978-1-4724-2504-1 (ebook)—ISBN 978-1-4724-2505-8 (epub)
 1. Utopias in literature. 2. Travel in literature. 3. Literature—Early modern, 1500–1700—History and criticism. 4. Travelers' writings—History and criticism. I. Title.
 PN56.U8H68 2014
 809'.93372—dc23
                                                                                    2013047653

ISBN: 9781472425034 (hbk)
ISBN: 9781472425041 (ebk – PDF)
ISBN: 9781472425058 (ebk – ePUB)

Printed in the United Kingdom by Henry Ling Limited, at the Dorset Press, Dorchester, DT1 1HD

Contents

Acknowledgements		*vii*
Introduction: The Utopian Mode in Dialogue		1
1	Copious Discourse: *Utopia* and Dialogue	15
2	'Godly Conversation': The Reformation of Utopia	41
3	'It is the man who speaks with God who knows more': Education and the Decline of Dialogue in *Christianopolis* and *The City of the Sun*	61
4	'Private Conference' and 'Public Affairs': Natural Philosophy, Dialogue and the Ideal Society in *New Atlantis*	89
5	'Counsel and Endevors': Millennium and Reform in the 1640s	119
6	'Instructive Discourses': The Proliferation and Rejection of Utopia in the 1640s and Beyond	141
Selected Bibliography		*165*
Index		*185*

Acknowledgements

It has taken me a long time to write this book, during which I have accrued many debts, both intellectual and personal. It goes without saying that for all that I owe, any remaining errors are entirely my own. I thank Stephen Clucas, who supervised my PhD at Birkbeck, University of London, for his generosity with his time, expertise and limitless knowledge of intellectual history. I am also grateful to many other staff and students at Birkbeck, and particularly Peter Forshaw, Tom Healy, Laura Jacobs and Sue Wiseman. I would like to thank David Colclough and Colin Davis for their valuable constructive criticism, and William Poole and Richard Serjeantson for their guidance.

This project has moved with me to the University of Reading via a brief stint at Queen Mary University of London, from which time I am grateful to David Colclough, Rosanna Cox, Pete Langman and Evelyn Welch for a number of useful conversations and references. At Reading I would like to thank many current and former colleagues in the Department of English Literature and the Early Modern Research Centre for their help with my research, especially David Brauner, Cedric Brown, Rebecca Bullard, Simon Dentith, Alison Donnell, Rachel Foxley, Mark Hutchings, Mary Morrissey, Michelle O'Callaghan, Peter Robinson and Adam Smyth. I am very grateful to a number of people who have read parts of the book in draft, including Dominic Baker-Smith, Eva Johanna Holmberg, Pete Langman, Michelle O'Callaghan, David Harris Sacks and Cathy Shrank. Erika Gaffney, Whitney Feininger and the team at Ashgate have made the production of this book a smooth and enjoyable process, and I am also indebted to the anonymous readers for a useful report. I thank the staff of the British Library, the University of London Senate House Library, and the University Library Cambridge for their helpful assistance over many years. The completion of the final draft of this book was enabled by a term of partial leave funded by the Research Endowment Trust Fund of the University of Reading, awarded by the Faculty of Arts and Humanities.

My deepest debts are to my family. My husband, Will Mandy, has lived with my utopian enthusiasms from their earliest days and without his unwavering confidence, love and encouragement I would never have been able to turn them into a book. My thanks are inadequate, but I offer them anyway. My parents-in-law, Geoff Mandy and Caroline Polmear, have also been a constant source of support and good cheer. I thank my family and friends for all that they have done to keep me reasonably sane during the writing process.

I dedicate this book to my parents, Kathy Williams and Tom Houston. I deeply appreciate the support of my father and my stepmother, Anne Houston, especially during my MPhil and PhD. Dad, I am sorry that Comenius did not play a bigger part in this book. I am more grateful that I can say to my mother for her abiding faith and belief in me. Finally I would like to thank Will and my beautiful sons, Edgar and Felix, for reminding me each day that real life is immeasurably better than utopia.

October 2013

Introduction:
The Utopian Mode in Dialogue

Utopia is ou-topos: nowhere. One might as easily state, reading the literary history of the Renaissance period: utopia is everywhere. It is in Prospero's island and the forest of Arden; ancient Rome and contemporary Venice; Ralegh's Guiana and Spenser's Ireland; Sidney's Arcadia and Milton's Eden; Plattes's Macaria and Winstanley's ideal commonwealth; it is even to be found in the Renaissance garden. Writings about all of these places – some real, all imaginary – have been read as utopian.[1] Utopian bibliographies, consequently, might be expected to be encyclopaedic. In order to be useful, however, such bibliographies have to exclude material and draw boundaries around what precisely constitutes a utopia.[2] Since recent studies have questioned whether utopia can properly be considered a literary

---

[1] On the utopianism of Gonzalo's speech in *The Tempest* (2.1.139–64) and of *As You Like It* see Dean Ebner in '*The Tempest*: Rebellion and the Ideal State', *Shakespeare Quarterly*, 16:2 (1965), 161–73; Jan Kott, '*The Tempest*, or Repetition', *Shakespearean Criticism*, 29 (1996), 368–73; Hugh Grady, 'Reification and *Utopia* in *As You Like It*: Desire and Textuality in the Green World', *Shakespearean Criticism*, 37 (1998), 43–58. On descriptions of the Roman republic and Venice as utopian, see Keith Thomas, 'The Utopian Impulse in Seventeenth-Century England', in *Between Dream and Nature: Essays on Utopia and Dystopia*, ed. by Dominic Baker-Smith and C.C. Barfoot (Amsterdam: Rodopi, 1987), pp. 20–46 (p. 28). On Ralegh, see Amy Boesky, *Founding Fictions: Utopias in Early Modern England* (Athens: University of Georgia Press, 1996), pp. 162–4. On Spenser see Nina Chordas in *Forms in Early Modern Utopia: The Ethnography of Perfection* (Farnham: Ashgate, 2010), pp. 75–6. On Sidney see Northrop Frye, *Northrop Frye on Literature and Society, 1936–1989: unpublished papers*, ed. by Robert R. Denham (Toronto: University of Toronto Press, 2002), p. 68. On Milton see Ana M. Acosta, *Reading Genesis in the Long Eighteenth Century: From Milton to Mary Shelley* (Farnham: Ashgate, 2006), p. 73. On Gabriel Plattes's *Macaria* and Gerrard Winstanley's writings, see Charles Webster, *Utopian Planning and the Puritan Revolution: Gabriel Plattes, Samuel Hartlib, and 'Macaria'* (Oxford: Wellcome Unit for the History of Medicine, 1979). On the utopianism of the Renaissance garden, see John Dixon Hunt, 'Gardens in Utopia: Utopia in the Garden', in *Between Dream and Nature*, pp. 114–38 (p. 132).

[2] Utopian bibliographies which cover the Renaissance period include: Raymond Trousson, *Voyage au pays de nulle part: histoire littéraire de la pensée utopique* (Brussels: Université de Bruxelles, 1975); Pierre Versins, *Encyclopédie de l'utopie des voyages extraordinaires et de la science fiction* (Lausanne: L'Age d'Homme, 1972); Glenn Negley, *Utopian Literature: A Bibliography with a Supplementary Listing of Works Influential in Utopian Thought* (Lawrence: Regents Press of Kansas, 1978); Arthur O. Lewis, *Utopian Literature in The Pennsylvania State University Libraries: A Selected Bibliography* (University Park: Pennsylvania State University Libraries, 1984); Lyman Tower Sargent, *British and American Utopian Literature, 1516–1985: An Annotated, Chronological Bibliography* (New York: Garland, 1988). See also the useful bibliography compiled by Denis Bruckmann, Laurent Portes and Lyman Tower Sargent for the New York Public

genre at all, the scholar of Renaissance utopianism is further obliged to consider what kind of text a utopia is: if not a genre of literature, then perhaps a form, a mode or simply a concept.[3]

If the question of genre has been a thorny one in the process of understanding Renaissance utopias, then the question of form is equally problematic. Utopias were written in a number of different forms during the sixteenth and seventeenth centuries; this book charts utopia's development through the dialogue and the travel narrative until its appropriation of multiple forms of writing in the mid-seventeenth century. If it is possible to identify utopian elements in texts of diverse genres and forms – to see utopia on the stage, or to read it in an epic poem, or an account of a foreign city, or a political treatise – then it might follow that the relationship between utopia and form is not especially important. It is a premise of this book, however, that utopias are deeply engaged with the question of form, in terms of both their own literary forms and the creation and imagination of the social forms with which they are occupied. J.C. Davis, whose work on Renaissance utopia is the basis for current scholarship on the subject, addressed the question of form in a 1993 article in which he looked closely at the connection between contemporary understandings of the relationship between legal formality and liberty.[4] Noting ways in which utopian writers built on the formalities and formalizing aspirations of their own societies, Davis asserted that utopia may be understood as part of a changing discourse of human liberty. This study looks in detail at how utopias aspired to improve the forms of their own societies as part of a changing discourse of human perfectibility. It reads utopias in context in order

---

Library's 2000 exhibition 'Utopia: The Search for the Ideal Society in the Western World' [http://utopia.nypl.org/primarysources.html, accessed 17.10.12].

[3] The question of how to define the Renaissance utopia might fill a book in itself. The question has most recently and usefully been assessed by Chordas in *Forms in Early Modern Utopia*, pp. 1–8 and Fátima Vieira, 'The concept of utopia', in *The Cambridge Companion to Utopia*, ed. by Gregory Claeys (Cambridge: Cambridge University Press, 2010), pp. 3–27. See also Darko Suvin, 'Defining the Literary Genre of Utopia: Some Historical Semantics, Some Geealogy, A Proposal and A Plea,' *Studies in the Literary Imagination*, 6:2 (1973), 121–45, repr. in Darko Suvin, *Metamorphoses of Science Fiction: On the Poetics and History of a Literary Genre* (New Haven: Yale University Press, 1979), pp. 37–62 (p. 50, p. 52). The question of whether utopia is properly considered a genre of literature or a mode of discourse is addressed by William Poole in the introduction to his edition of Francis Lodwick's *A Country Not Named* (Tempe: The Arizona Center for Medieval and Renaissance Studies, 2007).

[4] J.C. Davis, 'Formal Utopia/Informal Millennium: The Struggle between Form and Substance as a Context for Seventeenth-Century Utopianism', in *Utopias and the Millennium*, ed. by Krishan Kumar and Stephen Bann (London: Reaktion, 1993), pp. 17–32 (p. 17). In his comprehensive history of Renaissance utopianism, *Utopia and the Ideal Society* (1981), Davis defined ideal-state fictions according to how they respond to the 'collective problem' of supply and demand. On this basis, he suggested five categories: utopia itself, the Land of Cockaygne, arcadia, the perfect moral commonwealth and the millennium. While adhering to his original typology, Davis's later work on utopias recognizes the difficulty of finding a model of utopia appropriate to the period.

to assess the changes to utopian forms and content which made the utopias of the seventeenth century so different from their 'founding fiction', More's *Utopia*.[5] Its interest in form and genre make this book a study of texts rather than, for example, other utopian projects, agendas or 'real-world experimentation', but both literary forms and social forms are central to its reading of utopia: in its understanding of utopias as imaginations of idealized societies and institutions, *The Renaissance Utopia* will look more closely at the social formalizing utopias undertake through describing new or improved societal forms.[6]

Understood most simply, in the Renaissance period a utopia is a text which portrays an ideal or seemingly ideal society in order to address the question of how to live well. That society may be a country, city or city-state, as it is in More's *Utopia* or Tommaso Campanella's *The City of the Sun* (1623), or it may be a single institution, such as Salomon's House in Francis Bacon's *New Atlantis* (1626) or the school in John Dury's *The Reformed School* (1650). It may be an idealized version of a society which already exists, though it is more often imaginary. Utopias often include descriptions of the journeys undertaken to reach this ideal society, whether through the device of a narrator or in reported conversation; this is especially common in earlier Renaissance utopias, and becomes less frequent in texts written in the mid-seventeenth century, as we will see in Chapters 5 and 6. A text may be classed as utopian when it contains a description of an ideal society, even if the text as a whole is concerned with other matters; it is on this basis that texts such as *The Tempest* and Michel de Montaigne's 'Of Cannibals' (1578–80) have been read within the utopian tradition.[7] This book, however, is neither a complete history of utopianism nor a history of the European utopia; many utopian texts, such as Anton Francesco Doni's *I Mondi* (1552) and Francesco Patrizi's *La città felice* (1553), are omitted, interesting though they are. My purpose is to examine the development of the utopian form from 1516 until its proliferation in the middle years of the seventeenth century, and my focus – with the exception of Chapter 3, on Andreae and Campanella – is its development in English literature. There is, I argue, something uniquely complicated and compelling about the transformation of utopia during the Renaissance, and detailed study of this transformation provides insight into how people thought about both the prospect of the ideal society and their own role in bringing it about.

---

[5] Boesky, *Founding Fictions*.

[6] There is more work to be done on Renaissance utopian projects and 'real-world experimentation', a phrase borrowed from Chordas, *Forms in Early Modern Utopia*. This area lies outside the scope of the present study; see *Forms in Early Modern Utopia* for current work in this field.

[7] Gonzalo's speech (*The Tempest* 2.1.139–64) and Montaigne's 'Of Cannibals' are described as utopias by Ebner in '*The Tempest*: Rebellion and the Ideal State'. Other scholars to consider Gonzalo's image of an ideal society as a utopia include William Rockett, 'Labor and Virtue in *The Tempest*', *Shakespeare Quarterly*, 24:1 (1973), 77–84 (78), and Maurice Hunt, '"Stir" and Work in Shakespeare's Last Plays', *Studies in English Literature 1500–1900*, 22:2 (1982), 285–304 (301–2). On 'Of Cannibals' and utopia, see also Walter Cohen, 'The Literature of Empire in the Renaissance', *Modern Philology*, 102:1 (2004), 1–34.

If each study of utopia must first decide how to define utopia, there is at least consensus on where to begin.[8] Thomas More's *Utopia*, first published in 1516, is widely recognized as the text which reinvented the ideal-state fiction for the Renaissance era. *Utopia* is also the starting point for this book's investigation into what happened to utopia in the period between the publication of More's 'little book' and the 'utopian planning' of the civil war years.[9] During this period, the utopia was transformed from an intellectual exercise in philosophical interrogation into a serious means of imagining practical social reform. In looking at why and how utopia changed in the wake of More's work, *The Renaissance Utopia* argues that the history of utopian literature is characterized by dialogue. Sixteenth-century English utopias were written entirely or partly in the dialogue form; this book will consider lesser-known examples by Thomas Lupton and Thomas Nicholls, as well as *Utopia*. In the early seventeenth century, the travel narrative became the conventional form for exploring alternative worlds, before the utopia set new boundaries in the 1640s. In the middle years of the seventeenth century, as millenarianism and radical politics focused attention on the question of the ideal society, utopian writers turned away from the conventional utopian forms of dialogue and travel narrative in their efforts to bring about the realization of the ideal worlds that they imagined in print. Nonetheless, dialogue remained present in much mid-seventeenth-century utopian literature, partly through its interest in the educational potential of conversation. This abiding relationship between utopia and dialogue is clearly founded in the fact that the most influential utopia of the period, More's, was written as a dialogue in the open mode: questioning, discursive and self-critical. Later utopian dialogues became increasingly closed as they grew more interested in the educational capacities of dialogue and less concerned with its potential for open-ended debate. Indeed, utopias replicate the pattern noted by Virginia Cox in relation to the Renaissance dialogue: they demonstrate an increasing tendency towards closure.[10] Utopian dialogues thus actively present challenges to the reader in assessing the ways in which they are meant to be read. Later utopias used or incorporated the dialogue form as a means of engaging directly with More's text, with the utopian tradition or with other utopian writing. But utopia and dialogue also share a deeply held concern with the question of how to live well; the dialogue form is useful to utopia precisely because of the dialogue's history of interest in the nature of the good life and its contemporary use to discuss and resolve social problems, a question to which we will return in Chapters 1 and 2.[11]

---

[8] Although, as Nina Chordas points out, *Utopia* is not the 'sudden irruption' it may seem to be; *Forms in Early Modern Utopia*, p. 15.

[9] Charles Webster, *Utopian Planning and the Puritan Revolution*.

[10] Virginia Cox, *The Renaissance Dialogue: Literary Dialogue in its Social and Political Contexts, Castiglione to Galileo* (Cambridge: Cambridge University Press, 1992).

[11] See Chapter 2. On dialogue and the question of the good life, see Janet Levarie Smarr, *Joining the Conversation: Dialogues by Renaissance Women* (Ann Arbor: University of Michigan Press, 2005), p. 23. On the use of Renaissance dialogue to debate issues of national concern, see Cathy Shrank, *Writing the Nation in Reformation England 1530–1580* (Oxford: Oxford University Press, 2006), p. 143.

The text with which this study begins, *Utopia*, emerged at a time of widespread reform across Europe. The Reformation, which began in the early sixteenth century, had its roots in attempts to reform the Catholic church by those concerned with what they saw as false doctrine and bad practice on behalf of the church as an institution, and evidence of the corruption of its hierarchy.[12] The wider move for reform in the early 1500s was not restricted to the emerging Protestantism; rather, reformation was a concern for late medieval Catholicism throughout Europe.[13] The rise in late fifteenth-century Florence of Girolamo Savonarola, who, like the early Protestant reformers, desired a return to apostolic simplicity and insisted on the importance of making Christianity the basis of everyday life through the reformation of every social institution, demonstrates the widespread nature of such attempts at reform and their focus on institutional change.[14] The European Reformation was concerned with the question of how to achieve the 'best state' of a commonwealth to which the title page of *Utopia* refers; this question reverberated on both an institutional and an individual plane, constituting both 'a demand for external reform to end abuses and pressure for a genuine spiritual renewal on the deepest level'.[15] The dispute over the path to Christian salvation was thus at the core of efforts to reform the church in the early sixteenth century and also at the core of utopian writing. It was a question that led would-be reformers, such as Egidio da Viterbo, who addressed the Fifth Lateran Council in 1512, to consider the ways in which the church as an institution could be improved. Egidio, who was, like Luther, an Augustinian, sought a restitution of the discipline and ideals of the church. In his address to Lateran V, he called on the Council to restore life to the church and to 'tear down, root up, and destroy errors, luxury and vice, and to build, establish and plant moderation, virtue and holiness' in its reforms.[16] These aims were to be articulated imaginatively in Hythloday's report of the Utopians' society, which he claims has achieved exactly these ends through communal living

---

[12] Lewis W. Spitz, *The Renaissance and Reformation Movements, Volume II: The Reformation* (Chicago: Rand McNally College, 1971), p. 301, and see Chapter 12, 'The Age of the Reformation'; Carl E. Braaten and Robert W. Jenson, eds, *The Catholicity of the Reformation* (Grand Rapids: William B. Eerdmans, 1996); Patrick Collinson, *The Reformation* (London: Weidenfeld and Nicolson, 2003), p. 13.

[13] See John C. Olin, *Catholic Reform: From Cardinal Ximenes to the Council of Trent, 1495–1563* (New York: Fordham University Press, 1990), pp. ix–xii, *et passim*. Historians of the Catholic Reformation have emphasized the continuities between late medieval and Renaissance reformist impulses; see Michael A. Mullett, *The Catholic Reformation* (London: Routledge, 1999), p. ix.

[14] For the similarities between Savonarola and the early Protestant reformers, see Lauro Martines, *Scourge and Fire: Savonarola and Renaissance Florence* (London: Jonathan Cape, 2006), p. 4, and Alison Brown, 'Introduction', in *Selected Writings of Girolamo Savonarola: Religion and Politics, 1490–1498*, trans. and ed. by Anne Borelli and Maria Pastore Passaro (New Haven: Yale University Press, 2006), pp. xv–xxxv (p. xv).

[15] Spitz, *The Renaissance and Reformation Movements, Volume II: The Reformation*, p. 326.

[16] 'Egidio da Viterbo's Address to the Fifth Lateran Council', in Olin, *The Catholic Reformation*, pp. 44–53 (p. 50).

and the removal of money: 'What a mass of troubles was then cut away! What a crop of crimes was then pulled up by the roots!'[17] Utopias, in turn, looked to institutional reform as the means of achieving or promoting the ideal society.

The issues of social and spiritual reform which were expressed across Europe were being raised in England by others besides More. Edmund Dudley's *The Tree of Commonwealth*, written while Dudley was imprisoned in the Tower of London in 1510, discusses the question of how the commonwealth should operate through the metaphor of a tree, which is rooted in justice, truth, concord and peace and brings forth fruits such as honourable dignity, worldly prosperity and tranquillity. Dudley's image of a stable yet dynamic commonwealth is founded in the belief that the proper organization of society will enable the prosperity of each individual, as well as the strength of the group as a whole:

> The comon wealth of this realme or of the subiectes or Inhabitauntes therof may be resemblid to a faier and mightie tree growing in a faier feild or pasture, vnder the couerte or shade wherof all beastes, both fatt and leane, are protectyd and comfortyd from heate and cold as the tyme requireth. In like maner all the subiectes of that realme wher this tree of comon welth doth sewerly growe are ther by holpen and relyved from the highest degre to the lowest.[18]

Dudley's treatise has often been read as having little of interest to say on the subject of politics, but in fact it had an important contribution to make to Tudor political thought.[19] In its discussion of the need for a moral understanding of kingship, its calls for clerical reform and its belief that each individual must be allowed and encouraged to fulfil his proper role, *The Tree of Commonwealth* is responding to the same early sixteenth-century drive for reform as More's *Utopia*.

That *Utopia* is the product of widespread interest in the question of social reformation, and more particularly of Christian humanism, has long been recognized.[20] Humanism, as is discussed in greater detail in Chapter 3, was

---

[17] *The Complete Works of St. Thomas More, Volume 4: Utopia*, ed. by Edward Surtz, S.J., and J.H. Hexter (New Haven: Yale University Press, 1965), p. 241, line 39; p. 243, lines 1–2, hereafter cited as *Utopia*, 241/ 39, 243/ 1–2. All further references will be to this edition and will be given in the text.

[18] Edmund Dudley, *The Tree of Commonwealth*, ed. by D.M. Brodie (Cambridge: Cambridge University Press, 1948), pp. 31–2.

[19] For *The Tree of Commonwealth* as 'curiously barren', see G.R. Elton, *Reform and Reformation: England 1509–1558* (London: Arnold, 1977), pp. 1–2. Brodie has argued that the text should be understood as a manual for princes rather than a 'comprehensive political treatise'; see 'Introduction' in *The Tree of Commonwealth*, pp. 1–17 (pp. 16–17). See also Tom Betteridge's reassessment of the work in *Literature and Politics in the English Reformation* (Manchester: Manchester University Press, 2004), pp. 7–9.

[20] See for example Quentin Skinner, *The Foundations of Modern Political Thought*, 2 vols (Cambridge: Cambridge University Press, 1978), I, 257–62; David Weil Baker, *Divulging Utopia: Radical Humanism in Sixteenth-Century England* (Amherst: University of Massachusetts Press, 1999); Hanan Yoran, *Between Utopia and Dystopia: Erasmus, Thomas More, and the Humanist Republic of Letters* (Lanham: Lexington Books, 2010).

concerned with the serviceability of knowledge and of learning; utopia suggested that learning could help ameliorate the human condition, that is, that the act of writing about a better society could assist in its achievement. As utopias developed in the seventeenth century, their subjects and concerns were very different from those of *Utopia*, but they continued to manifest humanist ideals, both in their abiding interest in the capacity of knowledge and education to improve society, and in the practical ways in which education could be institutionalized and human knowledge organized. Few today would question the significance of these origins and the importance of reading Renaissance utopias in context; since Davis's *Utopia and the Ideal Society* there have been a number of useful studies of utopia in the sixteenth and seventeenth centuries.[21] *The Renaissance Utopia* is to some extent a reexamination of the utopian 'tradition', if that is not too vague a word, in English Renaissance literature; although it does not seek to impose a teleological order which suggests that such a tradition had a definite ending, it finishes in the mid-seventeenth century, as utopian literature proliferated and the achievement of the ideal society seemed a genuine prospect. I hope that this book will contribute to the study of Renaissance utopianism in three ways. Firstly, it will examine a series of utopias in context from 1516 to the 1650s in order to explain how the utopia changed from a playful, intellectual mode of philosophical enquiry to a serious attempt at describing and achieving practical social reform. Secondly, it will read utopias as dialogues, arguing that the utopian literature of this period is characterized by an engagement with dialogue in the wake of More's *Utopia*, and that the concept of dialogue continued to be central to utopian literature even as it ceased to employ the conventional forms of dialogue and, eventually, utopia itself. Finally, in doing so, it will argue that the utopian literature of the Renaissance period merits reassessment. Chapters 5 and 6 will show that the 1640s represented a uniquely active and idealistic period in the history of utopian literature, constituting a utopian moment which was perhaps never to be repeated. Paying attention to the utopian literature of the preceding period not only sheds light on this explosion of utopianism in the mid-seventeenth century, but demonstrates how the sociopolitical and literary conditions of the preceding period shaped utopian literature in new and distinctive ways.

In tracing the changing nature of utopia, then, I argue that there are two forms which are particularly important to its origins and development during the Renaissance. The first of these is the travel narrative. It is impossible to attempt to understand the emergence and development of utopia in the sixteenth and seventeenth centuries without appreciating the degree to which these were shaped by global travel and its literature, and in recent years the relationship between utopia

---

[21] See, for example: Marina Leslie, *Renaissance Utopias and the Problem of History* (Ithaca: Cornell University Press, 1998); Dorothy F. Donnelly, *Patterns of Order and Utopia* (Houndmills, Basingstoke: Macmillan, 1998); Baker, *Divulging Utopia*; Robert Appelbaum, *Literature and Utopian Politics in Seventeenth-Century England* (Cambridge: Cambridge University Press, 2002); Christopher Kendrick, *Utopia, Carnival, and Commonwealth in Renaissance England* (Toronto: University of Toronto Press, 2004); Chordas, *Forms in Early Modern Utopia*.

and travel has been reassessed.[22] The journey is, of course, inherent to utopia, which must always exist at a distance from the author's own society, and one reason for the explosion of utopian writing in the sixteenth and seventeenth centuries, alongside the renewed interest in classical literature and ideals, was the increase in travel and the concomitant increase in writing about travel. The travel narrative is itself a naturally ironic form of writing, often making untenable claims to truth or claiming to do something which it does not in fact do, and the potential for the literature of travel to sustain many layers of meaning has been richly explored in recent decades. In utopia, the journeys and encounters depicted are not usually real, a fact which the texts themselves may or may not recognize openly. *Utopia* may look like a genuine early sixteenth-century travel narrative, with its inclusion of maps, commendatory letters and samples of the Utopian language, but the text simultaneously signals its fictional status. More's use of place names which seem to contradict their own function, such as 'Anydrus' or 'waterless' for a river, and indeed, 'Utopia' or 'no place' for a country, are an example of such signalling. Utopias, like travel narratives, can seem at once authentic and unreal, and, as travellers' tales, they have an unstable relationship with the truth.[23] Furthermore, as a written account of an actual encounter, travel writing substitutes text for experience. It attempts to convey the author's (real or pretended) experience of a foreign location, communicating that experience without actual corroborative proof of its truth or validity. In so doing, the travel narrative draws attention to the reader's rôle in the production of meaning, as it requires the reader's consent to or belief in its own reality in order for its communications to have any worth. Moreover, the journey described in the travel text itself serves as a metaphor for the act of reading, which maintains a suggestive parallel between traveller and reader in Renaissance travel literature.[24]

---

[22] For the relationship between utopia and travel in the Renaissance see Chloë Houston, 'Travelling Nowhere: Global Utopias in the Early Modern Period', in *A Companion to the Global Renaissance 1550–1660: English Culture and Literature in the Era of Expansion*, ed. by J. Singh (Oxford: Blackwell, 2009), pp. 82–98; Chloë Houston, ed., *New Worlds Reflected: Travel and Utopia in the Early Modern Period* (Farnham: Ashgate, 2010); Chordas, *Forms in Early Modern Utopia*; Peter Womack, 'The Writing of Travel', in *A New Companion to English Renaissance Literature and Culture: Volume I*, ed. by Michael Hattaway (Oxford: Wiley-Blackwell, 2010), pp. 527–42.

[23] So enduring was the association between travel literature and mendacity that Renaissance travel writers experienced what William Sherman has called 'acute problems of authenticity and credibility,' thus creating a grey area between fact and fiction which utopian literature exploits. As Andrew Hadfield has noted, the reiteration of the various valuable functions of travel literature to both individual and state had become 'common currency' in travel accounts by the early seventeenth century. William H. Sherman, 'Stirrings and Searchings (1500–1720)', in *The Cambridge Companion to Travel Writing*, ed. by Peter Hulme and Tim Youngs (Cambridge: Cambridge University Press, 2002), pp. 17–36 (p. 31); Andrew Hadfield, *Literature, Travel, and Colonial Writing in the English Renaissance, 1545–1625* (Oxford: Oxford University Press, 2001), p. 39.

[24] On travel as a metaphor for reading in the period, see Georges van den Abbeele, *Travel as Metaphor: From Montaigne to Rousseau* (Minneapolis: University of Minnesota Press, 1992).

The second of the forms from which utopia arises is the dialogue, another type of literature which notoriously plays with the boundaries between fact and fiction. The dialogue, like both utopia and travel writing, is difficult to define in generic terms, with an ambiguous position between a narrative form and drama.[25] Dialogues were produced in large numbers in the sixteenth century and on a wide array of topics; in his study of the formation of English Renaissance dialogue, K.J. Wilson has suggested that its appeal to humanists was its natural capacity for debate, allowing writers to 'dispute ideas without making a commitment to them, without being held responsible'.[26] As with travel literature, the writer of a dialogue has an ambiguous narrative position. In a dialogue it is possible to dramatize the discursive processes of thought and assert opinions without committing to them. The writer's position is that of eavesdropper, recording a conversation in which he may or may not have had a part, and representing an act of communication and debate into which the reader is also frequently drawn, '"actively engaged in the production of meaning" and implicated, with the author, in the peculiar "instability" of the form'.[27] Dialogue, then, like travel writing, asserts that it is conveying a real experience – the act of witnessing the recorded conversation – in text. As a 'representation of a communicative process', Virginia Cox has argued, the 'oral exchange depicted in a dialogue acts as a kind of fictional shadow to the literary transaction between the reader and the text,' and thus 'each word, each argument in a written dialogue is simultaneously part of a fictional conversation and an actual literary exchange'.[28] Like the literature of travel, the dialogue draws attention to the reader's role in making sense of the text by maintaining the parallel between the experience recorded – be it physical journey or oral conversation – and the reader's act of reading. The Renaissance utopia, both travel narrative and dialogue, is thus rooted in forms of writing which contain multiple layers of meaning, maintain an uncertain relationship with the truth and draw the reader into the process of making sense of the text, paralleling the reader's experience of reading the text and the author's experience within it.

---

[25] See K.J. Wilson, *Incomplete Fictions: The Formation of English Renaissance Dialogue* (Washington: The Catholic University of America Press, 1985), p. lx. Michel Le Guern has distinguished between dialogue and drama; see Le Guern, 'Sur le genre du dialogue', in *L'automne de la Renaissance*, ed. by J. Lafond and A. Stegmann (Paris: J. Vrin, 1981), p. 142. On the difficulties of defining travel writing as a genre, see Sherman, 'Stirrings and Searchings (1500–1720)', pp. 31–2.

[26] Wilson, *Incomplete Fictions*, p. 180. On the popularity of the dialogue form in the Renaissance and its pervasiveness in the sixteenth century, see Roger L. Deakins, 'Tudor Prose Dialogue: Genre and Anti-Genre', *Studies in English Literature*, 20 (1980), 5–23, and Cathy Shrank, 'Stammering, Snoring and Other Problems in the Early Modern English Dialogue', in *Writing and Reform in Sixteenth-Century England: Interdisciplinary Essays*, ed. by John Blakeley and Mike Pincombe (Lewiston: Edwin Mellen Press, 2008), pp. 99–120 (pp. 99–100).

[27] Cox, *The Renaissance Dialogue*, p. 3.

[28] Cox, *The Renaissance Dialogue*, p. 5.

The Renaissance Utopia thus charts two main developments in utopian literature. The first marks the transition from utopia as philosophical satire to utopia as an imaginative means to achieve social reform. The second traces the movement from utopias primarily being written as dialogues to utopias primarily being written as narratives. These two developments are directly related: as writers of utopias increasingly sought to use the utopian mode to criticize and improve society, they turned away from the discursive, ironic dialogue form in favour of a more straightforward narrative form. For the later utopian writers considered in this book, the dialogue form would have hindered, rather than helped, their aims: by the mid-seventeenth century, as the dialogue form itself declined in use, to choose the dialogue form to put forward ideas of social reform would be a conscious archaism. As they sought to reach wider readerships and to speak directly to those readers, writers of utopias rejected dialogue, prompting a shift from a reliance on the dialogue form in the sixteenth century to the adoption of a narrative form in the mid-seventeenth century.

Also crucial to this shift was the rise in number and in popularity of the travel narrative during the period in question. By the end of the sixteenth century, the travel narrative was the natural form in which to describe the experience of encountering a new world. As increasing numbers of Englishmen journeyed abroad, so travel narratives were printed in ever larger numbers, until 'Europe was deluged with materials on the overseas world'.[29] For writers of utopias seeking to reach wide and varied audiences and wishing to convince those audiences of the potential reality of the ideal society, the travel narrative represented a richer and more attractive prospect, even as they continued to engage with aspects of the dialogue form.

Charting the move from dialogue to narrative, this book will begin by examining how sixteenth-century utopian dialogues use the dialogue form in a variety of ways that show their interest in contemporary use of the form and its classical roots. After More's *Utopia*, however, utopia starts to move away from the dialogue form and its multiple voices in favour of a less ironic and more didactic presentation of the ideal society. In reading More's *Utopia* as a dialogue, the first chapter argues that dialogue is important for *Utopia* in terms of both form and content. As well as facilitating the presence of multiple voices within the text, and thus contributing to its ambiguity and irony, the dialogue form serves three main functions in *Utopia*. Firstly, drawing on its roots in education and humanist argument, dialogue is used as a textual strategy for debate and discovery, ultimately offering a choice between a life of active service and the independent pursuit of happiness. These alternatives, represented by the persona of Thomas More and the traveller Raphael Hythloday, respectively, dramatize the position in which More found himself in 1515, as he decided whether to commit himself to a life in service of the state. Secondly, the position of the dialogue form between the literary and non-literary worlds, and its well-known tendency to blur the boundaries between truth and fiction, both develops More's playful extension of his fictional personae into the

---

[29] Donald F. Lach, *Asia in the Making of Europe: Volume I: The Century of Discovery* (Chicago: University of Chicago Press, 1994), p. 204.

'real world' and complicates the lessons that the dialogue itself purports to teach. Thirdly, the tendency of the dialogue form to self-criticism facilitates *Utopia*'s interrogation of its own ideals and rhetoric, as the text questions the usefulness of both the dialogue and the ideal-state exercise. In order to demonstrate the broader use of the concept of dialogue in *Utopia*, this chapter suggests that dialogue also provides a useful model for reading More's *Utopia* as itself being in conversation with other texts, and specifically those of Plato, Lucian and Augustine. Ultimately sceptical about the prospect of the ideal society, the first Renaissance utopia uses dialogue in a variety of ways that later sixteenth-century utopias would draw on, but it treats ironically questions that its successors would take seriously.

Chapter 2 considers two neglected utopian fictions of the later sixteenth century. Bibliographies of Renaissance utopia tend to suggest a gap in English utopian fiction between *Utopia* and the upsurge in utopian writing in the early seventeenth century. This chapter, however, suggests that Thomas Nicholls's *A pleasant Dialogue between a Lady called Listra, and a Pilgrim. Concerning the gouernement and common weale of the great prouince of Crangalor* (1579) and *Sivqila, Too Good to be True*, by Thomas Lupton (1580), play an important role in the development of the Renaissance utopia. In common with contemporary polemical dialogues, these utopias are 'Reformation fictions', demonstrating the ongoing process of consolidation of Protestantism in English society. They represent societies which their authors saw as genuinely ideal in an effort to promote the adoption of certain of their customs and systems and to garner patronage for the authors themselves. In so doing, these utopias start to close down the dialogue form's capacity for multiple voices and to develop a polemical stance. By placing these utopias in context and examining the afterlife of More's *Utopia*, this chapter shows that the later sixteenth century represented a crucial shift in the use of utopia, as it became associated with social amelioration rather than satire and philosophical enquiry.

The third chapter turns to the European context for the development of utopian writing in the early seventeenth century. Reading two texts which often appear in studies of Renaissance utopianism, Johann Valentin Andreae's *Reipublicae christianopolitanae descriptio* or *Christianopolis* (1619) and Tommaso Campanella's *La Città del Sole* or *The City of the Sun* (1623), it begins from the premise that this period witnessed both the rise of the utopia and the decline of the dialogue form. In these two utopias, the concept and form of the dialogue are useful primarily for their didactic associations: in Campanella, to recall an ideal classical age and a contemporary society which is both perfect and achievable; in Andreae, to portray an ideal city which represents the 'Protestant brotherhood' he wishes to make available to every reader. These utopias offer practical visions for the ideal society as well as spiritual ideals, and, crucially, present their utopian societies as direct models for the reader. Both – in different ways – presented as travel accounts, these early seventeenth-century European utopias also signal the increasing importance of travel and encounters with the wider world to the development of the utopia.

Bacon's *New Atlantis*, the subject of Chapter 4, also demonstrates the interrelated nature of utopia and travel writing in the early seventeenth century, as the travel narrative, rather than the dialogue, became the appropriate form for describing encounters with other worlds. *New Atlantis*, in referring obliquely to *Utopia*, points to the growing awareness of utopias as texts with a common capacity to be read as handbooks for living. In Bacon's 'fable', the central laboratory of Salomon's House is the utopia, rather than the wide society of Bensalem; writing in the utopian mode, and using elements of dialogue, allows Bacon to conjure a society which is at once like and unlike his own, in order to imagine the conditions that would be required for the proper and necessary institutionalization of natural philosophy. This chapter examines the ways in which *New Atlantis* incorporates elements of dialogue in its representation of both Bensalem and Salomon's House. It suggests that the incorporation of these elements, which include the use of spoken conversation and its role in the practice and dissemination of natural philosophy, demonstrates the continued importance of dialogue to utopian literature, even when the dialogue form is no longer in use. The dialogue form was to become increasingly less important to utopia during the mid-seventeenth century, in part because it suggested a distance between utopia and reality that the authors of utopias wished to deny.

Bacon's influence on Samuel Hartlib and his associates has long been recognized. In their efforts to establish ideal institutions that would promote the organization of knowledge and the reformation of society, the Hartlib circle contributed to the utopianism which has been widely identified in England in the 1640s. The concept of conversation was important to the Hartlibians, who saw themselves as a group of interlocutors whose discussions via letters and pamphlets, as well as in person, could bring about the social changes they wished to see. As such arguments took place, literary forms of debate became obsolete and utopia diffused into other forms. The last two chapters of the book thus contend that the unique religious and political context of this period changed the form of the utopian discourse, as the utopia developed in two opposite though related ways and proliferated beyond the traditional forms of utopia and dialogue. Chapter 5 looks at millenarian utopian writings during this decade, as Hartlib, John Dury, Gabriel Plattes and others channelled utopia into unconventional forms, turning away from both the dialogue and the travel narrative. It argues that the mid-seventeenth century constitutes a utopian period during which the achievement of the ideal human society genuinely appeared possible, and any literary forms that suggested a distance between utopia and reality were rejected. When the dialogue form was used in Plattes's *Macaria* (1641), it was in the briefest of ways, but utopian texts were in immediate dialogue with each other as they sought to promote and achieve the ideal society. Hartlib and his associates both read and wrote utopian literature as direct models for change, and in so doing they epitomized the sincere and fervent optimism about reform which characterized this period.

The final chapter looks further at how utopias rejected the traditional utopian form, though the concept of dialogue, through the use of conversation as narrative device and metaphor, continued to remain an important feature of utopian literature. It begins with a brief consideration of the variety of ways in which the utopian mode of discourse was being used in the middle years of the seventeenth century, including picaresque, early science fiction, satire and political treatise. Its main object, then, is to explore the development of the imaginative strand of utopianism, the forerunner of the utopian novel, in its reading of Samuel Gott's *Nova Solyma* (1648). In demonstrating the points of communication between this imaginative utopia and contemporary utopian reformist literature, it contends that these shared features themselves represent a form of dialogue between texts which was important to the ways in which the utopian mode was to develop; such utopias also reflect the ways in which the utopian form had changed by the end of the period considered by this book. By the mid-seventeenth century, utopian dialogues took place between rather than within texts, a fact which, as Chapter 6 makes clear, reflects their attempts to access a wider and more diverse public audience. By this point, the traditional dialogue form is largely absent from utopia; but the existence of the utopian tradition, and the utopian dialogues of the past, means that all writing which suggests the possibility of a better society or an improvement in the human condition risks being seen as sharing *Utopia*'s '*Heterodoxal* novelties, and imaginary whimseys'.[30] The presumption that utopias had a mutual and impracticable optimism about human nature meant that later utopian thinkers often avoided writing texts that could be construed as utopias. At the same time, reformers associated with the Hartlib circle were already beginning to realize that the conditions necessary for the achievement of the ideal society were unlikely to materialize.

Nonetheless, for Hartlib and his colleagues in the 1640s, utopia was no longer 'ou-topos', and the utopian society was not a distant, foreign location, but one perceived to be immediately achievable. For Thomas More, the true path to a godly life was represented by the spiritual City of God, which, by its very nature, could not be achieved on earth through social reform. For John Dury, writing in 1646, the City of God represented a practical way of achieving salvation for those who lived according to its ways: it was 'the way of government which the Word of God doth prescribe unto spirituall men, to assure them of Gods favour, to get their names written in Heaven'.[31] For More, the ideal society was a matter for investigation and discourse, not for realization on earth; for Dury, it could be achieved by men working under divine will to undertake institutional reform. Despite the difference in their responses to the question of the ideal society, both men were engaged in contemporary debates about that question to which they contributed utopias. It is the aim of this book to bring such disparate texts into dialogue with one another in order to trace how the utopia changed from an ironic interrogation of the notion of the ideal society to a tool employed in a fervent attempt to make it real.

---

[30] John Webster, *Academiarum Examen, or the Examination of Academies* (London, 1653), Bv ('The Epistle to the Reader').

[31] John Dury, *Israels Call Ovt of Babylon Unto Jerusalem* (London: 1646), p. 35.

Chapter 1
Copious Discourse: *Utopia* and Dialogue

Introduction: *Utopia* and the Dialogue Form

The contraction of the title of Thomas More's ideal-state dialogue from *De optimo reipublicae statu, deque nova insula Utopia, libellus vere aureus, nec minus salutaris quam festivus* to *Utopia* inevitably not only results in a simplification of the text's name, but diminishes the text's complexity. Dominic Baker-Smith argued in his 1991 study of *Utopia* that the common reduction of the title to a single word has the effect of concentrating attention on 'the monologue of Book II' at the expense of 'the debate of Book I'; this attention to monologue over debate is symptomatic of a former tendency in scholarship to neglect the discursive, ironic elements of *Utopia* in favour of its portrayal of an idealized society.[1] As well as focusing on the 'single voice' of Book II, such scholarship has sought to locate More's own real opinion amongst the many ideas and positions that the text offers. In recent decades, scholars of *Utopia* have preferred to consider its many layers of meaning, and Quentin Skinner's assertion that the text is deliberately enigmatic represents the critical consensus.[2] The potential for double meaning in the opening words of the title – 'Of the best state of a republic *and* the new island Utopia' – is symptomatic of *Utopia*'s propensity to deny the possibility of a single, cohesive interpretation. More's use of the dialogue form, with its multiple voices and shifting narration, exerts a rhetorical control over the reader which refuses to allow the identification of More himself with any one position: either with Raphael Hythloday or Hythlodaeus, the Portuguese sailor who describes the seemingly ideal island he encountered on his travels, for example, or with the

---

[1] Dominic Baker-Smith, *More's* Utopia (London: HarperCollins, 1991), p. 228.
[2] Quentin Skinner, *The Foundations of Modern Political Thought*, 2 vols (Cambridge: Cambridge University Press, 1978), I, 255–62, and Quentin Skinner, 'Sir Thomas More's *Utopia* and the language of Renaissance humanism', in *The Languages of Political Theory in Early Modern Europe*, ed. by A. Pagden (Cambridge: Cambridge University Press, 1987), pp. 123–57 (pp. 123–4). On the irony of *Utopia*, see also Dermot Fenlon, 'England and Europe: *Utopia* and its Aftermath', *Transactions of the Royal Historical Society*, 5th series, 25 (1975), 115–35; Brendan Bradshaw, 'More on *Utopia*', *Historical Journal*, 24:1 (1981), 1–27; George M. Logan, *The Meaning of More's 'Utopia'* (Princeton: Princeton University Press, 1983), pp. 268–70; Damian Grace, '*Utopia*: A Dialectical Interpretation', in *Miscellanea Moreana: Essays for Germain Marc'hadour*, ed. by Clare M. Murphy, Henri Gibaud and Mario A. Di Cesare (Binghamton: State University of New York at Binghamton, 1989), pp. 273–302 (p. 273); Baker-Smith, *More's* Utopia, pp. 217–18, p. 232.

persona of Thomas More or Morus, who debates with him in Book I. *Utopia*'s use of irony can be related directly to its dialogue form, an aspect of the text which, while it has not been ignored, merits further study.[3]

The dialogue's association with didacticism and enquiry, its unlimited potential for playfulness (including self-identification as truth and fiction) and its tendency to self-criticism contribute to *Utopia*'s many layers of meaning. Furthermore, the concept of dialogue provides a useful model for reading More's *Utopia* as itself being in conversation with other texts. *Utopia*'s dialogue with the works of Plato, Lucian and Augustine, for example, elucidates its position on important questions concerning travel, the good life and the ideal society. The ways in which *Utopia* uses the dialogue form, and the dialogues it opens up with other texts, demonstrate its criticism not only of the ideal society and the prospect of human perfectibility, but of its own chosen form: the utopian dialogue itself.

Utopia is not, of course, the only dialogue that Thomas More wrote; it is the earliest in a series of explorations in the form which continued with the *Dialogue Concerning Heresies* (1528) and *A Dialogue of Comfort Against Tribulation*, written during his imprisonment in the Tower in 1534. In each of these More pairs one or two younger men and an older man in the primary Socratic situation.[4] In *Utopia*, after civilities have been exchanged, More and his friend Peter Giles take Hythloday to More's house in Antwerp, where they sit and talk in the garden, 'on a bench covered with turfs of grass'.[5] The conversation is interrupted by the evening meal, after which the three men return 'to the same place, sat down on the same bench, and gave orders to the servants that we should not be interrupted' (*Utopia* 109/ 29–34). The younger and older male interlocutors, the grass-covered

---

[3] Treatments of *Utopia* that have considered it as a dialogue include: David M. Bevington, 'The Dialogue in Utopia: Two Sides to the Question', *Studies in Philology*, 58:3 (1961), 496–509; Richard J. Schoeck, 'Correct and Useful Institutions: On Reading More's *Utopia* as Dialogue', in *Essential Articles for the Study of Thomas More*, ed. by Richard S. Sylvester and G.P. Marc'hadour (Hamden: Archon Books, 1977); John D. Schaeffer, 'Socratic Method in More's Utopia', *Moreana*, 69 (1981), 5–20; Skinner, 'Sir Thomas More's *Utopia* and the language of Renaissance humanism'; Grace, '*Utopia*: A Dialectical Interpretation', pp. 273–302; Christopher J. Warner, 'Thomas More's *Utopia* and the Problem of Writing a Literary History of English Renaissance Dialogue', in *Printed Voices: The Renaissance Culture of Dialogue*, ed. by Dorothea Heitsch and Jean-François Vallée (Toronto: University of Toronto Press, 2004); Jean-François Vallée, 'The Fellowship of the Book: Printed Voices and Written Friendships in More's *Utopia*', in *Printed Voices*; Cathy Shrank, *Writing the Nation in Reformation England 1530–1580* (Oxford: Oxford University Press, 2006); Nina Chordas, *Forms in Early Modern Utopia: The Ethnography of Perfection* (Farnham: Ashgate, 2010).

[4] K.J. Wilson, *Incomplete Fictions: The Formation of English Renaissance Dialogue* (Washington: The Catholic University of America Press, 1985), p. 139.

[5] *The Complete Works of St. Thomas More, Volume 4: Utopia*, ed. by Edward Surtz, S.J., and J.H. Hexter (New Haven: Yale University Press, 1965), p. 51, lines 27–8, hereafter cited as *Utopia*, 51/ 27–8. All further references will be to this edition and will be given in the text.

bench, the meal and subsequent conversation and the reference to the changing time of day are elements of the dialogue inherited from the classical form, such as Cicero's *Tusculan Disputations* and Plato's *Symposium*. The ancient dialogues of Plato, Cicero and Lucian were, for Renaissance humanists, the models of the form, and their desire to imitate and reproduce these models explains why the dialogue became one of the most popular genres of the period.[6]

Book I of *Utopia*, the so-called dialogue of counsel, incorporates two dialogues: the 'outer' dialogue relates the conversation between More, Hythloday and Giles in Antwerp in 1515, while the 'inner' dialogue recounts a conversation which takes place while the Portuguese sailor is a guest of Cardinal Morton in England.[7] The question of multiple voices in the text is further complicated by *Utopia*'s contention that it has two authors rather than one, a fiction maintained in the commendatory letters preceding the 1518 edition, which praise More's eloquence in relating Hythloday's tale. As Nina Chordas has noted, it is principally Book I that gives *Utopia* the character of a dialogue, 'not only by staging its own protracted dialogue on the advisability of counseling princes, but by allowing the monologue of Book II to read like an extension of that dialogue, carrying over with it both the speaker and his implied audience.'[8]

Utopia's dialogue form has long been recognized as important, and is usually identified as marking it as a text with 'deeply humanist features'.[9] Even those who see More's use of the dialogue as the invention of a new form tend to see this as itself characteristic of Renaissance humanism.[10] More recently the interplay between utopia and dialogue has been reassessed and the importance of dialogue to *Utopia* reasserted. Chordas's *Forms in Early Modern Utopia* (2010) argues that utopia not only has 'an affinity for dialogical settings, but that both dialogue and utopia share the quality of simultaneously functioning in fictional and extra-fictional realms, and that dialogue, both as form and sub-genre, functions as an important component of early modern utopia'.[11] The connections between the dialogue form

---

[6] See Heitsch and Vallée, eds, *Printed Voices*, p. ix. For dialogues as humanist texts, see also Shrank, *Writing the Nation*, p. 20.

[7] The terms 'inner' and 'outer' come from Grace, '*Utopia*: A Dialectical Interpretation'.

[8] Chordas, *Forms in Early Modern Utopia*, pp. 23–4.

[9] Mary Thomas Crane, 'Early Tudor Humanism', in *A Companion to English Renaissance Literature and Culture*, ed. by Michael Hattaway (Oxford: Blackwell, 2000), pp. 13–26 (p. 22).

[10] Thus Joseph Levine describes More's 'dialogue with himself' as not only being 'unprecedented in English literature', but marking More out as the 'first English Renaissance individual', in Burckhardtian terms (Joseph Levine, 'Thomas More and the English Renaissance', in *The Historical Imagination in Early Modern Britain: History, Rhetoric, and Fiction, 1500–1800*, ed. by Donald R. Kelley and David Harris Sacks [Cambridge: Cambridge University Press, 1997], p. 9). See also Amy Boesky, *Founding Fictions: Utopias in Early Modern England* (Athens: University of Georgia Press, 1996), p. 46.

[11] Chordas, *Forms in Early Modern Utopia*, p. 17.

and the philosophical question of how to live a good life demonstrate the form's suitability for utopian writing.[12] As J. Christopher Warner has noted, discussions of English Renaissance dialogue tend to begin – and indeed sometimes end – with *Utopia*.[13] Thus, although most of the major studies of Renaissance utopianism spend little time considering the Renaissance dialogue, the dialogue form is not only an important part of the first Renaissance utopia, but also important to the continued development of the mode, particularly in the later sixteenth century.

With reference to *Utopia*, there are three major functions which the dialogue form fulfils. The first is related to its association with education and learning. As has been well documented, the dialogue form was central to Renaissance education, both in terms of the common use of dialogues in the classroom and in terms of its broader influence. Humanist education centred on the practice of rhetorical debate, or of arguing on both sides of an argument (*in utramque partem*).[14] There were many dialogues written specifically for the classroom in both the classical and Renaissance periods which were widely used in early humanist education.[15] Hence the dialogue form was to become 'a tool much favoured by humanist teachers [...] to provide instruction and edification at the same time'.[16] It was also replicated, of course, in the manner of legal debate in which More was learned. Arguably, the form influenced not only humanist educational practices but also Renaissance ways of thought. The practice of dialogue in the classroom, after all, involved not only debate, but the capacity of one pupil to argue both for and against a particular point.

---

[12] Janet Levarie Smarr has stated that the 'search for how to live the good life in its serious sense is a primary focus of the whole core of tradition in the dialogue genre'; see Janet Levarie Smarr, *Joining the Conversation: Dialogues by Renaissance Women* (Ann Arbor: University of Michigan Press, 2005), p. 23.

[13] Warner, 'Thomas More's *Utopia* and the Problem of Writing a Literary History of English Renaissance Dialogue', p. 63. On the links between dialogue and utopia, see also Smarr, *Joining the Conversation*, 'Introduction'.

[14] See Foster Watson, *The English Grammar Schools to 1660: Their Curriculum and Practice* (Cambridge: Cambridge University Press, 1908; repr. London: Frank Cass, 1968), pp. 91–7; Joel B. Altman, *The Tudor Play of Mind: Rhetorical Enquiry and the Development of Elizabethan Drama* (Berkeley: University of California Press, 1978), pp. 40–44; David Norbrook, *Poetry and Politics in the English Renaissance*, rev. edn (Oxford: Oxford University Press, 2002), p. 286.

[15] See T.W. Baldwin, *William Shakespeare's Small Latine and Lesse Greeke*, 2 vols (Urbana: University of Illinois Press, 1944), I, 724–6; K.J. Wilson, *Incomplete Fictions*.

[16] Ian M. Green, *Humanism and Protestantism in Early Modern English Education* (Farnham: Ashgate, 2009), p. 176. On dialogue in humanist education, see also Lisa Jardine, 'The Place of Dialectic Teaching in Sixteenth-Century Cambridge', *Studies in the Renaissance*, 21 (1974), 31–62; Peter Mack, 'The dialogue in English education of the sixteenth century', in *Le dialogue au temps de la Renaissance*, ed. by M.T. Jones-Davies (Paris: Centre de Recherches sur la renaissance, 1984), pp. 189–212; Thomas O. Sloane, 'Rhetorical Education and Two-Sided Argument', in *Renaissance-Rhetorik*, ed. Heinrich F. Plett (Berlin: Walter de Gruyter, 1993), pp. 163–78; K.J. Wilson, *Incomplete Fictions*, Chapter 3.

Thus the ubiquity of dialogue in Renaissance education arguably led to thinking itself being dialogic, or, as Jeffrey Dolven has termed it, 'an affair for two voices'.[17]

As an influential study of Renaissance dialogue explains, 'dialogue is a textual strategy for discovery, or, better still, it is a textual strategy for embodying dialectical discovery in discourse'.[18] In *Utopia*, this textual strategy is employed to think through a series of interconnected problems or questions relating to how to live a good life. Dialogue thus serves as a means of representing differing perspectives without authorial endorsement. In the conversations between More, Giles and Hythloday, and Hythloday's related conversations at Morton's table, we are offered a series of responses to the question of how best to serve in society, and particularly whether an active or contemplative life is better. So, for example, in Book I Peter Giles raises the issue of Hythloday entering court service, because this would provide a role in which he would be both entertaining and useful (*Utopia*, 55/ 15–20). Hythloday refuses to forward his own interests through an activity he abhors, and argues that there is little difference between service and servitude. In contrast to his cynicism, More presents potential service as virtuous: 'you will do what is worthy of you and of this generous and truly philosophic spirit of yours if you so order your life as to apply your talent and industry to the public interest' (*Utopia*, 57/ 10–13). Hythloday, however, counters this with scepticism, arguing that kings are more interested in winning new domains by violence than ruling well what they already possess (*Utopia*, 57/ 25–30). He portrays a royal council as being full of men who have an inflated sense of their own wisdom and above all else seek to please royal favourites, 'whose friendliness they strive to win by flattery' (*Utopia*, 57/ 35–6). As an example, he relates the conversation that took place while he was at the table of Cardinal Morton, aiming to show how little he would be regarded by councillors in a similar situation. Despite this, More is not persuaded. His emphasis remains on the social good to which Hythloday would be able to put his skills: 'I cannot change my mind but needs must think that, if you could persuade yourself not to shun the courts of kings, you could do the greatest good to the common weal by your advice' (*Utopia*, 87/ 7–10). More points out that such service is 'the most important part of your duty as it is the duty of every good man' (*Utopia*, 87/ 10–11); as Skinner notes, he responds to Hythloday by promoting the Ciceronian *vita activa* against the sailor's defence of *otium*.[19] Nonetheless, Hythloday comprehensively rejects the active life of service which Giles and More advocate.

Through the dialogue form, then, the reader is presented with a number of alternative answers to the questions of how best to live and whether it is better to dedicate one's life to civic service or to pursue one's own way, as Hythloday

---

[17] Jeffrey Andrew Dolven, *Scenes of Instruction in Renaissance Romance* (Chicago: University of Chicago Press, 2007), p. 49.

[18] Jon R. Snyder, *Writing the Scene of Speaking: Theories of Dialogue in the Late Italian Renaissance* (Stanford: Stanford University Press, 1989), p. 23.

[19] Skinner, 'Sir Thomas More's *Utopia* and the language of Renaissance humanism', pp. 132–5.

chooses to do. The text dramatizes More's own situation in 1515, as he hesitated over his decision to follow a career in state service.[20] Given his eventual decision to serve the king, it is tempting to identify More's position with that of the persona of More, who, in response to Hythloday's claim that there is no room for philosophy in the king's council, promotes instead an active life of civic service which is founded not on scholastic ('*scholastica*') philosophy, but on other more civil philosophy ('*alia philosophia ciuilior*') (*Utopia*, 98/ 6, 11, 99/ 5–8, 13–16). However, the text makes no such identification, and offers instead a rehearsal of the arguments for and against different options. The use of dialogue facilitates the offering of a series of potential solutions to a problem, rather than advocating a single course of action. Utopias used to be read as texts that advocated change; More's *Utopia* points to the necessity of improvement in a variety of ways, but it refuses to endorse a straightforward direction for that improvement.

The second element of dialogue that is crucial to More's *Utopia* is its playfulness, and in particular its tendency to blur the boundaries between truth and fiction and between the literary and non-literary worlds. As a textual representation of the act of conversation, dialogue is both explicitly a work of fiction and a supposed record of an actual event. The form suggests that it is a written witness of a discussion which really took place, often using descriptions of temporal and geographical location, for example, to lend verisimilitude. At the same time, it is fictional, and references to the appearance of the garden within which a conversation took place, and the decline of the sun as time passed, serve only to highlight this fact. Dialogue, like utopia, is located on the boundary between fact and fiction, and it commonly highlights and interrogates this location. It is a form which 'shuttles between the literary and the extra-literary, disrupts the boundaries between fiction and nonfiction, and explores the tension between figure and statement',[21] and confuses boundaries and distinctions 'between fiction and nonfiction, orality and literacy, or poetry, prose, and drama.'[22] Thus the dialogue is itself about the nature of fiction and the processes of communication, 'a kind of fictional shadow to the literary transaction between the reader and the text'.[23] The playful, self-referential nature of dialogue serves to complicate its function as a didactic tool. Dialogue's function is not simply to 'teach lessons'; it is to inculcate a way of thinking. Renaissance dialogues, in their literary playfulness, refuse to offer simple answers to the questions that they pose; More's *Utopia* is exemplary in this respect.

One example of *Utopia*'s playfulness is in More's continuation of his fiction into the *parerga* and especially the paratextual letters which surround the two

---

[20] See J.H. Hexter, '*Utopia* and Its Historical Milieu', in *Utopia*, pp. xxiii–cxxiv (pp. xxvii–xli).

[21] Snyder, *Writing the Scene of Speaking*, p. 9.

[22] Heitsch and Vallée, *Printed Voices*, 'Foreword', pp. x–xi.

[23] Virginia Cox, *The Renaissance Dialogue: Literary Dialogue in Its Social and Political Contexts, Castiglione to Galileo* (Cambridge: Cambridge University Press, 1992), p. 5.

books of the main text. The letter from the French humanist Guillaume Budé to Thomas Lupset, the student and assistant of both Erasmus and John Colet, who had delivered a copy of *Utopia* to Budé, provides a convenient example of *Utopia*'s blurring of the boundaries between fact and fiction. In 1515, Budé had begun a sometimes controversial correspondence with More's friend and colleague Erasmus which was to last for a number of years, and as early as February 1516, Erasmus had urged him to read *Utopia*. Having done so, Budé provided a commendatory letter which was printed in both the 1517 and 1518 editions of the text. Budé introduces Utopia as follows:

> Now, the island of Utopia, which I hear is also called Udepotia, is said, by a singularly wonderful stroke of fortune (if we are to believe the story), to have adopted the customs and the true wisdom of Christianity for public and private life and to have kept this wisdom uncorrupted even to this day. (*Utopia*, 11/ 4–8)

Budé presents an image of Utopia based on Christian ideals, and goes on to say that this has been achieved through community of property, love of peace and contempt for gold and silver. He asserts in his letter, as Hythloday will later maintain in describing Utopia, that the 'true wisdom' of Christianity amounts to little more than communality of possessions, an apparent simplicity which sounds a note of caution. In the same breath with which he commends the Utopians' Christianity, Budé puns on Utopia as 'Udepotia' or 'Neverland', and adds the cautionary aside of '*si credimus*' ('if we are to believe') Hythloday's story, which is obviously fictional. Here Budé touches on one of the central issues surrounding *Utopia*'s use of dialogue. The text pretends to represent a society structured in an ideal manner and open to Christianity, but in doing so it demands that we consider the true purpose and wisdom of that religion. Does true Christianity amount primarily to a disdain for material possessions, such as that of the Utopians? Is the ideal Christian society simply one in which people live rationally, as Hythloday suggests? Or, and this is in fact lacking in Utopia, must it also facilitate the individual's relationship with God and preparedness for God's grace, in readiness for the life to come? Budé goes on to wish that all societies could follow the basic principles of Utopian legislation, and asks what sort of holiness the Utopians had to possess not to fall victim to avarice and cupidity. But rather than ask God to address these points, he calls instead upon '*superi*' and '*diui immortales*' ('the powers above', 'the immortal gods'), referring to people as 'mortals' and to the devil as 'the Stygian adversary'. Budé's terms of reference are classical. He suggests that God has behaved in a less kindly manner to the states of Christendom: 'Would that the great and good God had behaved as benignly with those regions which hold fast and cling to the surname of Christian derived from his most holy name!' If Christian societies could live like the Utopians, Budé suggests that 'the golden age of Saturn would return', continuing to offer a confused frame of reference for Utopia which is at once Christian and classical; he looks forward to a classical ideal, not a Christian one. How can Utopia be, as Budé claims, simultaneously 'one of the Fortunate Isles, perhaps close to the Elysian Fields' of classical culture, and 'Hagnopolis', the holy city, 'leading a kind of heavenly life'?²⁴ By collapsing the difference between the Christian and classical frames of reference Budé opens up the question of how compatible the two really are, and, given that Utopia is a society that lives according to reason and without Christianity, he undermines his own straightforward presentation of Utopia as a purely Christian example of good living.

If Budé's letter subtly undermines a straightforward reading of *Utopia*, then so does More's own. In his letter to Giles, More emphasizes that he is writing about matters beyond his own knowledge and experience, claiming that he is only repeating 'what in your company I heard Raphael relate' (*Utopia*, 39/ 8). He makes a show of insisting that he has, in spite of this, been as truthful as possible in relating Hythloday's tale:

> Just as I shall take great pains to have nothing incorrect in the book, so, if there is doubt about anything, I shall rather tell an objective falsehood than an intentional lie – for I would rather be honest than wise ['*quod malim bonus esse quam prudens*']. (*Utopia*, 41/ 31–5)

But *Utopia* is a text which is anything but honest. Rather, it is making a claim for honesty which mirrors that of other dialogues of the period, which identify truth-telling with plain speech.²⁵ This in itself is clearly an ironic gesture, however; *Utopia* makes a joke of plain speech, with its Greek puns, use of litotes and a central character, Raphael Hythloday, whose name means 'peddlar of nonsense'.²⁶ The text's playfulness and blurred boundaries between truth and fiction result in a complication of any potential 'lessons' that it may seem to offer.

The third function of the dialogue form that has particular importance for *Utopia* is its capacity for self-criticism. Renaissance dialogues frequently engaged in social criticism while simultaneously pointing to their own inefficacy. This is a feature which Cathy Shrank has described with reference to the dialogues of More and others, who promote the notions of civic duty and of the writer as having a political role, but simultaneously suggest the pointlessness of such ideas: 'Subscription to a humanist project of education and public duty coexists with an awareness of the potential perversion, or impotency, of learning in practice.'²⁷ This can be read as unease about the humanist project in literature of the later Tudor period, but this element is also important in understanding the ways in which *Utopia* complicates any potential teachings it offers about how best to live. Dialogue, because it

---

[24] *Utopia*, 11/ 16–19, 26–30; 10/ 11, 18–19; 11/ 18, 20–21; 11/ 31–3; 11/ 36; 13/ 5–6, 8, 10–11.

[25] Shrank, *Writing the Nation*, p. 161. For the complicated meanings of honest/'*honestas*' in the early modern period, see Jennifer Richards, *Rhetoric and Courtliness in Early Modern Literature* (Cambridge: Cambridge University Press, 2003), pp. 27–8.

[26] On More's Latin style, see R. Monsuez, 'Le Latin de Thomas More dans *Utopia*', *Caliban*, 3 (1966), 35–78; Edward Surtz, 'Aspects of More's Latin Style in *Utopia*', *Studies in the Renaissance*, 14 (1967), 93–109. See also Elizabeth McCutcheon, 'Denying the Contrary: More's Use of Litotes in the *Utopia*', *Moreana*, 31–2 (1971), 107–22.

[27] Shrank, *Writing the Nation*, p. 255.

contains more than one voice, cannot help but be self-contradictory at times, and this is a feature which *Utopia* exploits. As the dialogue form developed in the later sixteenth century, so did its capacity for self-contradiction and self-criticism, in ways that sometimes demonstrated the influence of *Utopia*. Thomas Wilson's *A discourse uppon Usurye* (1572), for example, imitates *Utopia* through its 'disorientating tendency to mix fact and fiction' and its interest in the problems of giving counsel, as well as its setting.[28] Shrank argues that Wilson's allusions to *Utopia* give *A discourse uppon Usurye* 'additional satirical bite'; by signalling that his own discourse owes a debt to More's, Wilson 'underlines the potential futility of rhetoric'. For a text to advertise a connection to *Utopia* is, by 1572, a means of recognizing its own potential ineffectiveness. As Shrank comments,

> The use of dialogue to criticize the perpetuation of social ills does not just point pessimistically to their continued existence: it questions the efficacy of the genre as a mode of social criticism and instrument of change. Despite More's satire, avarice remains and charitable love continues to be eroded.[29]

But the ineffectiveness of utopianism – and the ineffectiveness of dialogue – are of course acknowledged in *Utopia* itself. Amy Boesky has commented that 'utopian fiction advocates a reorganization of human activity that initially seems liberal or progressive but is always set forth in self-critical or qualitative ways'.[30] In *Utopia*, this self-criticism is directly related to the use of the dialogue form, and particularly via the use of the persona of Thomas More.

Most obviously, the persona of More articulates scepticism about the possibility of idealistic political schemes. In his discussion with Hythloday about the role of philosophy at court, he exclaims that 'it is impossible that all should be well unless all men were good, a situation which I do not expect for a great many years to come!' (*Utopia*, 101/ 2–4). In his description of Utopia, however, Hythloday goes on to argue that men have indeed been made good by social organization; that, for example, 'all greed for money was entirely removed with the use of money' (*Utopia*, 241/ 39; 243/ 1). At the end of Hythloday's discourse, More's narrative persona expresses his desire to continue the conversation, in order 'to think about these matters more deeply and to talk them over with him more fully', given that 'I cannot agree with all that he said' (*Utopia*, 245/ 34–5, 39). More suppresses this desire, however, noting both Hythloday's tiredness and his tendency to censure those who oppose his ideas. More's interjections, and the framing of *Utopia* as an unfinished

---

[28] Shrank, *Writing the Nation*, pp. 217–18.
[29] Shrank, *Writing the Nation*, p. 218.
[30] Boesky, *Founding Fictions*, p. 9. This trait of utopian fiction is well documented beyond the Renaissance. It may usefully be compared to Tom Moylan's concept of the 'critical utopia' in relation to science fiction. Moylan writes that 'A central concern in the critical utopia is the awareness of the limitations of the utopian tradition, so that these texts reject utopia as a blueprint while preserving it as a dream'. See Tom Moylan, *Demand the Impossible: Science Fiction and the Utopian Imagination* (New York and London: Methuen, 1986), p. 10.

conversation, serve as reminders of the existence of real life beyond Utopia. To deny real life is to abnegate responsibility. In his commendation of practical philosophy, instead of the academic philosophy 'which thinks that everything is suitable to every place', More insists that duty to the commonwealth is paramount:

> If you cannot pluck up wrongheaded opinions by the root, if you cannot cure according to your heart's desire vices of long standing, yet you must not on that account desert the commonwealth. You must not abandon the ship in a storm because you cannot control the winds. (*Utopia*, 99/ 12–13, 31–5)

Hythloday, by implication, has taken the sailor's last course of action; he has abandoned ship.

More's role in the dialogue extends into the prefatory material. His letter to Giles, for example, describes his professed concerns over the accuracy of the text. Noting that 'I am not so confident as to believe that I have forgotten nothing', More refers to a disagreement between himself and his pupil John Clement, who was also present as Hythloday described Utopia. More and Clement cannot, in recollection, agree on the length of the bridge which spans the river Anydrus at Amaurotum: More thinks that Hythloday said it was five hundred paces, but Clement says that the river is only three hundred paces in breadth at this point. More calls upon Giles to 'recall the matter to mind' and adjudicate, for 'I shall take great pains to have nothing incorrect in the book' (*Utopia* 41/ 16–17, 25–8, 30–31). More worrying than the potential inaccuracy over the bridge is that 'we forgot to ask, and he [Hythloday] forgot to say, in what part of the new world Utopia lies' (*Utopia* 43/ 1–2). More points out that this omission means that those who wish to visit Utopia (including the enthusiast who wishes to be made bishop for the Utopians by the pope) cannot do so. The faulty memory of the persona of Thomas More and the consequent instability of the text, the letter says, means that access to Utopia is impossible. The figure of More is thus not a conduit for More's own views, but a reminder of the uncertainty of Utopia and the certainty of real life. His comment at the end of Book II, that 'there are very many features in the Utopian commonwealth which it is easier for me to wish for in our countries than to have any hope of seeing realised', is an acknowledgement both of the potential benefits that might follow from Utopian policies and their inapplicability to the real world (*Utopia* 247/ 1–3). As a dialogue, then, *Utopia* is relentlessly self-questioning and self-critical. It criticizes not only the very things it purports to praise or endorse, but also its own potential to contribute anything useful at all.

This utopian ambivalence was shared by other contemporary dialogues that addressed questions of the good Christian life (and the demands of politics). In his *Convivium Religiosum* of 1522, Erasmus, the 'master of dialogue', portrays the conversation between several friends who consider scriptural texts in order to try to arrive at true understanding.[31] Erasmus's dialogue, with its idyllic country

---

[31] Craig R. Thompson describes Erasmus as the 'master of dialogue' in his introduction to the *Convivium Religiosum*, in *Collected Works of Erasmus: Colloquies: Volume 39*, trans. by Craig R. Thompson (Toronto: University of Toronto Press, 1997), pp. 171–5 (p. 173).

setting in Eusebius's house and garden, is itself a reflection of an ideal world, but one which, in the words of David Weil Baker, is 'carefully circumscribed'.[32] The *Convivium* demonstrates the benefit of reading the Scriptures, and reflects Erasmus's desire that through translation and wider distribution, the Bible might be more widely available;[33] but the conversation itself can only take place at a remove from the real world. Eusebius emphasizes the accessibility of his home, with its door always open, but his garden and house represent ideals, not realities; hence Eusebius's guests note that there is 'something of the divine about this place', which is 'fit for a deity'.[34] This removal from reality is a shared element between utopia and dialogue, and, although *Convivium Religiosum* is a little later than *Utopia*, in both texts it is manifested in ambivalence about the benefits of the form being used. Dialogue thus does more than complicate the potential lessons of *Utopia* through playfulness; it calls their potential efficacy into doubt. Each of these features is crucial to the use of dialogue in *Utopia*; it is the simultaneous capacity to teach, to complicate the lessons taught and to question its own usefulness that dialogue brings to *Utopia*.

Utopia and the Greeks: Plato and Lucian

The dialogue form is a useful structure for *Utopia* because it enables the juxtaposition of a series of perspectives through the presence of multiple voices. *Utopia* can also be understood as being in dialogue with a series of Greek and Latin texts which not only inform the construction of More's imaginary society, but are in conversation with *Utopia* in different ways. Foremost among these is the most influential of all classical ideal-state fictions, the Platonic dialogue the *Republic*. Various comparisons have been drawn between particular features of *Utopia* and those of the *Republic*, but here I want to look in more detail at the ways in which Plato's presence in *Utopia*, his role in the conversation, demonstrates More's interrogation of Platonic ideals.[35] Books II to VII of the *Republic* deal with the development of an ideal city-state, governed by a well-educated military ruling class. As in Utopia, political stability is achieved through communality, including the state's practice of allotting each citizen a social task appropriate to his natural disposition. Although the *Republic* clearly conceives of an afterlife, in which men are rewarded or punished for their behaviour, and recognizes that the perfect city does not presently exist on earth, it nonetheless suggests that it could exist, were the circumstances favourable. In *Utopia*, the one person who unreservedly endorses the notion that his newly discovered society exemplifies the ideal state on earth is the traveller-narrator Hythloday. Hythloday is explicitly

---

[32] David Weil Baker, *Divulging Utopia: Radical Humanism in Sixteenth-Century England* (Amherst: University of Massachusetts Press, 1999), p. 47.
[33] Thompson, 'Introduction' in the *Convivium Religiosum*, p. 174.
[34] Erasmus, *Convivium Religiosum*, p. 205, p. 206.
[35] For Plato as a source of *Utopia*, see Edward Surtz, *Utopia*, pp. cliv–clx.

presented as a Platonic philosopher himself; indeed, Plato is his 'favourite author'. On several occasions he refers to Platonic philosophy in a commendatory tone: 'Plato by a very fine comparison shows why philosophers are right in abstaining from administration of the commonwealth', for example, and 'when I consider, I repeat, all these facts, I become more partial to Plato' (*Utopia*, 87/ 11; 103/ 16–18; 105/ 4–5). Utopia itself is introduced as 'being superior to Plato's republic' (*Utopia*, 21/ 19). The portrait of Utopia, then, comes to us through the eyes of an avowed Platonist and is associated with the *Republic* from the start. This introduction of a Platonic presence into *Utopia*'s dialogue has been read as an endorsement of Hythloday's view of the ideal society, but in fact it leaves the sailor's narrative open to interrogation and criticism.

Plato's insistence in the *Republic* on the importance of an educated ruling class for political and moral reform has been identified as one of the features that made him appealing to Renaissance humanists.[36] Although the Renaissance can no longer be understood simply as the 'Age of Plato', in contrast to the medieval 'Age of Aristotle', the recovery of Plato's works in the fifteenth century undoubtedly led to a renewal of interest in him as a philosopher and theologian. *Utopia*, in its imagining of an ideal state founded on classical philosophy, can be seen as part of this renewed attention to Platonic philosophy on the part of early Renaissance thinkers. Translations by fifteenth-century Italian humanists such as Leonardo Bruni and Marsilio Ficino, whose complete Latin edition of Plato's dialogues appeared in 1484, meant that sixteenth-century scholars like More had access to modern humanist editions. Plato's renowned elegance of style, his hatred of dogmatism and desire for harmony, as well as his reassuring religious doctrine, which had been described by Augustine as the closest of all pagan philosophies to Christianity, strengthened his appeal to Renaissance thinkers. However, an appreciation of the centrality of Platonic philosophy to the attention paid by the Renaissance to the classical age need not blind us to concomitant criticism of the great philosopher. For one thing, as Robert Bellarmine was to argue, the closeness of Platonic philosophy to Christian doctrine was precisely what made Plato a danger to the faith. As James Hankins argues in his study of Plato in the Renaissance, Plato's emphasis on the aristocratic philosopher, his banishment of poets from the Republic, his mistrust of the art of rhetoric and his belief in clearly unchristian tenets such as the transmigration of souls all placed him at odds with the ideals of Renaissance humanists. Humanists were, for the most part, courtiers involved with civic life and supportive of its systems, defensive of poetry and rhetoric and uncomfortable with some of Plato's religious writings, such as his account of creation.[37]

Consequently, fifteenth- and sixteenth-century humanists interrogated Platonic texts and ideals. Uberto Decembrio, for example, who composed his *De republica libri IV* around 1420, criticized Plato on several points, such as the community of

---

[36] For the Renaissance reception of Plato and contemporary translations of his works, see James Hankins, *Plato in the Italian Renaissance*, 2 vols (Leiden: Brill, 1990), I, 3–9, *et passim*.

[37] Hankins, I, 6, 13, 9–11.

goods which More was to adopt for *Utopia* a hundred years later. For Decembrio the *Republic* could be used in part as a convenient reinforcement of particular arguments or perspectives of his own. He employed Plato's emphasis on the need for an educated aristocracy to promote a programme of humanistic education for the upper classes, for example, although for Decembrio this meant those who are best fitted to rule, rather than those who are noble by birth. This diverse and selective use of Plato by his early translators and editors such as Decembrio makes it unsurprising that early humanists felt able to criticize Plato's philosophy quite openly. The fifteenth-century Venetian George of Trebizond, who declared his hatred of Plato in his writings from the 1420s onwards, attacked Plato's critique of rhetoric, amongst other things.[38] In his *Comparatio philosophorum Aristotelis et Platonis*, later published in Venice in 1523, George criticized Plato's political philosophy, and in particular his *Laws*. George argued that Plato's idealistic political arrangements, such as the system of working for no financial reward, were unrealistic. In refusing to allow private ownership, a feature which More was to emulate in *Utopia*, Plato suggested that the appetite for personal property and wealth would also be removed. Again, this is exactly what Hythloday suggests has taken place in Utopia. George, however, scoffed at such an idea, contending that the appetite for property was natural and could not be destroyed so easily.

George of Trebizond's criticism provides an important context for More's own use of the communality of property. In his attack on Plato, George writes:

> You [Plato] say, 'I lay it down that they [virtuous and capable men] shall be given the highest honours and most important magistracies.' But men regard as honours only those that carry some emolument. [...] In my view, to desire wealth is simply human [...] if we are not allowed to look after ourselves and our relations, if our labour brings us no private benefit, the soul is cast down and made effeminate, and ultimately is reduced to a mere counterfeit of its nature. This appetite must not therefore be pulled out by the roots. [...] You demand the impossible; even if it were possible, it would not be expedient. These things must be tempered by reason, not entirely prohibited.[39]

The persona of Thomas More states a similar case in the first book of *Utopia*, when he argues that individuals must have the motivation of personal gain if they are to work. In the description of Utopia, however, it is alleged that just such a removal of the appetite for private property has been achieved. Hythloday claims: 'In Utopia all greed for money was entirely removed with the use of money. What a mass of troubles was then cut away! What a crop of crimes was then pulled up by the roots!' (*Utopia*, 241/ 39; 243/ 1–2). The phrase that is translated in the last

---

[38] On Decembrio's use of Plato's *Republic* and George's reaction to Plato, see Hankins, *Plato in the Italian Renaissance*, I, 110–17, 165–86. On George's critique of Plato in the *Comparatio*, see John Monfasani, *George of Trebizond: A Biography and a Study of his Rhetoric and Logic* (Leiden: Brill, 1976), pp. 157–8.

[39] I am indebted here to the translation and commentary of James Hankins, *Plato in the Italian Renaissance*, I, 176.

sentence of this quotation is '*quanta scelerum seges radicitus euulsa est*', just as George of Trebizond refers in the passage quoted from his *Comparatio* to appetite being 'pulled out by the roots' or, in the original Latin, '*Non ergo hic appetitus euellendus radicitus est*' (*Utopia*, 242/ 1–2).[40]

Ultimately George resents Plato's attempt to decide for the whole of society what the common good should be, denying that such a thing can truly exist: 'The common good cannot be the ultimate good of anyone unless all should be of the same mind and will, which is extremely foolish even to imagine taking place in this life.'[41] The persona of More takes a comparable approach to the possibility of idealistic political schemes: 'it is impossible that all should be well unless all men were good, a situation which I do not expect for a great many years to come!' (*Utopia*, 101/ 2–4). There is a shared sense that such optimism regarding human character must be saved for the afterlife. For George of Trebizond, it is vital that each citizen should decide for himself the nature of his own good or '*vero bono*'. George rails against the moral and political guidance of Plato, despite his ancient authority. In implicitly criticizing Hythloday's portrayal of the ideal society, More follows the same impulse. Indeed, George's criticisms of Plato's ideal society are reminiscent of the complaints that have often been made about More's Utopia: there is too much coercion and not enough individual liberty.[42] Hence the interrogations of Platonic philosophy by early humanists like George of Trebizond provide an important background for our reading of *Utopia*. In presenting central aspects of the Utopians' society, such as their community of property, as being similar to Plato's ideal society of the *Republic* and the *Laws*, *Utopia* was engaging with a tradition of criticizing Plato that was as endemic to the early Renaissance as admiring and imitating him.

This tradition influenced other English dialogues of the period. Thomas Starkey's *A Dialogue between Pole and Lupset*, believed to have been written largely between 1529 and 1530, has become a classic of English political thought.[43] Like Plato, Starkey favoured education for the upper classes, envisioning an oligarchic system of government in England. In this dialogue Reginald Pole, who was eventually to become Archbishop of Canterbury and later Cardinal, seeks to persuade Lupset to give up the contemplative life and adopt the active life instead. In the course of their debate the two men discuss political philosophy, with reference to a series of classical sources, some of which are viewed in a critical light. Plato's *Republic* is no exception. Pole announces that they will endeavour to 'serche out as nere as we ca*n*, what is the veray & true Co*m*myn wele' as the basis

---

[40] George of Trebizond, *Comparatio philosophorum Aristotelis et Platonis* (Venice, 1523), Book III, Chapter 12, repr. in Hankins, I, 176.

[41] *Comparatio*, Book 3, Chapter 12, repr. in Hankins, I, 178.

[42] George of Trebizond, *Comparatio philosophorum Aristotelis et Platonis*, Book III, Chapters 12, repr. in Hankins, I, 179.

[43] The *Dialogue* was first published in 1535. For its date, see Thomas Starkey, *A Dialogue between Pole and Lupset*, ed. by T.F. Mayer (London: Royal Historical Society, 1989), pp. x–xii. It was solely available in MS. until 1871.

for their discussions. Lupset agrees with this aim, but beseeches Pole not to take Plato for his model:

> but here of one thyng I pray you take <hede that> in <thys> your devyse of your co*mm*unycatyon thys co*mm*yn wele <& you> folow not the exa*m*pul of plato, of whose ordur <of co*mm*yn wele> no pepul upon erth to thys days could ev*er* yet attayn, wherfor hyt ys reputyd of many me*n* but as a dreme, & vayne imygynatyon wych nev*er* can be brought to effect.[44]

Pole concurs with his colleague's opinion, which is later repeated.[45] Thus while Starkey evidently did not dismiss all Platonic philosophy, he maintained a robust scepticism regarding the idealism with which Plato imagined the best state of a commonwealth. Hence *Utopia*'s dialogue with Plato reflects the text's uncertainty about the prospect of the ideal society and the perfectibility of humankind.

Another Greek voice present in *Utopia* is that of the rhetorician and satirist Lucian, whose writings on imaginary travel and societies and philosophical-satiric dialogues also influenced *Utopia*. Dominic Baker-Smith has classified three features of the 'Lucianic temper' that marks *Utopia*: the interpenetration between the real and imaginary worlds, the introduction of fanciful names and a hostility to social custom and its capacity to distort our understanding of the world.[46] Each of these is important to a reading of *Utopia*'s dialogue with Lucian; I wish to focus here on the first of these features, and especially with reference to Lucian's portrayal of travel writing and ideal worlds. In the *True History*, Lucian undertakes a playful attack on tall travellers' tales, and in particular their representations of seemingly ideal societies. He scoffs at the claims at truth made by the writers of classical travel narratives, such as the travel stories of Ctesias and Iambulus, and the genre of travel writing they spawned:

> [His tales] were obviously quite untrue, but no one could deny that they made a very good story, so hundreds of people followed his example and wrote so-called histories of their travels describing all the huge monsters, and savage tribes, and extraordinary ways of life that they had come across in foreign parts.[47]

---

[44] *A Dialogue between Pole and Lupset*, p. 18.

[45] *A Dialogue between Pole and Lupset*, p. 108.

[46] Dominic Baker-Smith, 'Reading *Utopia*', in *The Cambridge Companion to Thomas More*, ed. by George M. Logan (Cambridge: Cambridge University Press, 2011), pp. 141–67 (pp. 143–5). See also Alistair Fox, *Thomas More: History and Providence* (Oxford: Blackwell, 1982); Arthur F. Kinney, *Humanist Poetics: Thought, Rhetoric, and Fiction in Sixteenth-Century England* (Amherst: University of Massachusetts Press, 1986), pp. 78–80; Carlo Ginzburg, 'The Old World and the New Seen from Nowhere', in *No Island Is an Island* (New York: Columbia University Press, 2000), pp. 1–23 (p. 11, p. 2). David Marsh sees *The True History* as 'the birth of Western utopian fiction' and considers its influence on *Utopia* in *Lucian and the Latins: Humor and Humanism in the Early Renaissance* (Ann Arbor: University of Michigan Press, 1998), pp. 193–7.

[47] *The True History*, in *Lucian: Satirical Sketches*, trans. by Paul Turner (London: Penguin, 1961; repr. Bloomington: Indiana University Press, 1990), pp. 249–94 (p. 249).

Lucian is explicit about the fictional nature of his own travel story: 'I am writing about things entirely outside my own experiences or anyone else's, things that have no reality whatever and never could have. So mind you do not believe a word I say.'[48] Although he never speaks to the reader so directly in his own voice, More also emphasizes that he is writing about matters beyond his own knowledge and experience, claiming in his letter to Peter Giles that he is only repeating 'what in your company I heard Raphael relate' (*Utopia*, 39/ 8). This play at verisimilitude reminds the reader of the falsity associated with the genre of travel writing from classical times onwards: More's account of Utopia is based entirely on the experiences of another, and so his claim to be telling the truth is self-consciously false. Later, in conversation with Morus and Giles, Hythloday makes his own claim for truthfulness, asserting the authority of the eyewitness: 'you should have been with me in Utopia and personally seen their manners and customs as I did, for I lived there more than five years' (*Utopia*, 107/ 19–21). In doing so he calls to mind the similar declaration of Lucian in the *True History*, where he claims the traveller's privilege of superior knowledge: 'Well, that is what it was like on the Moon. If you do not believe me, go and see for yourself.'[49] The similarity of these two claims reminds us that neither Lucian nor Hythloday has been to the society he imagines, and that neither society really exists. Like Lucian, who describes the 'Saladfowls' and the 'Garlic-gassers' he encounters, More uses comic names for the people and landmarks of Utopia, such as the river Anydrus ('waterless') and Utopia itself ('no place') (*Utopia*, 251 *et passim*).[50] In doing so, and in his ostentatious claims for truthfulness, he allies his text with Lucian's travel satires, in which descriptions of the ideal society are so hyperbolic as to be ridiculous. Reminding us of the tradition of satirizing travel literature, More strengthens the ironic and playful tone of his dialogue, but he also calls to mind Lucian's attempts to urge reform through jest and satire.[51]

As Baker-Smith reminds us, Plato is notably absent from Lucian's own 'Isle of the Blest'; instead, he is living in his own republic, 'lost in mental space'.[52] Lucian's voice in *Utopia*, and the presence of both Lucian and Plato in the text, strengthen More's criticism of the notion of the ideal society and the benefits of travel. More places *Utopia* in conversation with Plato and Lucian by bringing them into his own dialogue either directly, for example through Hythloday's voluble praise of Plato, or indirectly, such as through using Lucianic humour in naming the places and peoples encountered by Hythloday. Perhaps the most significant predecessor with whom More was in conversation, however, was Augustine, whose writings on the ideal society and the best way to live profoundly influenced More's own conceptions.

---

[48] *The True History*, p. 250.
[49] *The True History*, p. 262.
[50] *The True History*, pp. 254–5.
[51] Kinney, *Humanist Poetics*, p. 79.
[52] Baker-Smith, 'Reading *Utopia*', p. 143.

Christian Dialogue: *Utopia* and Augustine

Unlike Plato and Lucian, Augustine is not actively present in the text of *Utopia*; but his writings about how best to live, and in particular his *De civitate dei contra paganos*, or *Of the City of God against the Pagans*, stand behind all Christian humanist thinking about the ideal society. A central pillar of the Christian church to whose work More turned throughout his life, Augustine was concerned primarily not with the outward running of the state but with the inward running of the soul, and his voice, in both *De civitate dei* and his early dialogues, is as audible in *Utopia* as Plato's or Lucian's, despite the lack of direct reference. Listening to *Utopia*'s conversation with Augustine shows how More's interrogation of the 'best state of a commonwealth' recognizes the impossibility of achieving a perfect society on earth, and demonstrates the importance of considering the theological as well as the classical forebears of ideal-state writing. It also highlights the ways in which Utopian society seeks to deal with social, rather than individual, ills, which from an Augustinian perspective is a crucial failing. This question of social versus individual sin was to become a central focus for later sixteenth-century utopias, as the next chapter will show.

De civitate dei, like *Utopia*, tackles the question of how best to live in this world. The Utopian society that Hythloday describes in Book II might initially seem like the ideal Augustinian commonwealth, centred as it is on the need to restrain sinful humanity and the paramount danger of the sin of pride. In *De civitate dei* Augustine establishes that the purpose of society is to restrain the naturally sinful tendencies of human beings, for 'if man were left to live as he chose and act as he pleased', he would be unable to avoid sinning constantly, just as children must be physically disciplined if they are not to grow up untamed.[53] At the end of his discourse, Hythloday explains how the Utopians' establishment of community of property has defeated the sin of pride, and by removing the opportunity for this sin has created a successful society:

> They have adopted such institutions of life as have laid the foundations of the commonwealth not only most happily, but also to last forever, as far as human prescience can forecast. At home they have extirpated the roots of ambition and factionalism along with all the other vices. (*Utopia*, 245/ 6–10)

Hythloday is adamant that pride is the 'one single monster, the chief and progenitor of all plagues', a 'serpent from hell' (*Utopia*, 243/ 30–31, 39). His rant against pride is resonant of the more measured but equally absolute verdict in *De civitate dei*, in which Augustine identifies pride as the love of the self over the love of God, and concludes that 'the beginning of all sin is pride' (*DCD*, 12.6, 477). In fact, the Utopian solution to the problem of pride, total community of property, could be seen as a ratification of the Augustinian tenet that the basis

---

[53] Augustine, *Concerning the City of God against the Pagans*, trans. by Henry Bettenson (London: Penguin, 1984), p. 1065 (Book 22, Chapter 22), hereafter cited as *DCD*, 2.1, 1065. All further references will be to this edition and will be given in the text.

of happiness for the individual and the community are one and the same: 'For the source of a community's felicity is no different from that of one man, since a community is simply a united multitude of individuals' (*DCD*, 1.15, 25). A reading of More's *Utopia* as a straightforward portrayal of *De civitate dei* on earth might be encouraged by the fact that More was greatly influenced by Augustine throughout his lifetime. In the Yale edition of More's works, no writer is referred to in his religious writings more often than Augustine, whom he considered the pre-eminent Christian authority after the Bible.[54] *De civitate dei* was a particularly important text for More, who gave popular lectures on it at St. Lawrence Jewry in 1501, early in his career.[55]

In recent years there have been several assessments of the relationship between Augustine's *De civitate dei* and More's *Utopia*, which have concluded variously that the similarities between the two texts indicate More's personal approval of Utopia and that their differences indicate that we should treat Hythloday's narrative with some caution.[56] When one writer is as steeped in the work of another as is More in Augustine, it is difficult to isolate particular aspects of this relationship as it is manifested in a single text. Another predicament involved in assessing Augustine's influence on More is the difficulty of achieving a precise definition of the concept of Augustinianism. One scholar has presented the problem thus:

> Augustine was a singularly complex and unsystematic thinker who presents many different faces to his readers. He has been compared to a turbulent stream into whose rushing waters an abundance of silt has been washed, with the result that, although its waters are opaque, it deposits much rich nourishment along its banks for the support of a wide variety of life.[57]

---

[54] Richard C. Marius, 'Augustinianism and Carnival in More's *Utopia*', *Moreana*, 35 (1998), 129–50 (131); Thomas More, *The Complete Works of St Thomas More, Volume 9: The Apology*, ed. by J.B. Trapp (New Haven: Yale University Press, 1979), p. 320.

[55] William Roper, *The Lyfe of Sir Thomas More*, ed. by E.V. Hitchcock (London: printed for the Early English Text Society by H. Milford, Oxford University Press, 1935), p. 6. See also Peter Ackroyd, *The Life of Sir Thomas More* (London: Chatto & Windus, 1998), pp. 100–101.

[56] Edward Surtz considered the relationship between the *City of God* and *Utopia* under-researched; *Utopia*, p. clxvi. Though traditionally less common than interest in the relationship between More's writing and Plato, studies of Augustine's influence on *Utopia* have become more frequent. See Richard C. Marius, 'Thomas More and the Early Church Fathers', *Traditio*, 24 (1968), 379–407; Martin N. Raitière, 'More's *Utopia* and *The City of God*', *Studies in the Renaissance*, 20 (1973), 144–68, repr. in *The City of God: A Collection of Critical Essays*, ed. by Dorothy F. Donnelly (New York: Lang, 1995), pp. 253–76; Gerard Wegemer, '*The City of God* in Thomas More's *Utopia*', *Renascence*, 44 (1992), 115–35; István Bejczy, 'More's Utopia: The City of God on Earth?', *Saeculum*, 46 (1995), 17–30; Marius, 'Augustinianism and Carnival in More's *Utopia*'.

[57] William J. Bouwsma, 'The Two Faces of Humanism. Stoicism and Augustinianism in Renaissance Thought', in *Itinerarium Italicum: The Profile of the Italian Renaissance in the Mirror of its European Transformations*, ed. by Heiko A. Oberman with Thomas A. Brady, Jr. (Leiden: Brill, 1975), pp. 3–60 (pp. 7–8).

Nevertheless it is possible to conceive of Augustine's thought as a set of tendencies, if not a fully cohesive and coherent system. For *Utopia*, important Augustinian references are *De civitate dei*, Augustine's conception of the relationship of faith and reason, and his insistence on the need for divine grace for justification, as well as his early dialogues, including *De beata vita*. While Augustinianism is a pervasive influence in More's writing, it is possible to isolate in *Utopia* some particular features that provide both a new understanding of the relationship between *Utopia* and *De civitate dei* and a new way of reading More's text. In understanding this relationship, we must start by considering what Augustine has to say about the ideal life and the implications this has for More's presentation of the ideal society.

De civitate dei put forward the notion of two cities, one of men and one of God; this twofold division of the world originated in the fall of the angels from heaven. This was an idea that Augustine had discussed in earlier works, such as his *De Genesi ad Litteram*, where he writes that at the time of judgement these two currently intermingled cities will be separated, with one being joined to the holy angels and God and the other to the wicked angels and hell.[58] In Book 19 of *De civitate dei* Augustine considers the members of the city of God in the present age, who are not capable of achieving a truly ideal society in this life but long for its realization after death in the 'Heavenly City' (*DCD*, 19.13). For Augustine, the present life is a form of living hell in which the members of both cities are bound together (*DCD*, 22.22). The members of the city of God are like pilgrims ('*peregrini*') in that they reside in a land which is not their own (*DCD*, 19.17); they have no permanent home on this earth, but long for the achievement of the heavenly commonwealth or truly ideal society.

Utopia has often been read as the manifestation of More's ideas on what the ideal society might look like, and it is easy, when reading Hythloday's account of Utopia, to understand why it is often perceived as a genuinely ideal state. There are many aspects of Utopian society that appear right and fair by contemporary standards, particularly when read alongside Hythloday's criticisms of Tudor England, and some that we might imagine More himself might have advocated, such as effective agricultural systems, efficient town planning and the opportunity for study for all (*Utopia*, 115/ 22–31; 117/ 8–22; 121/ 1–12; 129/ 2–8). Utopia seemingly runs so smoothly that throughout the history of its reception, readers have complained that it is too ideal and could only be inhabited by saints.[59] David Hume thus categorizes *Utopia* in his essay 'Idea of a Perfect Commonwealth': 'All plans of government, which suppose great reformation in the manners of mankind, are plainly imaginary. Of this nature, are the *Republic* of *Plato*, and the *Utopia* of Sir Thomas *More*.'[60] Complaints such as Hume's insinuate, implicitly or

---

[58] Carol Harrison discusses the origins of the 'two cities' idea in *Augustine: Christian Truth and Fractured Humanity* (Oxford: Oxford University Press, 2000), pp. 200–202.

[59] A point established by Gerard Dudok, *Sir Thomas More and His Utopia* (Amsterdam: H.J. Paris v.h. Firma A.H. Kruyt, 1923), p. 142.

[60] David Hume, *Political Discourses*, 3rd edn (Edinburgh: Sands, Murray and Cochran, 1754), p. 252.

explicitly, that Utopia's extraordinarily good citizens and the consequent lack of realism constitute a failure on the part of the text. However, closer attention to the Utopians' 'reformation of manners' demonstrates that this feature is not a chance side effect of More's social planning, but is intricately involved with what the text has to say about human nature and perfectibility. The Utopians' lack of sinful behaviour is an intriguing feature of their presentation. Hythloday's account of the organization of their society describes the provisions made for the punishment of various crimes, such as adultery, and describes the presence of people who have been enslaved in punishment for crimes, so it is assumed that such sins could theoretically take place. But such a crime is never apparently witnessed, despite Hythloday's five years in Utopia. Indeed, the Utopians demonstrate no inclination to transgress the established customs and laws of their society. Thus no Utopians indulge in the frowned-upon activity of playing with dice, 'whose madness they know not by experience but by hearsay only' (*Utopia*, 171/ 7–9). No opportunity for sinful deviation from these customs is permitted: 'nowhere is there any license to waste time, nowhere any pretext to evade work – no wine shop, no ale house, no brothel anywhere, no opportunity for corruption, no lurking hole, no secret meeting place' (*Utopia*, 147/ 21–5). Hythloday identifies the cause of the Utopians' good behaviour as their community of property:

> In Utopia all greed for money was entirely removed with the use of money. [...] Who does not know that fraud, theft, rapine, quarrels, disorders, brawls, seditions, murders, treasons, poisonings, which are avenged rather than restrained by daily executions, die out with the destruction of money? (*Utopia*, 241/ 39, 243/ 1–6)

Hythloday reduces all sins to the sin of desire or *cupiditas*, and the Utopians are presented as not sinning because they have no motivation or impulse to do so: their *cupiditas* has been removed.

Like the superstitious pagans whom Augustine attacks in *De civitate dei* for believing that the fall of Rome was a consequence of the spread of Christianity, the Utopians are discouraged from forsaking their unchristian beliefs owing to an accident that once befell a Utopian who was considering changing his religion. Other than these references, however, there is little indication that the Utopians are concerned that their way of life may be wrong. Certainly on an individual basis there is no sign that they indulge in any self-doubt or self-criticism. The Utopians' attitude is most thoroughly exposed in Hythloday's relation of how he told them about Christ, his life, teaching and miracles and the martyrs who had drawn others to Christianity. Hythloday reports that the Utopians were 'readily disposed' to 'join' Christianity, and gives the following reasons:

> whether through the rather mysterious inspiration of God ['*secretius inspirante deo*'] or because they thought it nearest to that belief which has the widest prevalence among them. But I think this factor, too, was of no small weight, that they had heard that His disciples' common way of life had been pleasing to Christ and is still in use among the truest societies of Christians. (*Utopia*, 219/ 2–8)

The Utopians are therefore drawn to Christianity because they recognize their own society in Christ's preferred way of life. In effect, Christ appeals to the Utopians because he resembles them; they make no effort to resemble him, as Christians should. Again, they are influenced by the dictates of reason in the absence of revelation. The fact that strikes the Utopians is not Christ's immortality, his existence as God made flesh, but a mundane aspect of his mortality, in which he was joined by others. They favour his social teaching, rather than his spiritual value.

In presenting the Utopians in this way, through the smokescreen of Hythloday's approving narrative within the dialogue form, More critiques the Utopians' seemingly idealized society. When the characteristics of Utopian religion are assessed in Augustinian terms, they reveal a people who have failed to achieve a proper relationship with God or true self-understanding. A brief glance at Augustine's writings demonstrates the extent of this failure. Augustine's preference for faith over reason and his insistence that belief must precede understanding is particularly evident in his later works. Speaking of unbelievers, Augustine emphasizes the need for faith as the foundation of understanding in a statement that reverses the Utopian practice of founding all beliefs in rationality:

> Since they have indeed an unshakeable faith in the Sacred Scriptures as the most reliable witnesses, let them by prayer, study, and a good life seek to understand, that is, that what is retained by faith may be seen in the mind, insofar as it can be seen. [...] Let them first be illuminated by the gift of God that they may be faithful [...] then let them be built up to see what they believe, so that they may be one day able to see.[61]

Augustine had previously explained that 'the right purpose is that which proceeds from faith,' because 'a certain faith is in some way the beginning of all knowledge'.[62] It has been suggested that during his lifetime Augustine became increasingly pessimistic about humanity's potential to reach the truth through unaided reason alone, and came to stress the importance of humility against pride, of faith rather than reason as the means of accessing truth, a development which may be located in his development of a doctrine of the fall of humanity and his increasing conviction of man's sinfulness.[63] In Utopia, attention is paid to social ills rather than individual ones; the creation of successful social institutions has, in Hythloday's eyes, created a happy people. But the text implicitly criticizes the notion that humanity can perfect itself through effective city planning and the imposition of institutional life. As an Augustinian reading of *Utopia* demonstrates, the Utopians' self-sufficiency is not necessarily a marker of a successful society.

In challenging the suggestion that man can be self-sufficient, More was in keeping with other late medieval and Renaissance thinkers. In *Mons Perfectionis*,

---

[61] *Saint Augustine: The Trinity*, trans. by Stephen McKenna (Washington: Catholic University of America, 1963; repr. 1970), p. 520 (Book 15, Chapter 27), hereafter *Trinity*.

[62] *Trinity*, p. 270 (Book 9, Chapter 1).

[63] Harrison, *Augustine: Christian Truth and Fractured Humanity*, p. 21, p. 25.

for example, a text aimed at the educated layperson as well as the clergyman, Bishop Alcock had emphasized the necessity of reliance upon God (which for Alcock meant the Scriptures and the clergy): 'No man what condicion so euer he be of wyll thynke [that] he be suffycyent of hymselfe w[ith]out the grace of almighty god which is the pryncipal [and] first meuer to vertue in our soules without our meryte.'[64] This tradition of emphasizing man's insufficiency, and specifically the danger of relying on reason, stretches back to Augustine. In *De civitate dei*, Augustine had similarly castigated classical philosophy for proudly relying on its own reason rather than humbly confessing faith in Christ and acknowledging the authority of his teaching: 'and so let human weakness yield to divine authority' (*DCD*, 10.31, 420). Augustine's own renunciation of his classical rhetorical training in favour of Christian doctrine, as narrated in the *Confessions*, repeats this pattern. It is only after he has learned to love and to have faith in God through knowledge of the Scriptures that Augustine is able to understand that the Platonist books which he has read cannot provide the path to salvation.[65]

When it comes to the issue of living happily on this earth, Augustine is adamant in his insistence that the prospect of achieving the good life here is vain and misguided: 'life will only be truly happy when it is eternal' (*DCD*, 10.25, 590). Augustine returns in *De civitate dei* to the concept of the Supreme Good, or *summum bonum*, the achievement of which is the goal of classical philosophy. For Augustine, to desire happiness on earth through one's own efforts is 'amazing folly', the result of blindness and pride in those who refuse to humble themselves by admitting their error (*DCD*, 19.4, 854, 855). He repeats that the *summum bonum* cannot be reached in this life; rather, the most we can do is continue in hope of salvation and future happiness. The Utopians' manifested belief that they can live happily in the present through their own efforts is like that of the pagan philosophers whom Augustine derides and condemns: 'they attempt to fabricate for themselves an utterly delusive happiness by means of a virtue whose falsity is in proportion to its arrogance' (*DCD*, 19.4, 857). Elsewhere in Augustine's writings, evidence can be found of this belief that it is impossible to live a happy and sinless life as the Utopians appear to do:

> we need not be too disturbed by those who maintain that any man lives or has lived in this world entirely without sin: we must press them to establish their assertion if they can. [...] No man in this life, free though he be to choose, is ever found without sin.[66]

---

[64] John Alcock, *Mons Perfectionis: otherwyse in englysshe the hyl of perfeccon* (London, 1497), A.ii(2), quoted in Tom Betteridge, *Literature and Politics in the English Reformation* (Manchester: Manchester University Press, 2004), p. 5.

[65] *Saint Augustine: Confessions*, trans. by R.S. Pine-Coffin (London: Penguin, 1961), pp. 154–5 (Book 7, Chapter 20).

[66] *Augustine: Later Works*, ed. by John Burnaby (London: S.C.M. Press, 1955), *The Spirit and the Letter*, p. 196.

Augustine links the ubiquity of sinfulness with the need for self-dissatisfaction, such as in his *Commentary on the Gospel of St John*, where he says that 'each one of us discovers he's a sinner when he attends to himself'.[67] In his sermons in particular Augustine reiterates the need for self-examination and criticism, calling for the Christian to 'act as judge on yourself [...] observe yourself'.[68] Augustine's conception of sin is fundamentally not restricted to sinful behaviour. Rather, sin can also exist in the heart, within the self: 'As, therefore, one comes to sin by three steps – suggestion, pleasure, consent – so there are three varieties of sin itself: in the heart, in the act, in the habit.'[69] If sin can be present even in thoughts, then there is a duty to be constantly vigilant, and it is for this reason that Augustine says that the Lord's Prayer, with its request that debts be forgiven, must be repeated daily.[70] So it is vital to be aware of and ask forgiveness, not only for sins carried out in actions but also for sins committed within the self: 'we should also ask pardon for such thoughts, and we should strike our breasts and say: "Forgive us our debts".'[71] The Utopians' lack of self-consideration can thus be interpreted in an Augustinian light, not as the untroubled behaviour of a happy people, but as a lack of awareness of their own sinfulness and the state of what Augustine terms the 'wretchedness' of fallen humanity (*DCD*, 14.15, 575). Indeed, in an Augustinian sense, one could argue that the Utopians do not have 'selves' at all.

Augustine's own dialogue on the happy life, *De beata vita*, also puts forward the argument that happiness lies beyond the self; it results from having found rest in God, and true wisdom comes through Christ. Augustine's earliest dialogues, including *De beata vita*, were written during a period of reflection and seclusion at Cassiciacum in 386 CE, following his conversion to Christianity. As he prepared for baptism, Augustine was, like More when he wrote *Utopia*, in a liminal state, preparing to leave one kind of life for another and evaluating the benefits of different ways of living.[72] For Augustine too, the dialogue form suited this period of consideration and transition. In *De beata vita* he discussed some of the basic issues of Christianity and identified the same questions that dominate *Utopia*: what is true wisdom? Does the good life consist in material benefits? What should be the goals of a Christian life? As More did in *Utopia*, Augustine used the dialogue form to present various opinions on these subjects.

---

[67] *Augustine: Political Writings*, ed. by E.M. Atkins and R.J. Dodaro (Cambridge: Cambridge University Press, 2001), p. 104, hereafter *Political Writings*.

[68] *Sermon 13: On the Words of Psalm 2:10*, in *Political Writings*, p. 124. See also *Sermon 302: On the Feast of St. Lawrence*, in *Political Writings*, p. 115.

[69] *St. Augustine: The Lord's Sermon on the Mount*, trans. by John J. Jepson (London: Longmans, Green, 1948), p. 45 (Book 1, Chapter 12), hereafter *The Lord's Sermon on the Mount*.

[70] *The Lord's Sermon on the Mount*, pp. 115–17 (Book 2, Chapter 8).

[71] *Trinity*, p. 360 (Book 12, Chapter 12).

[72] Richard C. Marius describes this period of 'spiritual crisis' in More's life in *Thomas More: A Biography* (New York: Knopf, 1984), Chapter 3.

In *De beata vita* Augustine dramatizes a conversation that took place following his birthday celebrations, when eight participants were present (two of them have non-speaking roles in the dialogue). His prologue begins with an extended analogy between the pursuit of philosophy and travel at sea. He describes humanity as having been cast 'as into a stormy sea fortuitously and indiscriminately', ignorant of which way to turn: 'what man would know in what direction to strive or where to return unless some tempest, seemingly adverse to the foolish, push us unwilling, resisting, unwitting, and off our course, upon the land we longed to reach most of all?' Philosophers are, like Hythloday, 'seafarers' ('*nauigantium*'), and their attempt to determine the best way to live is like a journey 'to the land of the happy life'.[73] Augustine warns against taking an apparently beautiful location at face value. Those who would sail to the land of the happy life enter through the port, beside which stands a 'huge mountain'. This mountain, which appears 'resplendent', as if it would please the travellers and 'satisfy their desire for the happy land itself', is in fact dangerous, with 'hidden rocks underneath' and 'nothing substantial or solid within' (63, 65). Rather than delivering the happy life to the travellers, such a mountain draws them away from the harbour and destroys them, swallowing them up and flinging them into darkness (65). This description finds a parallel in Hythloday's picture of the only means by which the island of Utopia may be reached. In the centre of the bay which gives access to Utopia 'stands one great crag which, being visible, is not dangerous [...] The other rocks are hidden and therefore treacherous' (*Utopia* 111/ 20–21, 23–4). The mountain at the harbour to the happy land in *De beata vita* serves as a reminder that both visible and invisible threats can be dangerous; Augustine describes philosophy as a safe harbour in which to rest while assessing how to reach 'the part of the land which alone is really happy' (67). At the end of their debate on happiness, during which the participants agree that happiness is the goal of all and discuss the requisites of a happy life, the conversation concludes with Augustine's mother, Monica, quoting from Ambrose, 'Assist, O Trinity, those who pray' (115). The dialogue is resolved in the agreement that human life is the journey towards happiness, and that prayer and thanksgiving are necessary elements of the attempt to know God and thus be led to truth. Augustine's own early dialogue provides some interesting parallels to More's, not least in its emphasis on the perils of travel; Hythloday, we may remember, is described to the persona of More as being 'more anxious for travel than about the grave' (*Utopia* 51/ 12).

An Augustinian reading of More's *Utopia* further suggests that More uses the dialogue form to critique the genre of ideal-state writing as a whole. The Utopians' reliance on reason over faith is their greatest weakness. Augustine has sometimes been seen as one who emphasized faith over reason, but he also upheld the notion that man's rationality was his link to God:

---

[73] *De beata vita*, in W. M. Green and K.-D. Daur, eds, *Augustinus, Contra academicos. De beata vita. De ordine. De magistro. De libero arbitrio.*, Corpus Christianorum Series Latina 29 (Turnhout: Brepols, 1970), p. 61, p. 63, hereafter *De beata vita*.

> Heaven forbid, after all, that God should hate in us that by which he made us more excellent than the other animals. Heaven forbid, I say, that we should believe in such a way that we do not accept or seek a rational account, since we could not believe if we did not have rational souls.[74]

In this letter to Consentius, Augustine makes clear his belief that reason precedes faith. However, as is dramatized in the *Confessions*, Augustine maintains that the truth cannot be reached by reason alone. Etienne Gilson, in his authoritative examination of reason and revelation in the medieval period, has defined the reaching of this conclusion in the *Confessions* as manifesting a complete break from classical philosophy, 'opening a new era in the history of western thought'.[75] Augustine's letters also demonstrate his privileging of faith for the individual believer: 'If faith had not come first, would we not have heard the truth to no purpose?'[76] So for Augustine, the facility of reason is not to be denied or diminished, but must be assisted by Christian faith in an effort to achieve understanding, as Robert Hoopes elaborates:

> Men do not choose between reason and faith in accepting the truth of this relation [between God and man]. They are compelled to acceptance by inner and unconditional assent, so that they are able to say: 'Next to myself, I know God.' Believe, says Augustine, in order that you may understand.[77]

Through his Augustinian presentation of the Utopians, More shows that whatever social or economic improvements can be made in the imagination of an ideal society, it will never be possible to create an ideal people. The Utopians appear to have been perfected by the social and economic structuring of Utopia in Hythloday's eyes, but the interrogation of the best state of the commonwealth in Augustinian terms argues that perfection will only be achieved in eternal life, through the grace of God, and thus it is the relationship of the individual believer with God that is most important. Hence *Utopia*'s Augustinianism is to some extent pessimistic, expressed perhaps in the judgement of the persona of More that 'it is impossible that all should be well unless all men were good, a situation which I do not expect for a great many years to come!' (*Utopia*, 101/ 2–4). Yet the text's Augustinianism is also realistic and practical: it does not argue that no attempt should be made to improve earthly societies, but shows that the harder battle is fought in the individual soul, in the effort to improve the self.

---

[74] Augustine, Letter 120 [Augustine to Consentius], *The Works of Saint Augustine: Letters 100–150 (Epistulae)*, Volume 2, Part 2, trans. by Roland Teske (New York: New City Press, 2003), p. 131.

[75] Etienne Gilson, *Reason and Revelation in the Middle Ages* (New York: Charles Scribner's Sons, 1950), p. 17.

[76] Letter 120, p. 134.

[77] Robert Hoopes, *Right Reason in the English Renaissance* (Cambridge, MA: Harvard University Press, 1962), pp. 66–7.

Conclusion

The dialogue of Book I of *Utopia* demonstrates how desperately social reform is needed in More's own society, a land where sheep devour people and a poor man can find no work. The intensity and originality of More's social criticism in *Utopia* cannot be overestimated, but social reform is clearly not sufficient in itself; it is people who must be improved if reform is to be effective. Social reform, then, may be necessary; but equally it may not be successful. *Utopia*, as is widely recognized, is concerned not with political reform or social amelioration, but with philosophical enquiry and satire: it is an intellectual exercise in philosophical interrogation. These functions are enabled by its use of dialogue, because it is through its dialogue form that *Utopia* undertakes a criticism of utopia by showing the failings of ideal-state fiction. Later Renaissance utopias were to concern themselves more directly with the question of social reform. Nonetheless the fact that *Utopia*, via Augustine, calls to mind the importance of paying attention to the individual self reflects an interesting point of continuity between *Utopia* and later sixteenth-century utopian writing. Later utopian literature was to mark a movement towards an interest in individual rather than social sins in writing about the ideal society; but this interest is also present in More's dialogue. The centrality of the concept of original sin to More's theology and character has long been recognized. Marius, for example, saw him as 'saturated with pessimism about a frail humankind weakened by original sin'.[78] G.R. Elton believed that More's theological position was determined by his consciousness of original sin, 'because he had not been able to follow the call to abandon the flesh' himself; More's Christianity is thus one in which 'the other world is the only thing that matters'.[79] The very Augustinian concept of original sin is inevitably central to More's discussion of the good life. It is ultimately because of original sin in its various forms that any attempts at perfection will fall short. Those who choose to commit themselves to the active life (which Augustine would have said they must do) must nonetheless prepare themselves for disappointment. *Utopia*, sceptical about the prospect of the ideal society, establishes various features, subjects and qualities that later sixteenth-century utopias would draw on, such as the dialogue form, the travel narrative and the seemingly ideal society, but it treats with irony questions that later utopian literature would take seriously.

---

[78] Marius, *Thomas More*, p. 167.

[79] G.R. Elton, *Studies in Tudor and Stuart Politics and Government, Volume IV* (Cambridge: Cambridge University Press, 1992), p. 150.

Chapter 2
'Godly Conversation':
The Reformation of Utopia

Introduction: Utopia after *Utopia*

Thomas More's *Utopia*, as might be expected, has dominated discussions of the literary utopia in the sixteenth century. More's own significance to the period, the influence of his text on its literature and politics and *Utopia*'s status as the foundation stone of Renaissance ideal-state writing have led to its eclipsing what can only be seen as lesser utopias by lesser authors.[1] Nonetheless, later sixteenth-century utopias merit study, not only as followers in *Utopia*'s wake, but in their own right as literary texts, as Tudor dialogues and as markers of the development of the utopian mode of discourse in the sixteenth century.[2] It was during this period that the mode became associated with social amelioration rather than satire and philosophical enquiry, due in part to the afterlife of More's *Utopia*. This chapter will examine this shift in the use of utopia by looking at two sixteenth-century utopian dialogues which have been little considered: *A pleasant Dialogue between a Lady called Listra, and a Pilgrim. Concerning the gouernement and common weale of the great prouince of Crangalor* (1579), by Thomas Nicholls, and *Sivqila, Too Good to be True*, by Thomas Lupton (1580). *A pleasant Dialogue* and *Sivqila* demonstrate how later sixteenth-century writers of utopia turned to the dialogue in order to interrogate contemporary society and suggest improvements. These utopias can be read as examples of Tudor humanists' desire 'to influence the political debate and do their bit for the commonweal', as Cathy Shrank has written of the dialogue form in this period. In this sense, they demonstrate the use of the dialogue as a construct for social reform, and, like contemporary polemical

---

[1] The best study of utopianism and political radicalism in the sixteenth century is David Weil Baker's *Divulging Utopia: Radical Humanism in Sixteenth-Century England* (Amherst: University of Massachusetts Press, 1999). See also David Norbrook, 'The "Utopia" and Radical Humanism', *Poetry and Politics in the English Renaissance* (London: Routledge & Kegan Paul, 1984), pp. 18–31.

[2] This chapter will confine itself to English utopias, but more work needs to be done on placing these in their European context. On the Continent, projections of ideal states were produced by Johann Eberlein von Günzburg (*Wolfaria*, 1521), Anton Francesco Doni (*I mondi*, 1552), Francesco Patrizi (*La città felice*, 1553) and Kaspar Stiblin (*Commentariolus de eudaemonensium republica*, 1555). On these see Luigi Firpo, 'Renaissance Utopianism', in *The Late Italian Renaissance, 1525–1630*, ed. by Eric Cochrane (London: Macmillan, 1970), pp. 149–67; Luigi Firpo, *L'utopia nell'eta' della controriforma* (Turin: Giappichelli, 1977); Miriam Eliav-Feldon, *Realistic Utopias: The Ideal Imaginary Societies of the Renaissance, 1516–1630* (Oxford: Clarendon Press, 1982).

Protestant dialogues, can be understood as 'Reformation fictions'.[3] Although they are concerned with social and individual reform rather than polemicism, later sixteenth-century utopian dialogues serve to demonstrate the centrality of religion to literature and life in the period and the ongoing process of consolidation of Protestantism in English society.[4]

***

Utopia was successful immediately upon its publication. Following the first edition, published at Louvain in 1516, Latin editions appeared in Paris in 1517, twice in Basel in 1518 and Florence in 1519, with later sixteenth-century editions produced in 1548, 1555, 1563 and 1565–66. Vernacular editions were also popular, with the first translation into German in 1524, Italian in 1548, French in 1550 and Dutch in 1553. The first English edition of the text arrived in 1551, in a translation by Ralph Robynson, which was itself published twice more in the sixteenth century, in 1556 and 1597.[5] This first English translation of *Utopia* marks an important change in the reception of the text and the meaning of utopia in the sixteenth century. Robynson and the other men involved in its production were active Protestants living and working in Reformation London, and Robynson was associated with the Protestant programme of the Duke of Somerset through his patron, George Tadlowe, and the dedicatee of his translation of *Utopia*, William Cecil.[6] Tadlowe's own interests in civic reform and social change, exemplified by his involvement in charitable projects such as the development of the Royal Hospitals, provide an important context for the reading of the Robynson *Utopia* as a text intended to

---

[3] Cathy Shrank, *Writing the Nation in Reformation England 1530–1580* (Oxford: Oxford University Press, 2006), p. 218. On the use of dialogue for social reform, see also Judith Deitch, '"Dialoguewise": Discovering Alterity in Elizabethan Dialogues', in *Other Voices, Other Views: Expanding the Canon in English Renaissance Studies*, ed. by Helen Ostovich, Mary V. Silcox and Graham Roebuck (Newark: University of Delaware Press, 1999), pp. 46–73 (p. 65).

[4] The term 'Reformation fictions' is taken from Antoinina Bevan Zlatar's *Reformation Fictions: Polemical Protestant Dialogues in Elizabethan England* (Oxford: Oxford University Press, 2011). This chapter seeks to contribute, with Zlatar, to the contention 'that religion – the Reformation – is at the heart of sixteenth-century English culture' (*Reformation Fictions*, p. 8). For the consolidation of Protestantism in the later sixteenth century, see for example Patrick Collinson, *The Birthpangs of Protestant England: Religious and Cultural Change in the Sixteenth and Seventeenth Centuries* (London: Macmillan, 1988); Peter McCullough, *Sermons at Court: Politics and Religion in Elizabethan and Jacobean Preaching* (Cambridge: Cambridge University Press, 1998); Philip Benedict, 'The second wave of Protestant expansion', in *The Cambridge History of Christianity, Volume 6: Reform and Expansion 1500–1660*, ed. by R. Po-Chia Hsia (Cambridge: Cambridge University Press, 2007), pp. 125–42 (pp. 138–40).

[5] For full publication information see David Harris Sacks, ed., *Utopia by Sir Thomas More, trans. by Ralph Robynson, 1556* (New York: Bedford/St. Martin's, 1999), 'Preface', p. lx.

[6] Sacks, *Utopia*, p. 61.

influence and contribute to efforts to promote social change through the creation of new institutions, or the reform of existing ones. They demonstrate the 'context of active citizenship and reform' which produced the first English translation of *Utopia* and which signal its interests in changing society for the better.[7]

Robynson naturally produced a very different sort of text from the original, creating a book which was 'strikingly different from the Latin editions' and which in consequence did much to promote the notion of utopia as a model for an ideal society.[8] Printed (and reprinted) at times of social unrest, Robynson's *Utopia* sought to respond to the uncertainty of such times with the clear lessons and models offered by a utopian ideal. In translation, then, *Utopia* quickly became associated with an interest in social reform. It was 'transformed', David Harris Sacks has argued,

> from a book primarily challenging the intellectual conventions and answering the philosophical questions of a learned international audience, to one offering commentary on current social, economic, and political ills focused mainly on England and directed to a mixed readership [...]. It was now a work more of social amelioration than of philosophical inquiry and political satire.[9]

Robynson's translation, the main means by which most English readers encountered the text until the twentieth century, thus reflects an influential shift in the use of utopia and a strategic move towards its use in projects for social reform.[10]

This change in the use and perception of utopia in the sixteenth century can clearly be associated with the rise of Protestantism. The later events of More's career, his disagreements with Henry VIII, his persecution of Lutherans and his execution in 1535 meant that he subsequently became 'a Catholic martyr for some and a traitor for others'.[11] Although, as Vibeke Roggen suggests, this was not necessarily an immediate polarization, *Utopia* was for Protestants an easy target. Critics of More's theology, for example, suggested that he drew his arguments '"out of Utopia, from whence thou must know, reader[,] can come no fictions, but all fine poetry", for Purgatory is not to be found "(unless it be in Master More's Utopia), as Master More's poetical vein doth imagine"'.[12] In his *Actes and Monuments* and elsewhere, as David Weil Baker has shown, John Foxe

---

[7] Jennifer Bishop, '*Utopia* and Civic Politics in Mid-Sixteenth Century London', *Historical Journal* 54:4 (2011), 933–53 (945).

[8] Sacks, *Utopia*, p. 61.

[9] Sacks, *Utopia*, p. 68.

[10] Sacks, *Utopia*, 'Preface', p. x.

[11] Vibeke Roggen, 'A Protean text: *Utopia* in Latin, 1516–1631', in *Thomas More's Utopia in Early Modern Europe: Paratexts and Contexts*, ed. by Terence Cave (Manchester: Manchester University Press), pp. 14–31 (p. 25).

[12] John Foxe, *Actes and monuments of these latter and perillous dayes [...]* (London, 1570), quoted in Anne Lake Prescott, 'Introduction', in Jackson Campbell Boswell, *Sir Thomas More in the English Renaissance: An Annotated Catalogue* (Binghamton: Center for Medieval and Renaissance Studies 1994), p. xvi.

equated Utopia with the denial of human nature and reality.[13] The pessimism of Protestant godly reform was not a natural fermenter of utopianism, and for its reformers, 'utopia' quickly took on connotations of negativity and uselessness. As Paul Slack has argued, by the 1560s 'there were evident risks in public discussion of what Sir Thomas Smith called "feigned common wealths", Utopias "such as never was nor never shall be"'.[14] For English Protestants, the fictional utopia could be a dangerous or disparaged mode of writing. This is not, of course, to suggest that *Utopia* itself had no Protestant interest or readership. In fact, as its later transmission demonstrates, it could be recognized as a model by Catholics and Protestants alike.[15] This chapter, however, is not concerned directly with the use and transmission of *Utopia*, but with later utopian dialogues, which sought to contribute to the reformation of English morals and society, and which had a significant place in Protestant writing of the later sixteenth century.

***

The dialogue was a highly popular genre in the sixteenth century. It has been calculated that there are extant some two hundred and thirty prose dialogues from this period, and the genre established a pervasiveness through literature that derives 'in part, from a vernacular tradition, represented in the main by comic verse dialogues and, in part, from the humanist education that by the mid-sixteenth century was the national norm'.[16] Recent decades have seen a growing interest in the dialogue form, which has established its centrality to humanist ways of thought and to the literary culture of the Renaissance.[17] Renaissance dialogues

---

[13] Baker, *Divulging Utopia*, pp. 129–30.

[14] Paul Slack, *From Reformation to Improvement: Public Welfare in Early Modern England* (Oxford: Clarendon Press, 1999), p. 13, quoting Thomas Smith, *De Republica Anglorum*, ed. by Mary Dewar (Cambridge: Cambridge University Press, 1982), p. 144.

[15] Kirsti Sellevold, 'The French Versions of *Utopia*: Christian and Cosmopolitan Models', in *Thomas More's* Utopia *in Early Modern Europe*, pp. 67–86 (p. 86).

[16] Roger L. Deakins, 'Tudor Prose Dialogue: Genre and Anti-Genre', *Studies in English Literature*, 20 (1980), 5–23 (9); Cathy Shrank, 'Stammering, Snoring and Other Problems in the Early Modern English Dialogue', in *Writing and Reform in Sixteenth-Century England: Interdisciplinary Essays*, ed. by John Blakeley and Mike Pincombe (Lewiston: Edwin Mellen Press, 2008), pp. 99–120 (p. 100). For the popularity of the dialogue in the Renaissance, see also Janet Levarie Smarr, *Joining the Conversation: Dialogues by Renaissance Women* (Ann Arbor: University of Michigan Press, 2005).

[17] See, for example, Deakins, 'Tudor Prose Dialogue: Genre and Anti-Genre'; K.J. Wilson, *Incomplete Fictions: The Formation of English Renaissance Dialogue* (Washington: The Catholic University of America Press, 1985); Jon R. Snyder, *Writing the Scene of Speaking: Theories of Dialogue in the Late Italian Renaissance* (Stanford: Stanford University Press, 1989); Virginia Cox, *The Renaissance Dialogue: Literary Dialogue in Its Social and Political Contexts, Castiglione to Galileo* (Cambridge: Cambridge University Press, 1992); Eva Kushner, *Le dialogue à la Renaissance: Histoire et poétique* (Paris: Librairie Droz, 2004); Smarr, *Joining the Conversation*; Shrank, 'Stammering, Snoring and Other Problems in the Early Modern English Dialogue'.

were written on such a diverse range of topics that to suggest the genre served a single function would be far too simplistic. Central to my interest in the dialogue form in this chapter will be its didacticism, a feature integral to many dialogues of the period.[18]

One of the multiple concerns of the dialogue form was to engage with the question of how to live well and the problems of social reform. Janet Levarie Smarr has located the roots of this interest in the good life in the dialogue's classical and medieval origins, some of which were discussed in the previous chapter: Plato, Cicero, Lucian, Augustine and Petrarch.[19] Other scholars of the genre have established the ways in which authors like Thomas Smith employed it 'to analyse, and seek solutions for, issues of national concern'.[20] The dialogue could be political, then, and critical of society. The form was 'imbued with a belief in both rhetoric and public service' and deeply interested in political debate, but it 'also held the propensity to interrogate the effectiveness of those processes of debate and decision-making'.[21] Dialogues, as I have suggested, could be both critical and self-critical. Shrank's study of English commonweal dialogues has shown how they question their own prospects of achieving actual change, as they display 'manifestations of hesitancy, as they question the effectiveness or ethical positions of their speakers, or – mired in specifics – postpone resolution, or retreat into nostalgic or evasive positions'.[22] In its simultaneous critique of its society and itself, the dialogue form can be likened to the utopia, which critically appraises both the social order and its own limited capacity to achieve change.

This chapter will demonstrate that the dialogue continued to be a useful form for utopianism for two main reasons. Firstly, as mentioned above, the dialogue had didactic associations which made it uniquely appropriate for the expression of utopian ideals. An important part of a humanist education, the use of debate and dialogue to work out ideas and put forward arguments was second nature to men like Nicholls and Lupton, and thus formed an obvious means of putting forward their own ideas on the improvement of human society. Secondly, the dialogue naturally incorporated dramatic elements that were employed by these two authors to bring to life the lessons and messages they wished to convey.[23] I argue that these utopian dialogues use these elements of dialogue for two related aims: firstly, as Antoinina Bevan Zlatar has written of polemical dialogues during the period,

---

[18] For didacticism in the Renaissance dialogue, see, for example, David Marsh, 'Dialogue and Discussion in the Renaissance', in *The Cambridge History of Literary Criticism, Volume 3: The Renaissance*, ed. by Glyn Norton (Cambridge: Cambridge University Press, 1999), pp. 265–70.

[19] Smarr, *Joining the Conversation*, p. 23.

[20] Cathy Shrank, *Writing the Nation*, p. 143.

[21] Shrank, 'Stammering, Snoring and Other Problems in the Early Modern English Dialogue', p. 101.

[22] Shrank, 'Stammering, Snoring and Other Problems in the Early Modern English Dialogue', p. 115.

[23] On the dramatic nature of dialogue, see Zlatar, *Reformation Fictions*, p. 21.

they sought to educate the 'unlearned' in the moral behaviour necessary for the achievement of the ideal society;[24] and secondly, they sought to further the aims of (and ingratiate themselves with) those interested in strengthening the Protestant Reformation in England. Thus both of the utopian dialogues considered in this chapter draw on the didacticism of the dialogue form in order to suggest examples for the improvement of both society and individuals through the dramatization of a conversation between an ignorant questioner and an experienced traveller who relates positive examples gathered from foreign societies. This chapter will suggest that these texts develop aspects of the utopian dialogue beyond More's *Utopia* and reflect a Protestant shift in focus from the sins of the society to the sins of the individual. It is clear that utopian dialogues of this period have primarily religious, as well as political, aims, and this chapter contends that later sixteenth-century utopian dialogues had a part to play in the consolidation of Protestantism which was taking place during this period.

A pleasant Dialogue

In her entry on *A pleasant Dialogue* for The Origins of Early Modern Literature project at the Humanities Research Institute, Cathy Shrank has suggested that its author is the Thomas Nicholls born in 1532, a ship-owner who travelled to the Canary Islands in the 1550s when he served as secretary to the new Muscovy Company.[25] By the 1570s Nicholls had begun to translate travel writings and had links to others who dedicated texts to Edward Dyer (the dedicatee of *A pleasant Dialogue*), and his Reformist tendencies (which led to his imprisonment in Tenerife in the 1560s) are in keeping with the tone of this text. Moreover, Nicholls's contemporary writings reveal an interest in the dialogue form; in 1580, for example, he published his translation of a piece from the *Coloquios y diálogos* (1547) of the Spanish humanist Pedro de Mejía, *A delectable Dialogue, wherein is contayned a pleasaunt disputation between two Spanish Gentlemen, concerning Phisick and Phisitions, with sentence of a learned Maister given upon their argument.*[26]

Nicholls returned to London in 1577 and the first of his translations of travel writings, *The strange and maruetlous Newes lately come from the great Kingdome*

---

[24] Zlatar, *Reformation Fictions*, p. 6.
[25] Cathy Shrank, Entry on *A Pleasant Dialogue between Listra and a Pilgrim*, 16 January 2007, The Origins of Early Modern Literature, Humanities Research Online [http://www.hrionline.ac.uk/origins/frame.html, accessed 11.1.2012]. For Nicholls's biography, see Alejandro Cioranescu, *Thomas Nichols, mercader de azúcar, hispanista y hereje. Con la edición y traducción de su Descripción de las Islas Afortunadas* (La Laguna: Instituto de Estudios Canarios, 1963) and R.C.D. Baldwin, 'Nicholls, Thomas (1532–1601)', in *Oxford Dictionary of National Biography*, Oxford University Press, 2004; online edn, January 2008 [http://www.oxforddnb.com/view/article/20124, accessed 11.1.2012].
[26] Francisco Javier Castillo, 'The English Renaissance and the Canary Islands: Thomas Nichols and Edmund Scory', *SEDERI*, 2 (1992), 57–70 (68).

of Chyna, which adioyneth to the East Indya, was printed in that year. The origin of this was a Spanish text no longer extant, probably authored by a Spanish merchant who had travelled to China.[27] Nicholls clearly saw himself as particularly well placed to introduce Spanish travel writings to an English audience, especially when describing lands he himself knew, as he wrote in his *Pleasant Description of the Fortunate Ilandes, called the Ilands of Canaria* (1583): 'Thus much have I written of these ilands by experience, because I was a dweller there, as I have sayd before, the space of seven yeares.'[28] The same argument and insistence on the importance of the traveller's direct experience was to be made by the travelling Pilgrim who is the informant in Nicholls's *A pleasant Dialogue*. The Pilgrim calls attention to his personal experience of the lands and people he describes, claiming that he 'will say no more then I have harde at their owne mouthes' and insisting to his interlocutor that 'if you had seene it as I did, you would have sayd so'.[29] In doing so, and in including in his account phrases such as 'I sawe' (1 B7v), 'I espyed' (1 C1r), 'I never saw the lyke' (1 C4r) and so on, the Pilgrim is employing the common travellers' technique of insisting on the authority of the eyewitness account. A travel narrative gained legitimacy from its author's capacity to describe 'what mine eyes have seen', and such writings frequently employed the language of direct experience in order to lay claim to this authority.[30] But, of course, mendacious travel narratives might make just the same claims, leading to the associations between travelling and lying which became so common.[31] Fictional travel narratives notoriously claimed first-person experience of fantastic and impossible sights and encounters; it is within this permeable boundary between fact and fiction that utopia is itself located. The Pilgrim's claims to direct experience and truth thus serve simultaneously to claim verisimilitude for his account and to undermine such assertions of veracity in a manner which links the text to genuine travel writing, 'false' travel writing and utopia.[32]

Like Hythloday in *Utopia*, the Pilgrim in *A pleasant Dialogue* speaks with the dubious authority of the traveller, and does so in conversation with an interlocutor

---

[27] Castillo, 'The English Renaissance and the Canary Islands' p. 68.

[28] Thomas Nicholls, *A Pleasant Description of the Fortunate Ilandes, called the Ilands of Canaria* (1583), p. 123.

[29] T[homas] N[icholls], *A pleasant Dialogue*, Part 1, sig. A5v; Part 2, sig. C4r. All further references will be to this edition, and will be given in the text in the form (1 A5v, 2 C4r).

[30] John Cartwright, *The Preacher's Travels* (London, 1611), sig. B2r, quoted in William H. Sherman, 'Stirrings and Searchings (1500–1720)', in *The Cambridge Companion to Travel Writing*, ed. by Peter Hulme and Tim Youngs (Cambridge: Cambridge University Press, 2002), pp. 17–36 (p. 31).

[31] See Sherman, 'Stirrings and Searchings (1500–1720)', p. 31.

[32] For the 'acute problems of authenticity and credibility' encountered by authors of Renaissance travel literature and the blurred boundaries between 'true' and 'false' travel writing, see Sherman, 'Stirrings and Searchings (1500–1720)', p. 31. On the relationship between travel and utopia, see Chloë Houston, 'Introduction', in *New Worlds Reflected: Travel and Utopia in the Early Modern Period*, ed. by Chloë Houston (Farnham: Ashgate, 2010), pp. 1–14.

who is ignorant of the places he has visited: the Lady Listra, who is the supposed author of the first dedicatory letter to Dyer and of the text. By asserting Listra's authorship in the preliminary material, Nicholls playfully maintains the fiction of her existence, just as the letters which prefaced early editions of More's *Utopia* discussed the island and Hythloday as though they were real. Claiming authorship of 'this little dialogue', '*Listra*, of *Corinth*' apologizes for her 'base stile' in English, the language which she has wished to learn above all others (1 A2r, 1 A2v). The dialogue itself, however, is delivered by an unknown narrator in the third person, and Listra appears in it on her way into Corinth from 'her sumptuous house in the Countrey' (1 A3r). The text falls into two parts, with the first consisting of Listra's meeting with the Pilgrim, who tells her about the city of Crangalor, a community of 'Christians in *East India*' which is portrayed as an ideal society (1 A4r). The second part is prefaced by a further dedicatory letter to Dyer, this time supposedly authored by the Pilgrim on Listra's behalf, and is again narrated by an unknown third person. The presence of multiple voices in the text (the Pilgrim, Listra, the narrator) calls to mind the many voices present in More's *Utopia*; indeed, both texts are ambiguous about the narrator's 'true' voice in a manner typical of the dialogue form, and this ambiguity has the effect of distancing the author from his text. (As Jon R. Snyder noted in his study of Italian Renaissance theories of dialogue: 'The dialogist leaves no signature within the work itself; its writing belongs, in a sense, to no one.')[33] In their second reported encounter and conversation, Listra and the Pilgrim discuss various other places that he has visited on his journey into Asia, namely Zanzibar, Pembay, Cananor, Quiloa, Coben and Benalcasar. The dialogue ends with the Pilgrim on his travels once more, having vowed to reach Ethiopia and leave his body 'at my returne in *Aden*, or in *Coryzo*' (2 C7r).

A pleasant Dialogue can be considered a utopia in that the first part of the text gives an account of a fictional ideal society, that of Crangalor; the rest of the dialogue offers examples of good practice from other societies. The Lady Listra – unusual in Tudor dialogue in being a female participant in the conversation – serves the function of the ignorant interlocutor, questioning the Pilgrim on his experiences and offering interpretations. This relationship between the Pilgrim and the Lady is typical of the basic model common to dialogue of late antiquity, in which the participants often took the roles of teacher and pupil.[34] The text employs other features common to the dialogue form, particularly in its efforts to set the scene of the conversation. In the first part of the text, for example, Nicholls describes the clothing of his interlocutors (1 A3r) and sets his scene on the road 'toward Corinth' (1 A3r), describing the passing of time as the conversation continues: 'the sunne declyneth apace' (1 B8v) and 'night approcheth on so faste' (1 C1v). The conversation of the second part takes place at Listra's house, after the Pilgrim has rested and while he is waiting for Listra's tailor to make him new clothing (2 A4v–B1r). *A pleasant Dialogue* also particularly calls to mind aspects of More's

---

[33] Snyder, *Writing the Scene of Speaking*, pp. 27–8.
[34] Rudolf Hirzel, *Der Dialog: ein literarhistorischer Versuch*, 2 vols (Leipzig: S. Hirzel, 1895), II, 364–5; see Smarr, *Joining the Conversation*, p. 21.

Utopia, in both its content and its paratext. The dedicatory letter in the voice of one of the interlocutors, for example, evokes the letters with which More prefaced the two books of his own dialogue, while the title of Nicholls's dialogue recalls that of More's *De optimo reipublicae statu*.³⁵ Indeed, the character of the Pilgrim himself seems a version of More's Hythloday. The Pilgrim, like Hythloday, has 'travelled over many countries', is 'a man well growne in yeeres', just as Hythloday is 'a man of advanced years', and both men wear long beards and long cloaks (1 A3r).³⁶ More particularly, certain aspects of the society of Crangalor call to mind the practices of the Utopians; for example, their mutual distaste for sumptuous clothing (1 A5v).³⁷ Although *A pleasant Dialogue* thus evokes its utopian forebear in a number of ways, its deviations from *Utopia* – most especially Nicholls's preference for calling a spade a spade, a habit of which no one could accuse Thomas More – mark the disparity between Nicholls's genuinely idealized images of human society and More's ironic, complex portrayal of Utopia.

Nicholls's dialogue is explicit on the benefits of travel and its status as a godly activity. The Pilgrim explains to the Lady that the more he travels, the more he sees of God's works, and the more reason he has to give praise: 'I and suche other poore Pilgrimes doo often see by Lande and Sea, the admyrable workes of the almightie [...] I dooe dayly more and more, praise God, who is so great' (1 A3v). His pilgrimage is the work of his life, ending 'when my body is layed in the Grave', and all lives are pilgrimages: 'truely, al mankinde hath but a pilgrimage in this worlde: yea although they live at home in their native Countrey and delectable houses, an ende they must have of their pilgrimage' (1 A3v). This exchange, which takes place directly before the Pilgrim describes Crangalor, establishes the value of the traveller's stories and their application to all people, even the 'foolish' who 'wyll holde me for a lyar' (1 A3v). The insistence on the benefits of travel, the truth of the traveller's tale and the universality of pilgrimage set the tone for the following 'godly conversation' (1 B8v), in which the Pilgrim's observations on the practices of foreign lands are intended to have direct application to the readership in England.

Listra, as the ignorant questioner of the knowledgeable traveller, stands in for the reader in her conversation with the Pilgrim. Her frequent promptings of his narrative ('tell me father Pilgrime' [1 A3v], 'I pray you say' [1 B8v], etc.) mimic both the act of reading, in which curiosity stimulates the reader to keep turning the pages, and the act of conversation, which is the subject of dialogue. *A pleasant Dialogue*, like other Renaissance dialogues, is both 'a representation of a communicative process' and a communication itself. Here, as Virginia Cox has remarked of the dialogue form, the 'oral exchange depicted in a dialogue acts as a kind of fictional shadow to the literary transaction between the reader and the text'.³⁸ The reader is clearly intended to follow Listra's example in finding the

---

³⁵ Shrank, 'Stammering, Snoring and Other Problems in the Early Modern English Dialogue', p. 113.
³⁶ *Utopia*, 49/ 20–22.
³⁷ *Utopia*, 127/ 1–5, 167/ 27–39.
³⁸ Cox, *The Renaissance Dialogue*, p. 5.

Pilgrim's conversation edifying as well as interesting. Her comments reflect the enriching effect of the exchange, modelling the education which Nicholls offers to the reader. Thus, following the Pilgrim's description of a 'Tragicall show' he saw in Pembay, in which the child-performers were killed by 'lurking Death' (2 B4r) in order to demonstrate the ubiquity of death, Listra interprets the 'blessed exercise' as demonstrating how 'God hath endued this people with the lyght of his holie spirite' (2 B5r). Periodically she reflects on her process of education and enjoyment of it: 'I have father Pilgrime throughly understood all your talke' (1 B5r); 'loth I am to leave your godly conversation' (1 B8v).

By the end of the second conversation, the friendship between the Pilgrim and Listra is such that she wishes to maintain him in Corinth on a stipend, and, when he insists on continuing his travels, both weep at their parting. The strength of the Pilgrim's impression on the Lady – her offered payment no doubt hints at a desire for patronage which Nicholls himself would not have refused – and the benefit she gains from his conversation reflect an emphasis on the edification of the individual which characterizes the text as a whole. The text offers examples of good people who, as a result of their goodness, perform their civic roles well. Listra herself is a model of Christian charity, calling her assistance to the Pilgrim a duty to God (2 B1r). Elsewhere, the text recounts the importance of the personal qualities of the individuals encountered and offers these qualities as exempla to the reader for both good and ill. So, the Pilgrim recalls an honest judge, who refused to be swayed by bribes from an apothecary and a butcher when judging their case, recounting 'this merry tale' so 'that you may know how in this happy Lande, it prevaileth not for the ritch to say I have a fat purse' (1 B2r–B2v). In contrast is the example of a bad judge, who accepts a goose stuffed with gold as a bribe, and in consequence has his leg 'sawen off, with a woodden sawe, in the open Market place' (1 A7v). The Prince of Crangalor then asks the judge, 'sirra is the stuffing of a Goose good meate'?, to which the judge makes no reply; the example is so effective, 'that bribes were cleane banished' (1 A8r). The Lady's interpretation of this latter anecdote is that 'this Prince may welbe called the Deputie of God', and the judges are 'so upright in Justice' (1 A8r). The effectiveness of the society, and the good behaviour of its people, depend on the presence of morally upright individuals in positions of power who are kept in check by a good and worthy Prince. Social institutions (with the exception of prisons, in which Nicholls presumably had a personal interest, having spent time in jail) are largely ignored in favour of anecdotes recounting the correct behaviour of individual office-holders, such as judges, lawyers and clergymen. It has been suggested that Nicholls uses the fictive society of Crangalor to 'castigate English society for not living up to its potential as a Christian commonwealth', but the text does not in consequence call for social reform, or even suggest practical ways in which that reform might be undertaken.[39] Rather, *A pleasant Dialogue* 'does not re-envisage society; it populates it with idealised incumbents'.[40] It is as a result of these idealized incumbents that Crangalor emerges as an ideal society: 'a blessed

---

[39] Deitch, '"Dialoguewise": Discovering Alterity in Elizabethan Dialogues', p. 54.

[40] Shrank, 'Stammering, Snoring and Other Problems in the Early Modern English Dialogue', p. 114.

Lande' (1 B7r), a 'Terrenall paradise' (1 B7v). And lest the reader conclude that the fault with England is in its monarch, rather than the moral qualities of its populace, a fulsome encomium on Elizabeth is inserted. At the end of the first part of the text, Listra asks her informant whether he has ever been in England. He has, once, been briefly in London 'to take shipping into *Scithia*' (1 C1r), and his sole comment on England is on the glory of its monarch, 'a vertuous Mayden Queene, whose beautye and rare vertues, whose wisdom and synguler learning: yea her wonderful knowledge in sundry languages and the like, I never heard nor knewe in in any parte of the worlde where I have traveiled into' (1 C1r). No fault can be found with such a monarch, and no serious criticism is offered of her institutions; but her people may have something to learn from the virtuous examples offered in the *Dialogue*.

A pleasant Dialogue's focus on individual rather than social sin marks its Protestant character and its alignment with contemporary Protestant writings and sermons. In his book on public welfare in Renaissance England, Paul Slack has contended that there was a shift in interest in the Elizabethan period from social sins to individual ones, which he suggests could be attributed to Protestantism and the revival of classical satire.[41] This shift has been noted by other historians of Reformation England. Patrick Collinson, for example, describing the religious and cultural change in the period in *The Birthpangs of Protestant England*, posits that there was an alteration in the kinds of sins that were addressed in the pulpit. Firstly, he notes,

> *sins* are the target, rarely institutions. This was preaching which assumed and underwrote the social and political order, offering no challenge to it. There may have been a perceptible shift from the 'social' sins complained of in Edward's days, in a word 'covetousness', to the 'moral' and personal offences which exercised the Jacobean pulpit: drunkenness, whoredom, Sabbath violation, swearing.[42]

Collinson contends that these personal misdemeanours were criticized because to 'indulge in such sins was to expose the entire community to divine retribution'.[43] The sins of individuals mattered because they risked the wrath of God; for Protestant preachers and reformers alike, then, an essential means of improving the community was to improve the moral character of the individuals within it. As Antoinina Bevan Zlatar has more recently argued: 'In the sixteenth century, offences in the commonwealth were invariably understood to generate from individual failings, and framed in explicitly religious terms – they constituted a violation of the Ten Commandments.'[44]

A pleasant Dialogue marks this progression towards a focus on '"moral" and personal offences'. And, as one would expect, it delivers explicitly Protestant teachings to its readership. As Shrank comments, 'the bent of the work is unmistakably reformist, with its approval of "godly conuersation" (B8v) and the

---

[41] Slack, *From Reformation to Improvement*, pp. 10–11, n. 29.
[42] Collinson, *The Birthpangs of Protestant England*, pp. 18–19 (emphases Collinson's).
[43] Collinson, *The Birthpangs of Protestant England*, p. 19.
[44] Zlatar, *Reformation Fictions*, p. 9.

emphasis placed on preaching by the clergy in the exemplary commonweal of Crangalor (A5r), in contrast to the derision of relics (A3v) and of the one "papist" community ("Coben") the pilgrim encounters in his travels ([2]C3r–4r).[45] So, for example, the citizens of Crangalor reject the notion of purgatory and embrace a Protestant vision of eternal life:

> P: The people in the Countrey are fully perswaded, that there are but two wayes of eternitye, the one leadeth unto perpetual ioy and everlasting, felicity, and the other to everlasting, horrible and unquenchable hell fier, the which bothe places, shall have no end, whilest God is God.
>
> L: The name of Jesus be praised for such a Country and people. (1 B3v)

In a manner typical of the dialogues of this period, Nicholls dramatizes the messages of the pulpit for his readership. The Pilgrim takes on the role of preacher, offering moral guidance and biblical exegesis, while the Lady acts as his congregation, chiming in, as above, with 'The name of Jesus be praised' and similar responses at the end of his speeches. At times, this dramatization of the preacher's voice is barely disguised, as in the relation of a practice of the people of Quiloa, who, on the feast of Mary Magdalene, gather together 'all the light women and common harlots' at a 'feast' attended by other members of the community (including, on this instance, the Pilgrim). On this occasion,

> an excellent learned man dyd preach the conversion of *Mary Magdalen*, declaring of her wantonnesse, and worldly delyghtes. But quoth he: when she has tasted of the sweete doctrine of Christ our maister, her eyes were then opened, where shee sawe that fylthie puddell of sinne, that she was entered into. And then calling for grace, the spirit of the Lorde was not denyed her. (2 C2r–C2v)

The Pilgrim describes the 'lowde voyce' of the preacher and his rhetorical skill in achieving the 'conversion' of fifteen of the women. His report reproduces not only parts of the sermon preached, but also the reaction of the congregation, as an example to the Lady and thus the reader: 'Truely Madame, if you had heard this Gospell preached, you woulde have sayd that a hart of stone would have gushed out, with teares and sobbes' (2 C2v). In this manner, Nicholls's dialogue establishes itself as a handbook of guidance for the individual reader, providing dramatic examples of both good and bad behaviour and offering lessons to be drawn from the Pilgrim's experiences. Thus, the description of the idealized society of Crangalor relies on anecdotes, brief narratives and moral readings of these occurrences (for example, for the various punishments which are meted out for antisocial behaviour). Again, the Pilgrim's speech frequently mimics the tone of the pulpit. He explains that Crangalor's divines, for example, are quick to find out faults 'by some honest meanes', because:

---

[45] Shrank, Entry on *A Pleasant Dialogue between Listra and a Pilgrim*, 16 January 2007.

they doo well know, that they themselves, shall come to judgement, and be Judged, so that according to the oppinion of *S. Jerom*, they have dayly the sound of the Trumpet in their eares, that shall call to Judgement. And this is the principall cause, that they do live in the feare of God, and are blessed. (1 B2v–B3r)

Making suitable response to this sermon-like speech, the Lady replies, 'I doo most highly praise this godly rule and order' (1 B3r).

The second part of *A pleasant Dialogue* increasingly incorporates such dramatic elements into the Pilgrim's narrative, most notably through occurrences such as the court of death and the play that he witnesses (2 C4v). In doing so it demonstrates the potentially dramatic qualities of the dialogue form, which it particularly shares with contemporary polemical dialogues. Antoinina Bevan Zlatar has characterized the Elizabethan polemical dialogue as 'intrinsically dramatic', 'with its cast of individualized types conversing in real time and space'; these are features shared by the utopian dialogues considered here.[46] Although not a polemical text, *A pleasant Dialogue* is fundamentally a religious and markedly Protestant one in its moral lessons to the reader and the methods by which those lessons are conveyed. The moral, reformist tone of the dialogue may have been partly motivated by a desire to appeal to its dedicatee; as Leicester's protégé, Dyer was part of a group (including Fulke Greville and Philip Sidney) whose own literary output often promoted the Protestant politics of the Leicester faction.

Sivqila

Christopher Hatton, the dedicatee of the other utopian dialogue to be considered here, was also an associate of Leicester. Not much is known about the life of Thomas Lupton, the author of *Sivqila: Too Good to be True* (1580), but his surviving publications suggest a tendency to moralistic nationalism and a strongly held belief in money as the root of all evil. Indeed, Lupton's distaste for a monetary economy (evinced by his suggestion in his 1578 morality play *All for Money* that money prevents people from behaving with good moral conduct) are reminiscent of Hythloday's belief that the removal of money leads directly to the eradication of crime.[47] Lupton's interest in social reform is reflected in other of his texts, such as *A Persuasion from Papistry* (1581), in which he recommends to the queen a form of national insurance scheme 'which would lead not only to the repair of broken bridges and coastal defences but also require the rich and noble to pay annual

---

[46] Zlatar, *Reformation Fictions*, p. 21.

[47] G.K. Hunter, 'Lupton, Thomas (*fl.*1572–1584)', *Oxford Dictionary of National Biography* (Oxford: Oxford University Press, 2004) [http://www.oxforddnb.com/view/article/17204, accessed 30.1.2012]; 'In Utopia all greed for money was entirely removed with the use of money. What a mass of troubles was then cut away! What a crop of crimes was then pulled up by the roots!' (*Utopia*, 241/ 39; 243/ 1–2).

sums for the support of the indigent and sickly'.[48] *A Persuasion from Papistry*, along with *The Christian against the Jesuit* (1581), engages with the controversy of John Nichols, a lapsed Protestant clergyman, who returned to England from Rome in 1581 and, following a period of imprisonment, was persuaded to return to Protestantism. The tone and content of such writings has been taken as evidence, as Elliot Rose has suggested, that Lupton was a man 'who expected credit and reward for denouncing things, like greed and popery, that everyone was against'.[49]

Whatever credit he hoped for, Lupton, like Nicholls, had powerful patrons in mind when dedicating his utopian writings. Christopher Hatton served as a privy councillor; a favourite of the queen, he was soon to be made Chancellor. Though not always a wealthy man, he was a rising star at court and was to become something of a spokesman for the queen, serving when an MP as a channel for her communications with Parliament.[50] During the preceding decade, Hatton, with his many Catholic connections, had come under suspicion as a crypto-papist, and, like his associate Richard Bancroft, has been identified as demonstrating anti-puritan tendencies.[51] Despite his rumoured Catholic sympathies, however, Hatton took a moderate approach to religious questions and is elsewhere listed as a dedicatee in a group of 'men of reformist sensibilities with influence in court and at government', who are enjoined in dedications to further advance the Reformation.[52] Lupton evidently thought of him as being possibly sympathetic to the reforming message of *Sivqila*, and interested in its efforts to demonstrate the failings of contemporary society in comparison to an ideal one.

The text which Lupton offered to Hatton relates the conversation between Sivqila ('Aliquis' backwards, i.e. 'Anyone') and Omen ('Nemo'/'no-one') about their respective countries. Sivqila, a native of Ailgna ('Anglia'/'England') has travelled amongst papists, Turks and cannibals before arriving at Mauqsun ('Nusquam'/'Nowhere') and meeting Omen. The ensuing conversation both lays bare the failings of Ailgna and holds the exemplary Mauqsun up for praise: Mauqsun has no equal in all the world 'for goodnesse, godlinesse, obediencie, equitie, vertuous lyving, plaine dealing, and true meaning'.[53] Like *A pleasant Dialogue*, *Sivqila* is dominated by conversation in which a naive listener questions an informed traveller and is educated, via a series of anecdotes and examples of

---

[48] Hunter, 'Lupton, Thomas'.

[49] Elliot Rose, 'Too Good to Be True: Thomas Lupton's Golden Rule', in *Tudor Rule and Revolution: Essays for G.R. Elton from His American Friends*, ed. by Dellroyd J. Guth and John W. McKenna (Cambridge: Cambridge University Press, 1982), pp. 183–200 (p. 185).

[50] Wallace T. MacCaffrey, 'Hatton, Sir Christopher (c. 1540–1591)', *Oxford Dictionary of National Biography* (Oxford: Oxford University Press, 2004) [http://www.oxforddnb.com/view/article/12605, accessed 30.1.2012].

[51] See Patrick Collinson, *Richard Bancroft and Elizabethan Anti-Puritanism* (Cambridge: Cambridge University Press, 2013), pp. 36–7, p. 52, p. 185.

[52] Zlatar, *Reformation Fictions*, p. 18.

[53] *Sivqila: Too Good to be True* (1580), p. 4. All further references will be to this edition and will be given in the text.

good practice, about an ideal society's customs. The text was evidently at least moderately successful, as at least two further editions were produced and *The second part and knitting vp of the Boke entitled Too good to be true* appeared in 1581. This second part was dedicated, like Robynson's *Utopia*, to William Cecil. Cecil, of course, was a powerful man at court and was committed to religious reform, though within the existing political and social order.[54]

Hatton and Cecil clearly seemed to Lupton to be suitable recipients of the barely disguised lesson of *Sivqila*, namely that England should try to be less like Ailgna and more like Mauqsun. Lupton puts forward the rather obvious and tediously lengthy argument that bad behaviour is bad for society, and the text explains how such behaviour can be punished and thus eradicated. In putting forward an ideal community in which good laws have achieved a moral society, Lupton probably sought to garner patronage, and it is possible that he was successful: little is known of him after the last of his published writings in 1583, after which, it has been speculated, 'he either died or got the appointment he was angling for, and so disappeared from the historical record'.[55] *Sivqila* is more obviously presented as social advice than is *A pleasant Dialogue*, and it is usually taken to be a straightforward model for social reform. So, William Sherman has noted that '[w]hereas the practical purpose of More's *Utopia* has been a matter for debate, Lupton's is painfully clear and firmly rooted in socioeconomic reform', and Elliot Rose has argued that, in spite of its title, *Sivqila* 'is clearly intended to impress as a model for real reforms [...]. This is the whole purpose of the book'.[56] In his categorization of Renaissance ideal societies, J.C. Davis places *Sivqila* amongst the 'perfect moral commonwealths', reflecting the fact that, like Nicholls, Lupton populates his ideal community with ideal citizens.[57] The text can be understood as a utopia due to its portrayal of an ideal society and, as in *Utopia*, this idealization is heightened through contrast to a real society.

Lupton evidently does seek to promote Mauqsun as a model for England; Sivqila makes this clear when he speaks of his desire to be allowed to visit Mauqsun, which no strangers are allowed to enter, in order 'to have seene the maners and orders therof, whereby I myght have revealed them in mine owne countrey, when I had bin come home, that they might have bin practised there' (5). His desire to improve Ailgna/England, however, that it might 'excel other

---

[54] Wallace T. MacCaffrey, 'Cecil, William, first Baron Burghley (1520/21–1598)', *Oxford Dictionary of National Biography* (Oxford: Oxford University Press, 2004) [http://www.oxforddnb.com/view/article/4983, accessed 30.1.2012].

[55] Rose, 'Too Good to Be True: Thomas Lupton's Golden Rule', p. 184. Lupton aimed ever higher with his dedications: *A Persuasion from Papistrie* was dedicated to no less a person than the queen herself.

[56] William H. Sherman, 'Anatomizing the Commonwealth: Language, politics and the Elizabethan social order', in *The Project of Prose in Early Modern Europe and the New World*, ed. by Elizabeth Fowler (Cambridge: Cambridge University Press, 1997), p. 112; Rose, 'Too Good to Be True: Thomas Lupton's Golden Rule', p. 185.

[57] J.C. Davis, *Utopia and the Ideal Society: A Study of English Utopian Writing 1516–1700* (Cambridge: Cambridge University Press, 1981; repr. 1983), p. 29.

in goodnesse and equitie' (5) is hampered by the equally pressing need not to criticize the English status quo too strongly. Thus, when discussing the clergy, Sivqila assures Omen that there are many godly preachers in Ailgna, who 'are very diligent in preaching the trueth of the Gospell, and do mightely thereby reprove sinne'. Due to the actions of the Devil, however, or the failings of the minsters' flock, 'theyr painefull preaching doth little prevaile' (5). The fault, then, lies not with the clergy, but with the congregation. Similarly, when discussing the punishment of crime, Lupton is careful to note that the magistrates and rulers are not to blame for high levels of misdemeanour:

> Thoughe we have mercifull Magistrates, godlye Governours, sage Superiours, pollitike Rulers, and wittie Counsailoures: yet we have a great sort that are so greedy of gaine, so madde of mony, and so mindeful of mischeef, that they are as much ashamed to committe these offences, as a horse is loath to eate his meate when he commeth newly from labour. (145)

A reluctance to criticize the ruling classes may be one reason why Lupton focuses on the sinful behaviour of the masses, but it is also telling of his primary concern in *Sivqila*, which is to identify and rectify individual moral failings. As in *A pleasant Dialogue*, the problems of society are seen to be rooted in individual sin, which must be corrected by a simple but effective moral code of laws. The text does seek to promote social reform, but its primary interest is the moral reform of the citizens via examples of good practice, which it encourages the reader to note by dramatizing the reader's response through the character of Sivqila. Like the Lady Listra, Sivqila functions as the equivalent of the reader in learning about Mauqsun, questioning Omen about its practices and offering comments and praise: 'Truely an excellent good order' (40), 'Oh happie people' (71), 'Oh that we had that lawe' (77), etc. The dialogue contains a third 'voice' in the frequent marginal comments, which draw the reader's attention to particular points with directions, such as 'Consider this' (31) and 'Marke this' (53), and offer moralistic interpretations, such as 'A covetous rich man wel served' (32), 'Stoute fighters are not good men' (53) and 'Faire women are snares for fooles' (60). In these ways the text signals its concern for the edification of the reader, who is not only the noble patron, in a position to motivate social reform, but the individual reader, who may benefit from the frequent exhortations to mark the moral lessons of the conversation.

In keeping with this focus on individual sin and its correction, *Sivqila* consists largely of the description of the sins of individuals in Mauqsun and the laws and practices which have been instituted to deal with them. Thus we learn of the vanity of elaborate clothing, which in Ailgna takes the form of 'excesse of apparell, suche gawdy going, and such peacockly and new fashions every day: (for all the preaching and teaching)' (20). In Mauqsun only one fashion is worn, a custom which is maintained not by a particular rule but by social pressure:

> if anye with us happe to chaunge the fashion of his apparell, and go otherwise than the auntient custome of our Countrey doth allow: he shall not onely be pointed at and mocked therefore, but also noted of such inconstancie, that he shall never after be called into any office or place of credite. (22)

Should the threat of such ignominy be insufficient, it is backed up by legal censure: 'furthermore, he shal loose half his goods, whiche shall be distributed for the reliefe of the poore' (22). Insubordinate children, quarrelsome men, disobedient wives, drunkards, diceplayers: all who behave antisocially in Mauqsun are obliged through severe punishment to mend their ways. Young people who are disobedient to their parents, for example, are beaten 'on theyr bare skin thirtie stripes with a whip' for thirty days, and, if their parents are rich, are disinherited (40). A poor man who is found drunk is displayed in the marketplace, must give to the ruler of his town a weekly account of his movements for a year afterwards, must not go in a tavern for that period and must wear a badge with a picture of a pig on it so that he may be identified; anyone who drinks in his company is subject to the same punishment (58–9). These are severe punishments indeed. As in *A pleasant Dialogue*, the text draws attention to the good behaviour of individual office-holders, such as humble members of the nobility (96), judges (112) and surgeons (121). As Siqvila learns about the idealized society of Mauqsun through these examples, he also undergoes a personal process of education and enlightenment. He tells Omen at their parting that 'your excellent discourse of youre Countrey customes, manners, orders, and lawes, hath bin suche a deliyghte to me [...] that it hath fed me as wel as any foode' (177). Sivqila represents the pious pilgrim, who at the end of the conversation puts his trust in God to lead him safely home. Omen responds:

> That same God guide you, that you give glory unto. I know you are faythfull, patient, and given to prayer: and therefore whosoever prayeth to him faithfullye, he will protect them most safely. [...] God blesse you and defende you in youre journey. (178)

The 'Amen' with which Sivqila replies to this prayer is a suitably pious conclusion to the moral education which the text has offered.

Lupton's utopian dialogue thus offers both a social lesson, which might be summed up as 'good laws make good people', and an individual one, which is that each person should follow Christ and behave in accordance with his teachings. Though Lupton undoubtedly favoured the level of social control described by Omen, he must have realized that its achievement was unlikely in his own society. It is hard to believe, for example, that he genuinely thought that the young women of England should be encouraged to tear their sexually active peers apart with their teeth, as the maidens of Mauqsun would do to an unmarried woman who lost her virginity or became pregnant (64). Rather, he seeks to strengthen the moral messages through example, and to focus the reader's attention on the life to come:

> though it be sweete here, it will be sower in hel: though it be pleasant here, it will be painefull there: and though it be delightfull here, it will be detestable there. Therefor none but fooles will choose short pleasures for long paines, and short solace for endlesse sorrowes. (63)

As in Nicholls's *Dialogue*, biblical exegesis is never far from the surface, as Omen quotes the 'sentence of Christ' that 'Whatsoever you woulde that men shoulde do to you, even so do ye to them' and 'The poore in spirite are so blessed, that theirs is the Kingdom of Heaven' (32, 33).

Like *A pleasant Dialogue*, then, the primary concerns of *Sivqila* are the individual moral failings of its readership and the possibility of reforming these through example. However, even at this level, the text seems to signal a lack of belief in its own potential efficacy. The subtitle, 'Too Good to be True', echoes through the conversation between Omen and Sivqila, who frequently opines that 'Truly me thinks it is too good to be true' (32). Mauqsun, restricted to strangers like Bensalem in Francis Bacon's *New Atlantis*, can be visited only by Omen 'No-one', and by no one who does not already live there (4), and is thus inaccessible to both Sivqila and the reader of the dialogue. Moreover, the central premise of the text, that antisocial behaviour can be eradicated through social control and suitable punishment, is undermined by the sheer volume of crime and bad behaviour that Omen relates to have taken place there. Far from being absent or confined only to memory, immoral behaviour seems to proliferate in Mauqsun. For example, Omen recounts detailed practices for the treatment of those who play at dice or cards, whilst denying that any such exist:

> Sivqila: Is there anye with you that use to play at Dice?
>
> Omen: None at all: But, if there were anye, they would not be swearing Dicers [...] we have a lawe with us, that everye one that playeth at Dice or Cardes for money, or for any other thing of any value, the winner shal forfeite so much and twice as much more as he winneth: and the loser shall forfaite as muche more as hee loseth [...] (93–4)

Omen goes on to detail the exact division of the monies thus obtained, and whence it is paid. In the next breath, however, he claims not to know if this law is 'strictly executed', 'but there is not one Dicer nor yet Carder in all our Countrey' (94). This is typical of the text's attitude towards crime in Mauqsun: it is claimed not to exist, and at the same time the manner of dealing with it is described in great detail. If the former claim is true, then why is the latter practice necessary? Like other dialogues of the period interested in reform, *Sivqila* thus signals its lack of belief in its own potential efficacy. It demonstrates what Shrank has described in English commonweal dialogues as 'manifestations of hesitancy, as they question the effectiveness or ethical positions of their speakers, or – mired in specifics – postpone resolution, or retreat into nostalgic or evasive positions.' This is exactly the position of *Sivqila*, and, as Shrank writes of the commonweal dialogues, '[r]ecurrently, it is prayer that offers the only solution.'[58]

---

[58] Shrank, 'Stammering, Snoring and Other Problems in the Early Modern English Dialogue', p. 115.

Conclusion

These utopian dialogues of the later sixteenth century articulate a shift in utopia, as the utopian mode of discourse becomes concerned with social and moral improvement rather than irony, satire and philosophical enquiry. The dialogue form was useful as a means of interrogating contemporary society and contrasting it with an ideal alternative; it also provided a didactic model for encouraging change. The change sought, however, was not primarily political. Rather, Nicholls and Lupton identified individual moral failings and offered examples of good behaviour to be followed. These 'Reformation fictions', in contributing to the ongoing process of consolidation of Protestantism in English society, demonstrate that the development of utopia in the later sixteenth century was religious in nature. This development was to form an important basis for utopian writing in the seventeenth century, as the utopian mode was used to articulate both political ideals and religious prophecies.

A pleasant Dialogue and *Sivqila* are usefully read as dialogues because the dialogue form, and the features they share with contemporary dialogues, are integral to our understanding of them. It is impossible to avoid concluding, however, that they are less truly dialogic than More's *Utopia*, with its multiple voices and myriad layers of meaning. To borrow Virginia Cox's formulation, they are less 'true dialogue' and more 'elaborate monologue' because, whilst they do dramatize the act of communication, they do not fully incorporate different voices.[59] Each dramatizes the conversation of two people, but, with both interlocutors always in complete agreement and synthesis, the effect is that both sound like mouthpieces for the author. It is the presence of this monologue beneath the dialogue that makes these utopias less complex, less ironic, less playful than More's; and this, too, contributes to the utopia's crucial loss of irony in the later sixteenth century.

---

[59] Cox, *The Renaissance Dialogue*, p. 104.

Chapter 3
'It is the man who speaks with God who knows more': Education and the Decline of Dialogue in *Christianopolis* and *The City of the Sun*

Introduction: The Rise of Utopia and the Decline of Dialogue

Utopias written in the early seventeenth century, like those considered in the last chapter, were by and large less interested in presenting ironic, complicated visions of seemingly ideal societies and more concerned with promoting the values, and specifically the institutions, imagined in their alternative worlds. Before returning to English utopianism via Francis Bacon's *New Atlantis* (1626), it will be useful to consider the European context for the development of utopian literature in the early seventeenth century, when utopias began to move away from the dialogue form. There are, of course, a number of continental European texts published prior to the early seventeenth century which draw on More's *Utopia* in various ways and might themselves be said to constitute or contain utopias, some of which do not present straightforwardly ideal societies but adopt the ironic and satiric elements of their utopian forebears. The five books of François Rabelais's *Gargantua and Pantagruel* (from 1532) are, like *Utopia*, interested in the interconnected nature of spiritual renewal and political affairs.[1] The description of the Abbey of Thélème that ends *Gargantua* has been read as a 'utopian discourse provid[ing] a theology that is also a politics', and a number of scholars have drawn attention to its complex relationship with *Utopia*.[2] Rabelais also drew on the traditions of dialogue and colloquy in composing his *Gargantua* series, and his dystopian Abbey, with its motto of 'Do as thou wilt', constitutes a complex response to *Utopia* and its projection of the monastery and the seemingly ideal society.

Although it is beyond the scope of this book to consider the development of the European utopian tradition in detail, it should not be inferred that English Renaissance utopian writing should not be read in a European context. The importance of that context for the development of dialogues between utopias in this period is demonstrated, for example, by the Rabelaisian elements of Joseph Hall's *Mundus Alter et Idem* (1605). Although he does not allude directly to Rabelais, Hall's dystopian lands and journeys display a landscape, and even a lexicon, that

---

[1] Timothy Hampton, *Literature and Nation in the Sixteenth Century: Inventing Renaissance France* (Ithaca: Cornell University Press, 2001), p. 67.
[2] Hampton, p. 74. See also Christopher Kendrick, *Utopia, Carnival, and Commonwealth in Renaissance England* (Toronto: University of Toronto Press, 2004).

drew on his French predecessor's work.[3] There is a rich tradition of influence and dialogue between European utopias during this period; this chapter, in attempting to flesh out the European context for the development of English utopian literature, will be restricted to two examples of utopian writing from the early seventeenth century, Johann Valentin Andreae's *Reipublicae christianopolitanae descriptio* or *Christianopolis* (1619) and Tommaso Campanella's *La Città del Sole* or *The City of the Sun* (1623). These utopias typify the move away from the dialogue form, but also the continued incorporation of elements of that form. They also display the utopia's developing engagement with the literature of travel. Whereas More satirized the notion that travel and travel writing were exclusively beneficial, and Nicholls and Lupton were largely uninterested in the context of travel and the wider world, by the early seventeenth century the travel narrative had become an increasingly widely read form of literature and one which was well suited to the critique of both foreign and domestic societies.

Combining elements of both the dialogue form and the travel narrative, *Christianopolis* and *The City of the Sun* are also important precursors to later English utopian literature, as Chapters 4 and 5 will demonstrate. These utopias share a number of aspects which were to feature prominently in later seventeenth-century utopian fiction; in particular, the presence of an ideal college or school which forms the institutional heart of the ideal society. In general terms, the seventeenth century saw a growth in the volume of utopian literature and a decrease in use of the dialogue. Although sixteenth-century utopias relied on the dialogue form, this relationship between utopia and dialogue was in decline by the early seventeenth century. Nina Chordas has recently noted this disunion of utopia and dialogue, arguing that, with the development of print culture, the worlds of discourse and of thought became increasingly detached, as 'without this grounding in speech as intrinsic to the process of reading, dialogue began to lose its *raison d'être*'.[4] As utopias sought to reach wider and more diverse audiences, they moved away from the dialogue form towards other means of expression.

The objective of this chapter is not to explain the decline of dialogue per se, but to consider how these two utopian texts used dialogue, and why the dialogue form became less useful to utopia during the early seventeenth century. As utopia became more practically focused and less interested in satire and philosophical enquiry, it had less use for the conventional structures of the dialogue form. Nonetheless, the two utopias considered in this chapter both make use of elements of dialogue; in *The City of the Sun* in particular, dialogue provides a useful means of expressing moral

---

[3] See Anne Lake Prescott, *Imagining Rabelais in Renaissance England* (New Haven: Yale University Press, 1998), pp. 112–13 and, for parallels between Rabelais and Mundus, Sanford M. Salyer, 'Renaissance Influences in Hall's Mundus Alter et Idem', *Philological Quarterly*, 6 (1927), 320–34.

[4] Nina Chordas, *Forms in Early Modern Utopia: The Ethnography of Perfection* (Farnham: Ashgate, 2010), p. 27. Virginia Cox analyzes the change and decline of the dialogue in the later Renaissance in Chapters 8 and 9 of *The Renaissance Dialogue: Literary Dialogue in Its Social and Political Contexts, Castiglione to Galileo* (Cambridge: Cambridge University Press, 1992).

teaching. *Christianopolis*'s rejection of the dialogue form signals the beginning of the breaking off of utopian literature from this form, which ceased to be crucial to utopia as utopia became increasingly focused on achieving the reforms it imagined; Campanella and Andreae wanted to motivate the construction of the utopian society in the author's own time and place, and their focus on the ideal institution was a means of realizing this aim. Despite this rejection, *Christianopolis* incorporates elements of dialogue in ways that demonstrate the continued usefulness of notions of conversation and discourse to utopian fiction. Their utopias share a belief in the capacity of education to achieve the ideal society through improving the individuals within it, which, like the dialogue form, is a product of Renaissance humanism.

Early humanist writing about education sought to demonstrate the practical benefits to society of educating its youth. For sixteenth-century humanists such as Rudolph Agricola and Erasmus, education was a way of making the individual serviceable to the community. This 'new philosophy' focused on the utility of education as a means of judging its success; utility was classified as producing 'the kind of competence which will make an individual a responsible, moral and active member of the civic community'.[5] Humanists drew on the classical tenet that a good education makes a man a good member of society, one who can 'really perform his function as a citizen, who is fitted to the demands of both private and public business'.[6] It contributed to a pragmatic brand of humanism which was to flourish during the later sixteenth century, with the development of the belief that the point of a classical education was not necessarily to produce only scholars and philosopher-kings, but useful and active members of a civil and political society. The focus on the utility of education, and the consequent reform of the education system necessary to produce useful citizens, is contemporary with the religious and social reform of the Protestant Reformation of the sixteenth century, and is manifested by humanists such as Vives and Erasmus, who were concerned with producing students who could become fitted for particular roles in society, so that the whole state, and not just the individual, would benefit from education.

These sixteenth-century reformers were themselves drawing on a tradition that stretched back to the earliest days of Renaissance humanism. The fifteenth-century Italian humanist Pier Paolo Vergerio, for example, had perceived the teaching of children as a social duty and found the answer to the question of how to live well in education. Early humanists were convinced that education should fit the individual for civic life; it was a way of usefully coordinating the individual into the social group, and benefitting the whole of society.[7] Thus humanism, as

---

[5] Anthony Grafton and Lisa Jardine, *From Humanism to the Humanities: Education and the Liberal Arts in Fifteenth- and Sixteenth-Century Europe* (London: Duckworth, 1986), p. 168, pp. 163–4.

[6] Grafton and Jardine, *From Humanism to the Humanities*, p. 5, quoting Quintilian, *Institutio oratoria*, 1. pr. 10.

[7] Craig W. Kallendorf, ed. and trans., *Humanist Educational Treatises* (Cambridge, MA: Harvard University Press, 2002), p. 3, p. 5, p. vii; Kenneth Charlton, *Education in Renaissance England* (London: Routledge & Kegan Paul, 1965), p. 297.

it moved away from the scholasticism of the monasteries, showed an interest in instructing administrators, teachers and so on, rather than exclusively priests and aristocrats, and so became focused on the serviceability of learning.

During the sixteenth century, the utility of education was to remain a central theme of pedagogical writing. Following the Reformation it became fundamental to Protestant thinking and formed a core of the Lutheran tradition. The 1520s letters of Martin Luther, for example, reflect his belief that a good society depends on a well-taught citizenry:

> the highest welfare, safety, and power of a city consists in able, learned, wise, upright, cultivated citizens, who can secure, preserve, and utilize every treasure and advantage. [...] Thus, in all the world, even among the heathen, schoolmasters and teachers have been found necessary where a nation was to be elevated.[8]

Similarly, Philip Melanchthon, who was to have considerable influence on the ideals of the Further Reformation of the early seventeenth century, wrote in his orations on the subject that education is for the good of society, not just the individual: 'your studies do not concern only you, but also the state.' Melanchthon reminds his audience of young men, who are learning about the arts, to pay attention to the lower arts as well as the higher, because 'each art has been devised because of its certain usefulness'.[9] Johann Sturm's pedagogical writings evince a similar assurance that society flourishes through schooling, and the best-lived life is one devoted to civic matters. Sturm's belief in education as a vital part of the civilizing process reflects the attitude of humanists in general towards the educability of man.[10] Of central importance to this tradition was the interconnected nature of the reformers' intentions and methods of improving education and their commitment to religious reform. As for later reformers like Andreae, and much later utopian writing, these were goals which went hand in hand in achieving a better society.

Sixteenth-century reformers such as Sturm and Melanchthon not only conceived of education as socially useful but also tried to create or recreate institutions in which their ideal processes of instruction could take place, with the aim that these institutions would eventually equip society with the citizens it needed, graduates who had a basic theological grounding and were fitted for

---

[8] 'Letter to the Mayors and Aldermen of all the Cities of Germany in Behalf of Christian Schools' (1524), trans. by F.V.N. Painter, in Frederick Eby, *Early Protestant Educators: The Educational Writings of Martin Luther, John Calvin, and Other Leaders of Protestant Thought* (New York: McGraw-Hill, 1931), pp. 45–79 (pp. 55–6).

[9] Philip Melanchthon, 'On the order of learning' (1531), in *Philip Melanchthon: Orations on Philosophy and Education*, trans. by Christine F. Salazar, ed. by Sachiko Kusukawa (Cambridge: Cambridge University Press, 1999), pp. 3–8 (p. 5).

[10] Lewis W. Spitz and Barbara Sher Tinsley, *Johann Sturm on Education* (St. Louis: Concordia, 1995), p. 43, p. 49, p. 11.

civic roles. Melanchthon, for example, was called by Duke Ulrich to help with the reform of his and Andreae's alma mater, the University of Tübingen, in 1535. Melanchthon emphasized that Ulrich had asked his opinion on how the university could best fulfil the needs of the 'academic republic' and preserve religion. When he wrote to Jacob Brenz a year later, asking him to lend his help, Melanchthon's reasoning shows that he saw the reforms as having a religious and social purpose:

> I ask you on account of Christ and on account of the welfare of His church to move to Tübingen for a time. You ought to take this office first for the glory of Christ, then for the necessity of the church, lastly even for the country, which you should hold in high respect.[11]

Prior to his association with Tübingen, Melanchthon had already been involved with educational reform, both in theory and in practice, in keeping with his belief that a learned Christian nation must teach its people properly.[12] More than fifty-six cities asked for his help in establishing *gymnasia*, giving rise to the view that he was 'the builder of the first public school system since the days of ancient Rome'.[13] Reformist leaders and pedagogues like Melanchthon were strongly influenced by Christian humanism, and Melanchthon considered himself a biblical humanist in the school of Erasmus.[14] In Melanchthon's practical involvement with the reform of educational establishments and personal commitment to the teaching of classical studies as well as theology, he emphasizes the need for method and the proper compilation of knowledge, as well as a focus on the usefulness of all learning in bringing one closer to Christ. Both of these themes, the organization of knowledge and the concept of useful knowledge, were to play an important part

---

[11] Letter to Jacob Brenz (October 1536), quoted in Richard L. Harrison, Jr., 'Melanchthon's Role in the Reformation of the University of Tübingen', *Church History*, 47:3 (1978), 270–78 (275). Johann Sturm was also involved in the practical reformation of institutions, and developed a liberal arts curriculum for schools through to university level. See Spitz and Tinsley, *Johann Sturm on Education*, p. 12.

[12] See 'Introduction', in *A Melanchthon Reader*, trans. by Ralph Keen (New York: Lang, 1988), pp. 1–41 (p. 8).

[13] Keen, p. 9; Hans Engelland, 'Introduction', in *Melanchthon on Christian Doctrine: Loci Communes 1555*, trans. and ed. by Clyde L. Manschreck (New York: Oxford University Press, 1965), p. vii.

[14] Sachiko Kusukawa describes Melanchthon as a 'Christian humanist' according to the definition offered by Paul Oskar Kristeller: Christian humanists were those 'who applied their classical scholarship to biblical and patristic studies and who adopted and defended in their writings some tenets of Christian religion or theology'. Sachiko Kusukawa, *The Transformation of Natural Philosophy: The Case of Philip Melanchthon* (Cambridge: Cambridge University Press, 1995), p. 3, quoting Paul Oskar Kristeller, 'Humanism', in *The Cambridge History of Renaissance Philosophy*, ed. by Quentin Skinner and Eckhard Kessler, assoc. ed. by Jill Kraye (Cambridge: Cambridge University Press, 1988), pp. 113–37 (p. 133). For Melanchthon's view of himself as an Erasmian biblical humanist, see Melanchthon, *A Melanchthon Reader*, p. 8.

in the utopian writings of the early seventeenth century, including *Christianopolis* and *The City of the Sun*.[15]

The centrality of education to humanism and to reforming initiatives explains why education became such a crucial element of utopian literature during the early seventeenth century, as utopias began to represent societies which their authors wished to see constructed. Utopian literature, too, insisted on the interconnected nature of religious and educational reform; this applies both to the Protestant utopia considered here, *Christianopolis*, and its Catholic predecessor, *The City of the Sun*. The centrality of education to the tradition of social and religious improvement and to humanism in general may also explain why such utopias continued to incorporate elements of dialogue in full or in part: the association between educational practice and dialogue meant that features of dialogue continued to be useful to those creating fictional ideal societies during this period. The best-known utopian dialogue of the period is Campanella's *The City of the Sun*, a dialogue between a knight and a sailor in which the latter tells of his encounter with an ideal city discovered on his travels.

The City of the Sun: Poetical Dialogue and the Institutionalization of the Ideal City

Tommaso Campanella's 'poetical dialogue' *The City of the Sun*, first written in Italian in around 1602 and printed in Latin in 1623, demonstrates how early seventeenth-century utopian writing became increasingly focused on the practical workings and details of the ideal society. The dialogue form in *The City of the Sun* is used more as a narrative framework rather than to relate a realistic conversation; it serves as a structure for a description of how the institutionalization of every aspect of life achieves an ideal society which has education at its heart. The text is presented as a discussion between a 'Knight Hospitaler' and a 'Genoese' sailor who has travelled with Columbus. Thanks to this experience of travel he has encountered an ideal city, the knowledge of which he imparts through conversation. Originally appended to the *Politics*, *The City of the Sun* begins, with no introduction, when the knight asks the sailor to 'Tell me, please, all that happened to you on this voyage'.[16] The 'Genoese' responds with a full description of the city, which he encountered when forced to put ashore at Taprobana

---

[15] For Melanchthon's insistence on the importance of method, see Kusukawa, *The Transformation of Natural Philosophy*, p. 73. For his encyclopaedic approach to teaching and view of dialectics as the basis of all knowledge and method, see Deszo Buzogany, 'Melanchthon as a Humanist and a Reformer', in *Melanchthon in Europe: His Work and Influence beyond Wittenberg*, ed. by Karin Maag (Grand Rapids: Baker Books, 1999), pp. 87–101 (p. 94, pp. 98–9). For his emphasis on useful knowledge, and the use of dialectics for theological ends, see Buzogany, p. 87, p. 92. Engelland describes Andreae's belief that 'sciences all have a common theological task' ('Introduction', p. xxvi).

[16] Tommaso Campanella, *La Città del Sole: Dialogo Poetico/The City of the Sun: A Poetical Dialogue*, trans. by Daniel J. Donno (Berkeley: University of California Press, 1981), p. 27. All further references will be to this edition and will be given in parentheses.

(identified perhaps with a location on the island of Sumatra or with Ceylon).[17] As with the other utopian dialogues considered in this book, the discourse of travel is central to the construction of this imagined conversation; Campanella gives his imaginary city a realistic location and uses the convention of the shipwreck to explain the sailor's arrival at the City of the Sun, following his encounter with 'a large company of armed men and women' (27).

Although the text consists of a conversation between the two men, the bulk of the speech belongs to the sailor, and the knight's function is primarily to prompt disclosure of certain subjects. To this end, he makes specific requests for information, such as: 'tell me the manner of government you found among these people' and 'with whom do they make war and for what reason?' (31, 69). The use of the dialogue form also enhances the didactic nature of Campanella's utopia. The sailor sometimes takes a moral tone, commenting, for example, that 'when self-love is destroyed, only concern for the community remains' when describing the practice of communal property (39). The moral implications of such statements are enhanced when both the reader and the persona of the knight are addressed by the sailor as 'you': for example, 'I can tell you that the love they bear their country is an astonishing thing' (39). In identifying the reader of the text with the listening knight, who has never been to the City of the Sun, Campanella emphasizes the distance between utopia and reality, but he also highlights the universality of the lessons that his dialogue seeks to teach, as the knight's occasional reflections on the moral implications of the sailor's stories guide the reader's response to the text. *The City of the Sun* concludes with the sailor giving an astrological explanation for the reason why England, amongst other nations, is prone to heresy, while Spain and Italy 'have remained under the happy dispensation of the pure Christian law' (125). As he promises to discourse further on 'what is soon to happen in the world', the sailor refuses the knight's exhortations to 'Wait, Wait!' (127). The foreshortened conversation, typical of Renaissance dialogue, thus offers to the reader a tantalizing prospect of further information to come. Campanella's use of the dialogue form both facilitates this open-endedness and encourages the reader's active participation in wanting to know more about the City of the Sun, which is often read as a portrait of the sort of community Campanella would himself have liked to have built.

Giovanni Domenico Campanella was born in Stignano in Calabria in 1568. Upon joining the Dominican order at the age of fourteen, he adopted the name Tommaso in honour of Aquinas, and began a career of devotion to learning and commitment to religious, social and political change which was to see him spend the greater part of four decades in and out of prisons in Italy.[18] When Campanella wrote *The City of the Sun*, he was imprisoned in Castel Nuovo in Naples following his involvement with the Calabrian uprising, a plan to overcome Spanish rule in southern Italy and establish a republic in its place. *The City of the Sun* was first

---

[17] *The City of the Sun*, Introduction, p. 129. All further references to the introduction or notes will be given in the footnotes.

[18] For Campanella's life and prolonged imprisonments, see *The City of the Sun*, Introduction, pp. 1–14.

written in Italian and circulated in manuscript; Campanella had translated it into Latin by 1613, and this was the version printed in 1623 at Frankfurt. As the text first appeared shortly after the Calabrian insurgence, itself an effort to impose social reform, which it is believed Campanella led, it has become common to read *The City of the Sun* as a blueprint for the society he would have established in the wake of the uprising.[19] The text was also written at a time when such reform seemed both necessary and possible; Campanella believed that the year 1600 would herald a period of great upheaval leading to revolution, based on the evidence of recent disasters, astronomical calculations and old prophecies. Although the Calabrian uprising was easily put down, it had considerable backing at the time, being 'supported, or at least abetted, by several of the bishops and by most of the Dominican and Augustinian friars'.[20] Such support suggests that Campanella, like Johann Valentin Andreae, was part of a community that was interested in the prospect of achieving reform on a grand scale. His interest in social reform, if it did inform his writing of *The City of the Sun*, explains why this 'poetical dialogue' is exemplary of early seventeenth-century utopias' increasing interest in the practical workings of ideal societies.

In keeping with his interest in astrology, Campanella's City of the Sun is laid out as a replica of the solar system, 'divided into seven large circuits, named after the seven planets' (27).[21] The foundation of the city according to astrological principles means that it has its own star-chart, with 'the sun in the ascendant in Leo; Jupiter in Leo oriental to the sun; Mercury and Venus in Cancer', and so on (87). The astrological houses chosen here seem appropriate to the Solarians' aims in founding their city, as they are associated with foundations, religion and learning, cities in general and rulers.[22] The procreation of children and animals, and even the changing of clothing, is fixed according to the astrological calendar (55–7, 83, 51). The city's temple, which lies exactly in its centre, is a shrine to natural knowledge: 'Nothing rests on the altar but a huge celestial globe, upon which all the heavens are described, with a terrestrial globe beside it' (31). Solarian priests are astrologers, and religious worship takes place within an astrological context (113–15).

---

[19] For this view see, for example, Jon Snyder, '*The City of the Sun* and the Poetics of the Utopian Dialogue', *Stanford Italian Review*, 5 (1985), 175–87 (177); Stephen A. McKnight, ed., *Science, Pseudo-Science, and Utopianism in Early Modern Thought* (Columbia, MO: University of Missouri Press, 1992), 'Preface', p. ix; William Eamon, 'Natural Magic and Utopia in the Cinquecento: Campanella, the Della Porta Circle, and the Revolt of Calabria', *Memorie Domenicane*, n.s. 26 (1995), 369–402 (370); Sherry Roush, *Hermes' Lyre: Italian Poetic Self-Commentary from Dante to Tommaso Campanella* (Toronto: University of Toronto Press, 2002), p. 135.

[20] Eric Cochrane, *Italy 1530–1630*, ed. by Julius Kirshner (London: Longman, 1988), p. 170.

[21] On Campanella's astrology, see Peter J. Forshaw, 'Astrology, Ritual and Revolution in the Works of Tommaso Campanella (1568–1639)', in *The Uses of the Future in Early Modern Europe*, ed. by Andrea Brady and Emily Butterworth (London: Routledge, 2010), pp. 181–97.

[22] Donno, in Campanella, *The City of the Sun*, pp. 133–4.

These are just some examples of the pains Campanella has taken in order to enshrine knowledge at every level of his ideal state. Knowledge and learning are central to systems of power, and it is fundamental to the Solarians' system of government that they be ruled by the wisest man: 'We have a greater certainty than you do that a learned man does know how to govern [...]. [N]o one can master so many sciences unless he has a ready talent for all things. Therefore, such a person is always most able to rule' (45–7). In the City of the Sun, kings have become philosophers and philosophers kings. They may not have Christian revelation, but, as the Hospitaler observes, the Solarians both 'follow only the law of nature' and are 'so near to Christianity' (121). In this presentation of the Solarians as living by a kind of natural Christianity, Campanella creates an idealized society which is a non-ironic version of More's *I*. While More implicitly criticizes the notion that Utopia is a perfected society operating without God's grace, Campanella embraces the image of a people living by natural reason informed by scientific knowledge. This presentation manifests Campanella's conviction that reform could be achieved in the present; that people could be made good enough, through proper organization and without divine intervention, to live naturally virtuous lives.

As part of their idealized attitude towards learning and knowledge, the Solarians have created highly effective systems of education. They value learning above all things, and consider most noble those members of society who have learned most in skill and practice (43). Campanella details the practical organization of the education system, which is geared towards producing the most useful and cooperative citizens; children are given into the care of teachers when they are weaned, and are initially trained in all subjects before specializing (41–3). The ruler, Sun or Metaphysian, must know all mechanical arts, history, natural knowledge, mathematics; everything, in fact, except for languages, for he has translators to act as interpreters and grammarians (43–5). Children in the City of the Sun start to read at the age of three, and by ten years old have come to know all the sciences pictorially, learning natural sciences from the age of seven (41, 43). Such speed and depth of learning is made possible by the Solarians' approach to the teaching and representation of knowledge, which is vastly superior to that of their visitors: 'in our city the sciences may be learned with such facility, as you can see, that more may be gained here in one year than in ten or fifteen among you' (47). The walls of the city are covered in pictures and symbols to facilitate learning, showing the sciences of astrology and geography, languages, natural philosophy and so on (33–5). Thus the institutionalization of life in the City of the Sun results in the whole city becoming a school. The Solarians' dedication to learning and research is repeatedly shown to be of great benefit to their society. They have discovered liquids to cure nearly all infirmities; for example, they use astrology and eugenics to produce strong and healthy children, and have greater knowledge than their European counterparts (33, 35). Education and breeding are seen as vitally important because they affect the character of the child and consequently the nature of society (119).

The Solarians' learning, which continues in adulthood, extends beyond their own society throughout the known world: 'they explained to me that they understood the languages of all of the nations and that they dispatched ambassadors throughout the world to learn what was both good and bad in each of them' (37). It is travel which facilitates this level of knowledge and supremacy over other nations; *The City of the Sun* is an encomium for travel and the benefits it can bring, both to the city itself and to the knight – and by implication the reader – who hear of its wonders through the sailor's own travels. Thanks to their encyclopaedic knowledge of the world, the impression of knowledge in the City of the Sun is that nothing is unknowable or inexplicable; everything can be broken down and understood rationally, just as every social function can be identified and managed centrally. Based on astrological readings, the Solarians are even able to foretell future events. Their predictions hint at a new reformation in the Christian world:

> when the apsis of Saturn enters Capricorn, when that of Mercury enters Sagittarius and that of Mars enters Virgo, and when the superior conjunctions return to the first triplicity after the appearance of the new star in Cassiopeia, there will be a great new monarchy, reformation of laws and of arts, new prophets and a general renewal. They say that all this will be of great benefit to the Christians, but first the world will be uprooted and cleansed, and then it will be replanted and rebuilt. (121–3)

The Solarians' astrological readings demonstrate Campanella's interest in astrological ideas of apocalypticism that were current in the late sixteenth and early seventeenth centuries. The new star that he refers to here was first noticed in 1572, and was the subject of Tycho Brahe's *De nova stella* the following year. Noting that this was the first recording of a new star since 1264, Brahe imagined that the effects of this new star would be considerable, and would involve great political and religious changes.[23] Over the next ten years, a variety of texts were published on the new star, testimony to the excitement such occurrences could elicit.[24] As the observation of astrological phenomena frequently fuelled apocalyptic predictions of significant earthly changes, even the end of the earth altogether, Campanella refers to contemporary observations of the new star to add weight to his conviction that the time is ripe for reform.

The dialogue structure of *The City of the Sun* is primarily useful for its didactic associations, as the Genoese sailor elaborates on the wonders he has witnessed. The knight's occasional interjections demonstrate the potential for moral education provided by the dialogue form; towards the end of the conversation, for example, he reflects on the implications of the sailor's story for the spread of Christianity

---

[23] Tycho Brahe to Iohannes Pratensis, *Tychonis Brahe Dani Opera Omnia*, ed. by I.L.E. Dreyer, 15 vols (Hanuiae, 1913–29), I, 1–34 (34).

[24] For a list of texts published on the new star that were owned by the Elizabethan astrologer John Dee, and Dee's interest in the star, see Deborah E. Harkness, *John Dee's Conversations with Angels: Cabala, Alchemy, and the End of Nature* (Cambridge: Cambridge University Press, 1999), p. 135.

through globalization: 'I conclude from your report that Christianity is the true law and that, once its abuses have been corrected it will become the mistress of the world. I also conclude that for this reason the Spaniards discovered the rest of the world so as to unite it all under one law [...]. May [God] be praised' (121).[25] For the sailor, too, the Solarians have provided a process of education, and are themselves a source of knowledge, as he reiterates, 'How many things I learned [...]. How much I learned from these wise people [...] how much I learned' (125). At times the City of the Sun appears to hark back to an idealized classical age, with the Solarians often being compared to Romans – favourably, when it comes to their patriotism: 'the love they bear their country is an astonishing thing – as much greater than that of the Romans as their self-interest is less' (39). Amongst the men of note pictured on the outer walls are 'Caesar, Alexander, Pyrrhus, and all the Romans' (37). The Solarians' military procedures and celebrations are also described as Roman; their agricultural technique is based on texts called *Georgica* and *Buccolica*, reminiscent of Virgil's *Georgics* and *Eclogues* (73, 77, 85). They even assign names according to physical characteristics 'as the Romans did' (59). Some other practices, such as naked wrestling, are likened to those of the ancient Greeks, and to justify particular habits the Solarians turn to authorities such as 'Socrates, Cato, Plato', 'Aristarchus and Philolaus' (55, 109). Not only are the Solarians 'better' than their European visitors, but they seem to have selected the best practices from classical cultures in order to set up their philosophic community. Campanella's use of dialogue can be read alongside his inclusion of these idealized elements of classical culture as a means of anchoring his text in the classical past and thus highlighting its didactic potential. Although *The City of the Sun* reads more like a monologue in places, the dialogue form is nonetheless relevant to Campanella's effort to present his ideal society as a model for emulation.

Christianopolis and the Reformed Utopia

In *Forms in Early Modern Utopia*, Chordas argues that there are texts which should be read as 'dialogues in disguise', drawing on Mustapha Kemal Bénouis's argument for including Rabelais and Montaigne as '*dialogues déguisés*' in a study of sixteenth-century French dialogue.[26] In considering utopia, she includes within this category Johann Valentin Andreae's *Christianopolis*, which, 'though not written in dialogue form, [is] nevertheless so heavily permeated with its vestiges that they may almost, in whole or in part, be considered' to be a dialogue.[27] *Reipublicae christianopolitanae descriptio*, first published in 1619, takes the form of a narrative

---

[25] On Campanella's belief that Spain's conquest of the new world would lead to world evangelization, see John M. Headley, 'Campanella, America, and World Evangelization', in *America in European Consciousness, 1499–1750*, ed. by Karen Ordahl Kupperman (Chapel Hill: University of North Carolina Press, 1995), pp. 243–71.

[26] Chordas, *Forms in Early Modern Utopia*, p. 28.

[27] Chordas, *Forms in Early Modern Utopia*, p. 29.

of a traveller who has encountered the wonderful society of Christianopolis, and is encouraged to spread the news of this society in order to encourage others to join it and 'undertake the happy journey to Christianopolis'.[28] The vestiges of the dialogue form to which Chordas refers include reported conversations between the narrator and the various officials whom he encounters, in which the narrator is informed about Christianopolitan practices and thus educated not only about this ideal society but also about the principles of how to live well. Chordas's argument for considering the text as a dialogue in disguise draws attention to its dialogic elements, which, as well as reported conversations, include a playful attention to the borders between truth and reality in a text whose narrator is supposed to have sailed to Christianopolis across the 'Academic Ocean' in a ship named 'Fantasy' (155). Andreae's narrator presents his account as a report of his own journey around the city, and his narrative periodically returns to this structure ('it is time to take a walk in Christianopolis', 163; 'it is now time for us to enter the very heart of Christianopolis', 186). As in *The City of the Sun*, the experience of travel is thus the means by which the benefits of the ideal city are experienced and related. In this manner, too, *Christianopolis* recalls the scene-setting elements common to the Renaissance dialogue form. He also, like More, reflects on the inadequacy of his own memory as a record of his experience: 'I am very sorry that my memory has not been adequate for such a variety of things [...] you can easily see that I am no historian' (280). Calling attention to the potential gaps and errors in his narrative, Andreae positions his text as both truthful and potentially in error in a manner that is common to the dialogue and the travel narrative.

The fact that Andreae incorporated such aspects of dialogue into *Christianopolis* without actually adopting the dialogue structure suggests that he found the by-now familiar form of the travel narrative a more compelling medium for his fictional traveller's tale. Andreae's adoption of the travel narrative form may also suggest that he rejected the dialogue for other reasons: in favour of something more contemporary and more realistic, for example. Travel writings, while notorious for playing fast and loose with the truth, if not actually being made up of a pack of lies, did at least purport to relate tales of voyages that had actually taken place. The form of the travel narrative thus asserted the real existence of the location being described, which is its chief advantage over the dialogue for Andreae: central to Andreae's utopia is the notion that the ideal society can be easily accessed by all who read about it. For this reason, though he draws on the didactic and fictional elements of the dialogue form, he does so within the context of a first-person narrative in which he can directly exhort his reader to emulate the examples of the ideal society provided in the text. For Andreae, the concept of utopia need not be understood as beyond the reach of his readership. He urges his readers to emulate the principles of life in Christianopolis in order that they might finally achieve it; the implication is that this will be in heaven, but it is a journey for which the reader

---

[28] Johann Valentin Andreae, *Christianopolis*, ed. by Edward H. Thompson (Dordrecht: Kluwer, 1999), pp. 153–4. All further references will be to this edition and will be given in parentheses.

should at once 'make yourself ready' (283, 154). In his own life, Andreae was deeply engaged with the aims and ideals of the Reformation as they were carried forward into the seventeenth century, and his utopia, which appeared a century after the reforms instigated by Luther, was intended to further the work of the Reformation by promoting the principles of the ideally reformed society. For this reason, utopia was a place that each individual reader could and must strive to achieve.

Andreae was born in 1586 at Herrenberg, the son of a Lutheran clergyman and the grandson of Jakob Andreae, the 'Luther of Württemberg', and was educated at the University of Tübingen.[29] The list of his professors there, in the words of his biographer John Warwick Montgomery, 'read like a roll-call of Lutheran orthodoxy' and included Stephan Gerlach, Matthias Hafenreffer, Johann Georg Sigwart and Andreas Osiander (II). These men, who were occupied with the question of how to relate the theology of the Protestant Reformation to the needs and ideas of the new century, were to influence Andreae's thought and work for the rest of his life. As a Lutheran deacon and later as Superintendent in Calw, Andreae was at the centre of those committed to the ideology of what has been called the Second or Further Reformation, and this commitment was to influence his thought, and his utopia, in a profound manner.[30] The Further Reformation wished to complete the reforms of the Protestant Reformation, and demanded a *reformatio vitae* to follow Luther's *reformatio doctrinae*. Thus Andreae's utopian fiction, like More's, was the product of an individual working within a cultural set of like-minded men; it typifies the aims and interests of a group of fellow-thinkers interested in spiritual and political reform.

Andreae's deep and lasting commitment to social reformation is documented in his writings and in what we know of his attempts to alleviate the suffering of the poor and to establish a series of 'Protestant brotherhoods'. The intellectual circles in which Andreae mixed at Tübingen were involved with a variety of projects, including his *Societas Christiana* or *Civitas Solis*, or the *Unio Christiana*, which were critical of present-day society and sought to promote their own ideas for its reform. From approximately 1613, Andreae and other like-minded men at the university, such as Tobias Hess and Christian Besold, were actively engaged in attempts to found a Christian brotherhood, with the purpose of reforming society in general and renewing the inner life of the Lutheran church. These utopian societies were made up of interested parties who were concerned with both social and spiritual reform, although Andreae's was a society in the sense of a spiritual brotherhood, rather than a physical community. Andreae has also been linked to some of the major tracts of the hermetic brotherhood of Rosicrucians, whose reforming goals he praises in the opening letter to the reader that prefaces *Christianopolis*, although Montgomery argues against those who have seen

---

[29] For Andreae's biography, see John Warwick Montgomery, *Cross and Crucible Johann Valentin Andreae (1586–1654), Phoenix of the Theologians*, 2 vols (The Hague: Nijhoff, 1973), and Thompson in Andreae, *Christianopolis*, pp. 3–19.

[30] Montgomery, *Cross and Crucible*, I, 30–33.

Andreae as the 'spiritual father' of the Rosicrucian movement.[31] Indeed, in a letter written in 1642 and looking back on these early attempts at the creation of a utopian community, Andreae suggested that his efforts were not only distinct to those of the Rosicrucians, but directly opposed:

> It has been twenty-three or four years, since with the help and stimulus of Wilhelm Wense, Knight of Lüneberg, a most choice friend, I formed this *Image of a Certain Christian Society*, which, I had intended, we could place in opposition to the unworthy mockery of the fiction of the Rosicrucian fraternity.[32]

Nonetheless, Andreae's involvement with the composition of key Rosicrucian texts, including the *Fama fraternitatis* and the *Confessio fraternitatis*, suggests his long-term interest in the utopian ideals expressed in the Rosicrucian manifestos.

Despite the spiritual nature of this ideal community, his project for the improvement of society had practical intentions and functions, as Andreae made clear in his *Amicorum singularium clarissimorum Funera, condecorata* (Lüneberg, 1642), written after Wense's death. In this oration Andreae described his and Wense's intention to 'bring together in a kind of society a certain number of men who could and would work for the betterment of the age'. The purpose of this group was to be 'the cultivation of true religion, the improvement of dissolute morals, and the restoration of a literary culture with mutual encouragement'.[33] The fellowship's aims were to help Christians imitate Christ and live a truly good life, and while the reforms they proposed had a spiritual purpose they were nonetheless practical ideas, ideas they were intent on having carried out. The Lutheran deacon had also been engaged with practical efforts at social improvement through the physical rebuilding of a city, as a town in which he ministered was twice affected by fire, in 1617 and 1618, and he was involved in the projects for its restitution.[34] Two years after *Christianopolis* was first printed, Andreae was to found the Färberstift in Calw, a society which aimed to help the poor, educate the young and subvent

---

[31] On Andreae's involvement with Rosicrucianism and other Protestant fraternities, see Donald R. Dickson, 'Johann Valentin Andreae's Utopian Brotherhoods', *Renaissance Quarterly*, 49:4 (1996), 760–802. Frances Yates argued in *The Rosicrucian Enlightenment* (London: Routledge and Kegan Paul, 1972; repr. London: Ark, 1986) that Andreae originally welcomed the myth of Christian Rosencreutz as 'the vehicle for aspirations towards general reformation and the advancement of learning', an argument refuted by Montgomery in *Cross and Crucible*, I, 178–230. See also the introduction to Johann Valentin Andreae, *Gesammelte Schriften, Band 3: Rosenkreuzerschriften*, ed. and trans. by Roland Edighoffer (Stuttgart-Bad Cannstatt: Frommann-Holzboog, 2010).

[32] Letter from Andreae to Duke August, 27 June 1642, quoted in Donald R. Dickson, *The Tessera of Antilia: Utopian Brotherhoods & Secret Societies in the Early Seventeenth Century* (Leiden: Brill, 1998), p. 41.

[33] *Amicorum singularium clarissimorum Funera, condecorata* (Lüneberg, 1642), pp. 7–9, quoted in Dickson, *The Tessera of Antilia*, pp. 42–3.

[34] J.C. Davis, *Utopia and the Ideal Society: A Study of English Utopian Writing 1516–1700* (Cambridge: Cambridge University Press, 1981; repr. 1983), p. 74.

churches, an institution which he saw as a physical manifestation of the societies outlined in his utopian writings.[35] Other of his writings from this period, such as *Christianae societatis imago* (1619), *Christiani amoris dextra porrecta* (1620) and *Verae unionis in Christo Jesu Specimen* (1628), contributed to his vision of an idealized Christian way of life. His interest in social improvement was further developed by his own experience as a tutor and by a lifelong interest in education and its potential to transform both the individual and society.

By the time of the publication of *Christianopolis*, Andreae had been ordained for approximately five years and was pastor in the town of Vaihingen. This was a place and a period of his life which he later referred to as his '*Laboratorium*', during which he published a wide variety of books, including theological texts, drama, satire and poetry. *Christianopolis*, now the best known of these writings, began with a dedication to Johann Arndt, the Lutheran theologian whom Andreae greatly admired and whose name headed the list of the supporters of his 'Societas Christiana' in 1618–19.[36] In his dedicatory letter to Arndt, with which the text begins, Andreae addresses the older man as 'Reverend Father in Christ', claiming that Arndt is a foundation of 'this new community of ours', 'a very small colony taken out of that great Jerusalem that you have built up'. Andreae says that Arndt is to thank for the 'institutions and laws' of this community, and that he may also be looked to for advice on how to change or improve it. At the earliest stage, Andreae establishes the notion of a group of like-minded followers, for whom Christianopolis typifies a way of living that is both a new and real community and a 'great Jerusalem', a spiritual fellowship of those who follow Arndt in 'piety, probity and scholarship' (145).

It is surely this group of like-minded scholars whom Andreae has in mind when he addresses his 'Christian Reader' in the letter which follows his dedication to Arndt and precedes the main body of the text of *Christianopolis*. This letter itself comprises one of the elements of dialogue that are detectable in Andreae's utopia, as it frames the description of the ideal society as a direct communication with the like-minded reader. Andreae addresses this reader in terms which stress their mutual endeavour in trying to live well, in which he believes they can triumph, going on to claim that 'I wrote [my book] for my friends' (153). His letter begins with a description of two kinds of people: one who admires everything in the state uncritically and blindly attacks whatever it sees as dissent, and one who longs for something better than the current situation, enduring as far as possible but accepting improvements. Andreae offers types for these two categories. For the first category he suggests the Antichrist, 'who weighed down the church of Christ with abominable burdens', and for the second 'that invincible hero, our Doctor Luther', who took steps to achieve reform himself, when he could not do so by submission. It is quite possible, Andreae conjectures, that 'this drama may be repeated in our own time'. The 'light of a purer religion' has been restored

---

[35] Dickson, *The Tessera of Antilia*, p. 58.
[36] Montgomery, *Cross and Crucible*, I, 56.

to society and enshrined in scholarship, but Christians have learned that they are no different from worldly people, and still take pleasure in the sins which Christ detests (146–7). In this way Andreae places his work within the context of a renewed or second reformation of both church and society. Men who have zealously lifted their voices against sinful behaviour include Arndt himself, Martin Moller and Johann Gerhard; these men, with others, have sought 'to unite learning with uprightness' and to undertake a reformation of the church, politics and the university, although such attempts have met with resistance (148). There are those, Andreae notes, who prefer to have their sins concealed (149).

In this prefatory letter the author clearly aligns his purpose with those who sought to carry out further projects of reformation in religious and social institutions, and expresses optimism about the prospect of the achievement of such reform; there is nothing to stop his readership, he argues, from binding itself closer to Christ and proceeding under the direction of the Holy Spirit, living a Christian life rather than a worldly one. This is the 'inner certainty of the Christian' which has been made manifest in Christianopolis (152). The opening letter excoriates the three institutions of church, university and city square for their monstrous failings, which breed ignorance and sin, but it maintains that the solution is to demonstrate the correct example: 'not everyone is so averse to Christ as to reject his rules of life if someone will place them before them, and arrange their whole life accordingly' (150–51). *Christianopolis* is thus explicitly presented to the reader as a motivation to further reformation and an example of how a fully reformed society might function. At the close of the letter, Andreae insists that this society can be joined by anyone: 'the surest thing of all would be if you and your companions who are eager for a more honest life [...] with Christ as your leader on the journey, board the ship that flies a banner bearing the sign of Cancer and yourself undertake the happy journey towards Christianopolis' (153–4). In his claim that Christianopolis is open to all, Andreae suggests that reform is not only imaginable but possible; each reader is told to 'make yourself ready for the journey to heaven' (154). The letter to the Christian reader is Andreae's manifesto for further reformation and the aims of his utopian Protestant brotherhood.

The prefatory letters to Andreae's *Christianopolis*, like those preceding More's *Utopia*, are useful in establishing the way in which the reader is expected to approach the text. While the prefatory material to *Utopia* highlights its ironic tone, its ambiguity and its interest in the relation between classical and Christian values, Andreae's material is more explicit in positioning the text as a model for its readership. Andreae's direct address to his reader, his references to the contemporary theologians whom he admires, and his description of his book as 'an example' (152) demonstrate the way in which he intends his work to be read and establishes its context. Despite this, Andreae also claims that his book is in fact 'a less serious and less witty work' than that of More, and that it may in consequence 'be ignored more easily' (153). For all that his utopia is meant to display a portrait of simple Christianity, it is also 'a joke' to be shared amongst friends. The letter to the reader at once acknowledges the fictionality of Andreae's 'entertainment' and asserts that there is 'nothing artistic about it, but only simplicity' (153). Andreae both places his text within the tradition of utopian literature by comparing it to *Utopia* and distances it from that more 'serious' book, claiming that he would not 'have dared to write it for important people' (153). He recognizes that as a travel narrative, the text is open to questions regarding its authenticity, stating that any doubter as to the truth of his story should 'reserve his judgement until the truthfulness of all accounts of journeys by sea and land has been put to the test' (153). But the travel narrative nonetheless offers to Andreae a semblance of truthfulness which is lacking in the more explicitly fictional dialogue form employed by More for *Utopia*.

The prefatory letter is not the only point in his work at which Andreae makes reference to other utopian writings. His reference to his journey on 'the Ethiopian Sea' aboard 'the ship of Fantasy' (155) recalls Hall's *Mundus Alter et Idem*, in which the narrator also embarks on a journey (on the Ethiopian sea) aboard a vessel named 'The Fantasia'.[37] Indeed, Andreae also demonstrated the influence which this text had had upon him elsewhere in his writings. In his *Mythologiae christianae sive virtutum & vitiorum humanae imaginum libri tres*, also printed in 1619, Andreae included a section entitled 'Peregrinatio', in which a traveller also voyages on a ship named Phantasy and discovers places including Crapula, Yvronia, Viraginia and Moronia, which recall the locations encountered by Hall's narrator. *Mundus Alter et Idem* thus clearly made an impression on Andreae, alongside the *Republic*, which he mentions in his letter to the Christian reader, and *Utopia*, which is mentioned in his *Menippus* as well as implied by the reference to its author in the letter. Hall himself adopted a Lucianic tone in *Mundus*; John Millar Wands, his editor, has identified Hall's debts to both Erasmus and Lucian in his use of satire and jesting seriousness. In *Mundus*, however, Hall turned away from the dialogue form with which he had experimented in *Virgidemiae*. The text is composed of five books, each detailing the narrator's experiences of a different land. The first-person narration frequently includes direct conversation between the traveller and a number of interlocutors, with the same attempt to reproduce direct, colloquial speech that is common to the dialogue form, meaning that dialogue functions as a device within the text, if not as the actual form.

The Lucianic tradition which is so important to *Utopia* also provides a useful context for reading Hall's ironic utopia, in which the narrator naively encounters a series of foreign environments and describes them in seemingly admiring tones which highlight their absurdity. Both *Utopia* and *Mundus* rely on the convention that all is not what it seems in the travel narrative, which may be used to comment on the home society as well as the foreign environment. A recent editor of *Christianopolis*, Edward Thompson, suggests that Hall's text influenced Andreae by reinforcing his 'interest in the travel tale as a means of holding up to Europe a mirror in which her defects can be seen most clearly' (*Christianopolis*, 50). *Christianopolis* presents itself as a travel narrative that reflects on the failings

---

[37] Joseph Hall, *Another World and Yet the Same: Bishop Joseph Hall's Mundus Alter et Idem*, ed. by John Millar Wands (New Haven: Yale University Press, 1981), p. 17.

of the author's own society, but it also offers a very different kind of utopia from either More's or Hall's. Andreae's claims in his opening letter that his text should be treated as a joke, whilst in keeping with the utopian tradition, seem an inaccurate guide to the way in which he really intended his book to be taken. Any claims for a reading of the text in keeping with the tradition of '*serio ludere*' are rarely borne out in the main body of the work itself, which, while occasionally playful, more usually takes a sober and direct tone. As the letters demonstrate, Andreae in fact intended to use the utopian mode of discourse in a very different manner to More. Andreae thus responded to the nature of utopian writing as he understood it based on his reading of More and Hall (i.e., as an intellectual, witty, potentially playful form of writing), but his own work reflected little interest in this use of the utopian mode. In fact, Andreae's utopia is exactly the kind of idealstate writing that More's is be presumed to be by critics who read it as a genuinely ideal society; Christianopolis represents an ideal society which is explicitly held up in comparison to the author's and reader's own, with the aim of promoting its emulation. Like Hall, Andreae uses dialogue as a function within his narrative, rather than as the dominant form.

Andreae's rejection of dialogue as a structure for *Christianopolis* is particularly noteworthy, given his use of the form elsewhere. Like Hall, Andreae chose the dialogue form for satirical writings. Shortly before his utopian travel narrative, Andreae had published his *Menippus sive dialogorum satyricorum centuria* (1617), a book of one hundred satiric dialogues in the style of Menippus, a Cynic philosopher whose work (none of which survives) was reputed to ridicule the ideas of rival schools.[38] Menippus was the teacher of the great satirist Lucian, whose work has been shown to be an important influence on Renaissance utopian literature, and particularly *Utopia*. Andreae's satiric dialogues are influenced by those of Lucian, which Andreae had studied in Erasmus's translation, and by Erasmus's own dialogues; their speakers reveal their own individual sins or pass judgement on those of others.[39] That Andreae chose not to use the dialogue form for the ideal-society fiction that he composed directly after these satires suggests a deliberate rejection of satirical dialogue in favour of a more suitable form; this rejection of the dialogue form signals the move from Menippean satire to a constructive social criticism, intended to form a model for like-minded reformers.

Andreae's claim in his prefatory letter that he wrote *Christianopolis* 'for [his] friends' links the text to the group of scholars and reformers with whom he was involved at Tübingen and beyond, but it also depends upon the broad conception of friendship which Andreae described in other works dealing with

---

[38] Andreae's *Menippus* will appear as the ninth volume of his collected works, translated and edited by Carlos Gilly. For *Menippus* as satire, see Thomas Willard, 'Andreae's *ludibrium*: Menippean Satire in the *Chymische Hochzeit*', in *Laughter in the Middle Ages and Early Modern Times: Epistemology of a Fundamental Human Behavior, Its Meaning, and Consequences*, ed. by Albrecht Classen (Berlin/New York: De Gruyter, 2010), pp. 767–89 (pp. 778–81).

[39] Willard, 'Andreae's *ludibrium*: Menippean Satire in the *Chymische Hochzeit*', p. 779.

the concept of the ideal society. In *The Right Hand of Christian Love Offered*, which was translated into English by John Hall in 1647, Andreae describes a 'sacred amity' which 'ought to knit good men' and constitutes a 'fellowship' that any man, 'if he hath learned Christ, cannot but entertain.'[40] Wishing to extend 'this hand of faith and Christian love to all and every one of those, who being experienced in the bondage of the World, and wearied with its weight, do desire with all their hearts Christ as their deliverer', Andreae envisages this 'concord' as a potentially universal and ultimately unworldly community, which flies from earthly temptations.[41] In his *Societas Christiana*, also translated by Hall as *A Modell of Christian Society*, Andreae wrote of a community which would consist of those who had rejected the world and 'given their names to Christ', and could potentially include all those who had confessed the reformed Protestant religion.[42] In describing this 'Christian society', he detailed its various office-holders, including twelve 'Colleagues' or 'privy Counsellers', who, alongside the 'Head' of the society, would take responsibility for its running and advancement.[43] Andreae details the responsibilities and duties of each of these individuals, each in charge of an area of practical learning, including, for example, natural philosophy, economics and philology, and delineates a society which is based on the sharing of knowledge and understanding of a group of learned professional men. Although this model is for a real society in the sense that Andreae believes it can and should really exist, it is understood to be a society based on friendship and distant communication, rather than an actual community of people living and working together. Indeed, the fact that the members and officials of this society can exist at a considerable distance from one another is presented by Andreae as one of its advantages: 'sith most things are done by letters', there will be no necessity for any man to 'cast the care of houses and families, and leave our condition of life'.[44] Andreae's conception of a Christian society or brotherhood in such texts is one of a spiritually united community sharing knowledge, Christian aims and a Christian way of life. In *Christianopolis*, however, he extends his description of the ideal Christian society into a fictional utopia via an imaginary travel narrative, which describes a society that is supposed to exist and to be accessible to future visitors. Where Andreae's other writings discuss the ideal Christian community in general terms, *Christianopolis* describes the institutions and practices of the ideal society in specific detail, partly through reported conversation between the traveller-narrator and his interlocutors in Christianpolis.

---

[40] *The Right Hand of Christian Love Offered*, in G.W. Turnbull, 'Johann Valentin Andreae's *Societas Christiana*', *Zeitschrift für Deutsche Philologie*, 74 (1955), 151–85 (162).

[41] *The Right Hand of Christian Love Offered*, 165, 166.

[42] *A Modell of Christian Society*, in G.W. Turnbull, 'Johann Valentin Andreae's *Societas Christiana*', *Zeitschrift für Deutsche Philologie*, 74 (1955), 151–85 (153).

[43] *A Modell of Christian Society*, 154–60.

[44] *A Modell of Christian Society*, 160.

Andreae's utopia consists of the narrator's tale of his experience of a foreign society which he happens upon following a shipwreck. This narrator, who is so struck by the excellence of Christianopolis that he intends to commit his life to it, is especially impressed by the strength and excellence of the Christianopolitan system of education, which is explained through a detailed description of the organization of learning and its institutions. The College of Christianopolis, the discussion of which takes up by far the majority of the text, is described by its narrator as 'the very heart of Christianopolis', a position which is occupied geographically by the temple, and as 'the *primum mobile* of the community' (186). Within this College, which is home to the governors and Chancellor of the community as well as those directly involved with education, the narrator notes that he has 'never seen so much human perfection gathered in one place' (187). The humanist dream of the achievement of self-improvement through education has been achieved in this ideal institution at the heart of the ideal society.

The narrator observes that children in Christianopolis are educated from the age of six, and from that age live in the college itself, divided into three classes (219). During childhood, the school replaces the family unit and the institution of the College is placed at the centre of both social and individual development. The sexes are educated separately and the importance of education for girls is emphasized (221). Andreae details the functional aspects of education: the students' living arrangements and meals, the need for cleanliness, for supervision of morals and for careful inspection. He presents a comprehensive breakdown of the subjects that are studied in the various lecture halls: grammar, rhetoric, foreign languages, logic, metaphysics, theosophy, arithmetic, geometry, mystic numbers, music, musical instruments, the choir, astronomy, astrology, the Christians' heaven, natural history, civil history, church history, ethics, political science, Christian poverty, theology, the practice of theology and prophecies (221–51). Students progress through these subjects in turn, and can also access the halls of the more advanced studies of medicine and jurisprudence (253–6). Andreae even explains the punishment system, which involves abstinence and extra work and, very rarely, corporal punishment and detention (221). Every detail of the school and its staff is attended to, including the personal qualities needed in a good teacher: 'dignity, integrity, industry and generosity' (219).

Not only does Andreae focus on the practical aspects of the system of education, but he sees education itself as having a social purpose, understanding children as the community's investment and likening them to land which will offer a better crop if well prepared (218). The young people, Andreae states, are the miniature community which will one day replace the greater one, and as such education is critically important in the creation of a good society (219). Hence the narrator dwells on the practical aspects of the arrangement of education, such as the students' sleeping quarters, their bathing arrangements and their gardens, with an attention to detail which testifies to Andreae's deep personal interest in pedagogy and the organization of the practical side of learning and development. This awareness of physical detail and the practicalities of running a city is reflected throughout the text in the narrator's attention to useful technical innovations, such as systems for lighting the streets at night, for tending the communal gardens and for ensuring a good water supply (185, 273, 274). Andreae's concern with the day-to-day necessities of social life is evident in the attention he pays to the layout of living quarters, the precautions taken for avoiding the spread of fire and even the practical materials used for clothing and household equipment (182–4).

Throughout the description of Christianopolis, however, and especially in the delineation of the College and its numerous lecture halls, each devoted to a different subject, it is clear that Andreae wishes to focus his reader's attention on the spiritual functions and religious potential of the ideal human society. Education may have social functions, but its primary role is a spiritual one. For the students, learning is important, but intellectual development is not a top priority: 'the first and highest task they have is to worship God with a pure and devout mind; the second, is to achieve the best and most chaste morality; and the third is to develop their intellectual faculties' (220). In observing this, the narrator comments that this is the reverse of the usual order; in Christianopolis, all knowledge must be focused towards Christ and its purpose is to enable to students to live a good Christian life (200–201). The first educational figure the narrator discourses with in Christianopolis is the Scholar, who is responsible for knowledge and education, but whose most outstanding quality is not his wisdom, but his humility and kindness (199–200). He disapproves of any knowledge that does not bring the learner closer to Christ; he has progressed enough, the Scholar maintains, who can call himself a student of the Holy Ghost. Hence the narrator's first experience of learning in Christianopolis in fact serves to deny the importance of human knowledge and understanding. Only knowledge that has a spiritual end is important: 'Rise up, O sacred knowledge which teaches us about Christ, so that we learn nothing here which must be unlearned again, but learn only that which will be increasing and enduring through all eternity' (201). It is significant that the narrator learns these lessons through direct conversation with the Scholar; the elements of dialogue in the text are, like those in *The City of the Sun*, didactic in function.

Thus in *Christianopolis* conversation is an important method of learning for the narrator, and reporting that conversation is meant to be educational for the reader. Later, in discussion with the Presbyter, the narrator is able to discern the holiness and 'divinity' of his interlocutor through the act of conversation: 'when he spoke to me with a most welcome eagerness, I recognised in him the representative and intermediary of God' (192). The act of verbal communication is a means of assessing truth, and the report of this conversation thus serves to educate the reader in the holiness and humility that the Presbyter embodies, as 'he seeks no other satisfaction than the nourishment of Heaven' (193). During their conversation, the narrator records that he blushed to remember the behaviour of some people, who commit 'impieties against the sacred law' (193). His report of his physical response to his discourse with the Presbyter is meant to guide that of the reader, and the Presbyter himself to serve as an example of true Christianity. Conversations with other officials in the city function in a similar way, with the act of verbal communication central to these encounters and frequently made evident in the narrative: 'he always said', 'when I asked him', 'I certainly found him to be candid', etc. (200, 202). Elsewhere, such conversation is used to demonstrate the concept of the usefulness and serviceability of knowledge which was integral to the values of humanism and early seventeenth-century movements for further reformation. For Andreae, the serviceability of knowledge depended on its capacity to bring the individual closer to Christ and the Christian way of life. The Christianopolitans are clear about the importance of useful knowledge, and they welcome the narrator when he first arrives because he is able to recognize the paucity of what he knows. Ashamed at having called himself an educated person when discoursing with his examiner, the narrator confesses that he understands nothing of the subjects mentioned by this examiner, who exclaims, 'You are ours! You bring to us the cleanest of slates, as though purified by the sea itself' (161). The narrator's experience of shipwreck before arriving at Christianopolis represents a process of cleansing, a second baptism to prepare him for this heavenly community; Andreae adopts this feature of the travel narrative and turns it into a metaphor for entering the ideal society.

The notion of useful knowledge is epitomized in *Christianopolis* in the encyclopaedia, as the institutionalization of knowledge has enabled its organization on an encyclopaedic scale. Christianopolis possesses a huge amount of knowledge, which has been organized and classified in its library: 'the offspring of infinite great minds arranged in categories and according to subject matter'. The narrator is astonished to discover that it contains many texts considered lost by his own society. As in the City of the Sun, the learning on display is indeed encyclopaedic: 'there is no language on earth that has not contributed something of itself, and no great mind that has not paid its tribute, to this collection' (203). The Scholar is himself a human embodiment of the encyclopaedia image: 'One would believe of him that there was scarcely anything that he did not know' (199–200). Yet, the narrator observes, the citizens do not seem to make much use of the encyclopaedia that is their library, and the Scholar refuses to describe himself in such terms (200, 203). It is a mistake to believe, they would argue, that human knowledge can ever be encyclopaedic or paramount; instead, it is useful knowledge that leads to Christ which is important, which is why the Christianopolitans need only a few books. Instead of a secular encyclopaedia, the narrator is presented with the Bible as the true compendium of all knowledge: 'the one thing of value allowed to man by divine favour and also an inexhaustible source of secrets' (203–4). Similarly, when asked about the essence of knowledge, the Scholar replies that it is Christ, the Book of Life, 'in whom all things are unified'. On this basis, he rejects non-Christian learning: 'Only Christians have knowledge, and this comes from God. Other people utter empty words, because they come from within themselves' (200).

With Christian knowledge comprising all that is worth knowing, education in Christianopolis is at heart a religious experience. Just as the pupils' lessons begin with prayers, Andreae constantly refers to the centrality of God in all their studies. Thus the most important thing in the practice of rhetoric is to develop 'a taste for God's style', because 'whatever breathes the Spirit will have tremendous effect' (223). The conclusion of all reasoning, the narrator argues, is 'that we listen humbly to God, who is [...] always bound up most closely with the truth' (226). Likewise the learning of foreign languages should not be over-emphasized, because 'it is the man who speaks with God who knows more' (224). The metaphor of learning as conversation is used to promote talk with God over talk with other people. Even the narrator's description of Christianopolitan geometry is taken as an opportunity to repeat the central message: 'While [...] the people of Christianopolis measure many things, they are anxious first of all to take their own measure and to weigh themselves in the balance. In this way they can judge how great is God's mercy' (230). There is no academic subject that cannot be brought back to God. Rather than study philosophy, the Christianopolitans are taught theosophy, 'which recognises nothing that is the product of human invention or investigation, but owes everything to God', and is acquiescent where philosophy is questioning (227). Even the Christianopolitans' temple, located at the geographical centre of the city, is decorated 'with beautiful paintings of religious subjects or scenes from stories in the Bible', and used as a theatre for religious plays, which are performed in order to educate the young (258). Hence education, like every other activity in the city, has a religious function in drawing the student nearer to God, 'because the people of Christianopolis do everything in this world for the sake of the church' (242). For Andreae, life should be lived in the expectation of eternity, and education is the best means of so doing:

> There is never a more fortunate or profitable form of expenditure than this. [...] [I]t is the peak of good fortune to be able with one effort to ensure the security of the community and also the fitness of the young for future life, so that the children whom we bring forth here shall have been born not so much for the earth as for heaven. (218)

What is most important about Andreae's utopia in this context, both in terms of what it tells us about his own values and background and in the common ground it demonstrates between this and other Renaissance utopias, is that this essentially spiritual function of education is perceived as achievable through practical social reform and specifically through institutional reform. In Christianopolis, the correct structure of society has enabled the correct results for the individual; living within the ideal society, Christianopolitans have no option but to live reformed lives. Hence the sincere optimism of Andreae's utopianism relies upon the belief that it is possible to build or reform idealized institutions which will create perfect societies through the production of perfect citizens. Andreae highlights the important role of the individual in the process of reformation, making clear that it is the duty of each person to make Christ his model, which is why it is possible for anyone to decide to join him in this ideal community: 'with God's blessing you may go there with me very soon, if you are good' (283). Christianopolis is a spiritual utopia, while also demonstrating Andreae's understanding that the structure and practices of a society have a significant role to play in the process of individual betterment. In Andreae's view, there is such a thing as a good society to be instituted on earth, and the right laws and systems have the power to improve the people they control, but reform must happen on an individual basis. For this reason, Andreae's utopia is grounded on the positive conviction that reform is achievable, which evinces the characteristic optimism of the utopian writing of this period.

Andreae's optimism was clearly influenced by his own first-hand experiences of reformed institutions, like those in Calvinist Geneva. The principles of education as being intrinsically beneficial to both society and the individual were enshrined in Geneva, which Andreae had visited in 1611.[45] The Geneva Consistory, an ecclesiastical court which consisted of ministers and lay elders, in fact functioned as a form of educational institution, given its mission of ensuring that all citizens of Geneva had a basic understanding of the Reformed faith.[46] Geneva was a city devoted to education in practice and in influence; its academy, founded in 1559, played an important part in educating men who went on to minister across Europe. Calvin himself had focused at an early stage on the proper education of children, including in his *Ecclesiastical Ordinances* (1541) guidelines for their religious upbringing, and these principles of education and proper governance were at the heart of the Reformed church.

Alongside an insistence upon the importance of education, the cities and states which were controlled by the reformers relied upon a system of control or discipline which has come to characterize their means of social organization. Both Luther and Calvin had made social discipline a crucial part of their understanding of the definition of the true church.[47] Social discipline, a concept advanced by Gerhard Oestreich in the 1960s and more recently developed by Heinz Schilling, was closely associated in reformed thinking with the principles and practices of education. The role of the godly society was both to educate its citizens in the true faith and to impose Christian discipline on the whole community; even the ungodly could thus be obliged to obey God's laws. Moreover, the educational establishments founded in reformed cities such as Geneva, it has been argued, relied upon the same mechanisms of surveillance and discipline which underpinned Calvinist consistories. Such educational institutions spread the discipline of the reformed churches in their bid to impose a system of moral and social discipline which has been described as constituting a 'disciplinary revolution'.[48] Social control was thus integral to the functioning of Calvinist cities like Geneva, as 'instituting a Christian life through church discipline provided the internal impetus for the Calvinist movement'.[49] And the concern of Reformed regimes for social

---

[45] Montgomery, *Cross and Crucible*, I, 43.

[46] Robert M. Kingdon, 'The Geneva Consistory in the time of Calvin', in *Calvinism in Europe, 1540–1620*, ed. by Andrew Pettegree, Alastair Duke and Gillian Lewis (Cambridge: Cambridge University Press, 1994), pp. 21–34 (p. 24).

[47] Alastair Duke, 'Perspectives on International Calvinism', in *Calvinism in Europe, 1540–1620*, pp. 1–20 (p. 2).

[48] Philip S. Gorski, *The Disciplinary Revolution: Calvinism and the Rise of the State in Early Modern Europe* (Chicago: University of Chicago Press, 2003), p. 22.

[49] R. Po-Chia Hsia, *Social Discipline in the Reformation: Central Europe 1550–1750* (London and New York: Routledge, 1989), p. 28.

discipline was by no means an exclusively Calvinist phenomenon, but was equally present in Lutheran states in Germany.⁵⁰ In the words of R. Po-Chia Hsia, whose study of social discipline in the period demonstrates its importance in Reformation thought, 'the enforcement of church discipline functioned as an instrument of social control in the emerging territorial states of all three confessions'.⁵¹

The time that Andreae spent in Geneva was fairly brief, but the city appears to have made a lasting impression on him. In his own record of his experiences, he later observed:

> While I was at Geneva, I noted something of great moment which I will remember with nostalgia till the end of my days. Not only does this city enjoy a truly free political constitution; it has besides, as its particular ornament and means of discipline, the guidance of social life. By virtue of the latter, all the mores of the citizens and even their slightest transgressions are examined each week [...]. The resultant moral purity does so much honour to the Christian religion, is so consistent with it and so inseparable from it, that we should shed our bitterest tears that this discipline is unknown or completely neglected in our circles [...]. Indeed, if religious differences had not made it impossible for me, the harmony of faith and morals at Geneva would have bound me there – and so from that time I have striven with all my energy to provide the like for our churches.⁵²

The discipline which Andreae so admired in Geneva was not neglected when it came to constructing Christianopolis. As the text's most recent editor has noted, *Christianopolis* in part duplicates Genevan arrangements, as a component of Andreae's 'programme for the regeneration of Lutheran society'.⁵³ This is particularly evident in the narrator's description of his experience of and admiration for the kind of discipline and social control enshrined in Christianopolitan life. One of the narrator's earliest encounters is with an official who examines him as to his occupation and character. The purpose of this examination is clearly to gain understanding of the wanderer's inner state:

> He [...] questioned me very closely in a friendly way, while studying the expression on my face very keenly. [...] I could not help noticing that he was watching the calmness of my soul, the modesty of my expression, the hold I kept on my tongue, the steadiness of my gaze and the deferential posture of my body. (159–60)

Such observation calls to mind inspections by the Genevan Consistory, in which citizens were expected to demonstrate their spiritual fitness and social compliance by providing evidence of their understanding of the Bible or knowledge of prayers. In this process, the act of conversation is seen to be a means of discerning the truth

---

⁵⁰ Duke, 'Perspectives on International Calvinism', p. 15.
⁵¹ Po-Chia Hsia, *Social Discipline in the Reformation*, p. 28.
⁵² *Vita, ab ipso conscripta*, p. 23, quoted in Montgomery, *Cross and Crucible*, I, 43–4.
⁵³ Thompson in Andreae, *Christianopolis*, pp. 6–7.

about an individual's spiritual condition. It is a process which is clearly wholly successful as far as the narrator is concerned, as it is undertaken 'with such skill I felt he could scrutinise my very thoughts, yet he did it with so much kindness that I could hold back nothing, and with so much respect that I realised that I owed it to him to reveal everything' (160).

The practice of social discipline is elsewhere shown to be integral to Christianopolitan life. This is particularly true with regards to religious observation. The narrator notes that each citizen is obliged to pray three times a day; on each occasion they kneel and thank God for his help, praying for its continuation and for 'a happy death' (173). Everyone is assigned to a particular place for these prayers, it is observed, and 'No-one is allowed to be absent from these meetings, except for the strongest reasons' (174). Discipline is also observed in the matter of punishment, which is necessary given that 'human nature cannot be completely driven out anywhere' (178). Thus if human nature 'does not heed repeated warnings, or, if necessary, severe rebukes, then it must be beaten back by more severe measures' (178). In Christianopolis, human failings must be controlled socially, 'that God may not be offended by the sins of the people, and may be appeased by the distinguishing marks of faith' (196). Such discipline is perceived as being crucial to the Christianopolitans' success, and can only reflect badly on contemporary Europe. Despite the recent 'cleansing' that the European church has undergone, the narrator suggests, the church has not been convinced 'that she should put aside her pride and harshness, and accept a reasonable authority for her administrators' (181). It is for this reason that the church suffers and is unable to progress.

The presence of this kind of social control in Christianopolis, its relation to the universal system of contemporary education and the presentation of that system of education demonstrate the influence that the culture of the Further Reformation had on Andreae's life and writing. These elements are often portrayed by means of direct conversation between the narrator and an interlocutor, demonstrating the continued usefulness of aspects of the dialogue form. In its sincere belief in the possibility of the ideal society, *Christianopolis* reflects a development in utopian thought which was to form a turning point in how the utopian mode of discourse was used, and demonstrates an optimism about human perfectibility that was shared by other utopian writings of the period, such as *The City of the Sun*. Both texts demonstrate the centrality of the ideal institution, education and the reformation of learning to seventeenth-century utopian thought, and the degree to which the utopian form had changed from its Morean foundations. In terms of the relationship between utopia and dialogue, Campanella and Andreae both incorporate elements of the dialogue form to a greater or lesser extent, demonstrating that the form continued its association with the utopian mode. That the dialogue form itself was no longer integral to that mode, however, is signalled by Andreae's preference for the fictional travel narrative and the desire of both authors to represent the utopian society as one which can be physically accessed and copied. The very fictionality of the dialogue form, which had made it interesting to More, resulted in its distancing from the utopian mode in the early seventeenth century.

Conclusion

A brief consideration of these two utopias has demonstrated their mutual interest in practical education and ideal institutions as core aspects of the ideal society. Some of the similarities between these two early seventeenth-century utopias may be explained by the fact that Andreae, writing some years after Campanella, was familiar with the Dominican's work; the fact that Andreae had acquaintances who had visited Campanella in prison suggests that he was aware of his writings.[54] Certainly Andreae's utopia shows the influence of Campanella's, which Andreae could have seen in manuscript prior to its publication. Although this influence has been exaggerated in the past,[55] dissonant voices have been raised, arguing that the similarities between the two texts were superficial.[56] It is not intended here to weigh the similarities and disparities between the two utopias; for the purposes of this book, it is relevant that both Campanella and Andreae have an absolute conviction that reform can be achieved in the present, and that to this end they both offer practical social changes, which it is imagined will bring about such reform, notably in the field of education, and which focus on the reformed institution.

Christianopolis and *The City of the Sun*, we have seen, demonstrate common features which represent an important stage in the development of the Renaissance utopia, as they were written by men who were directly engaged with social and institutional reformation, and whose desire for reform was driven by deeply held religious and social concerns. Each utopia is presented as an educational experience for its narrator, demonstrating that reading the utopia is envisaged as an improving activity. A core element of this educational experience is conversation with initiates of the ideal society, and the reporting of such conversation constitutes a significant continued engagement between utopia and dialogue: conversation remains the main method by which information about the utopian location is obtained. Both of these texts manifest humanist ideals, in their interest in the capacity of education to improve society and in the practical ways in which education should be instituted and human knowledge organized. In so doing, each utopia brings the institution to the forefront of the ideal society and views the proper organization of social institutions as the means of achieving change. Moreover, the ideal societies in these utopian fictions represent communities which the author believes can and should exist in the present time, even if they do not yet exist. They present seriously the notion that More interrogated in *Utopia*, that humanity can improve itself, that an ideal society is possible and that it can be achieved through social reformation, and thus introduce a link between utopia, reform and the social institution which was to dominate utopian writing in the later seventeenth century.

---

[54] Frank E. Manuel and Fritzie P. Manuel, *Utopian Thought in the Western World* (Oxford: Blackwell, 1979), p. 290.

[55] See, for example, Frances Yates, *The Art of Memory* (London: Routledge & Kegan Paul, 1966; repr. London: Penguin, 1978), pp. 363–4.

[56] Marie Louise Berneri, *Journey Through Utopia* (London: Routledge & Kegan Paul, 1950), p. 104.

As they enshrine humanist ideals about the capacity of education to achieve an ideal society, Andreae and Campanella draw on elements of dialogue in a variety of ways, but in doing so they anticipate the division between the dialogue form and utopia that was shortly to take place in English utopian writing. Campanella uses the dialogue form for *The City of the Sun* because of its didactic associations, but for Andreae, this form was too imaginative, too explicitly fictional for the description of a society which he intended to appear real and accessible. Both of these texts are representative of the decline of dialogue and the weakening of the association between this form and utopian literature. Although the dialogue itself may have been in decline, however, elements of the dialogue continued to be important to the utopian mode, as this chapter has shown. Both texts also show the continued importance of the travel narrative as an influence on utopian literature, and this, too, is an important link between continental and English utopian writing of the period. While an understanding of the European context demonstrates how utopia continued to develop away from its roots in satire and philosophical enquiry and towards its later manifestations as a practical demonstration of how to achieve social improvement through ideal institutions, it also demonstrates the centrality of the dialogic concepts of conversation and discourse to early seventeenth-century utopian literature.

Chapter 4
'Private Conference' and 'Public Affairs': Natural Philosophy, Dialogue and the Ideal Society in *New Atlantis*

Introduction: *Utopia* and *New Atlantis*

Robert Burton's statement of his intention to build 'a Utopia of mine owne, a new Atlantis, a poeticall commonwealth' in the 1628 edition of *The Anatomy of Melancholy* links *Utopia* and *New Atlantis* as fictional ideal societies.[1] Connections between the writings of More and Bacon were made before the publication of *New Atlantis*; in the letter to Princess Elizabeth which prefaces his 1619 translation of Bacon's *De sapientia veterum*, Arthur Gorges states that these two 'worthie Chancellors of this famous Isle' share 'an admirable sympathy of wit and humour', attested to by their respective texts, 'the conceaved *Utopia* of the one, and the revealed *Sapientia Veterum* of the other'.[2] More, in Gorges's view, used the device of the imaginary ideal society to expose the failings of real ones: *Utopia* '(under a meere *Idea* of a perfect State goverment) contains an exact discoverie of the vanities and disorders of reall Countries'. Bacon, on the other hand, is unlocking the secrets of the world for public view: his book '(out of the foulds of the Poeticall fables) laies open those deepe Philosophicall mysteries, which had beene so long lockt up in the Casket of Antiquity'.[3] Both men 'discover' or 'lay open' truths for the edification of the reader, More by showing the failings of his contemporaries and Bacon by revealing the wisdom of the ancients.

By the time Bacon wrote his own 'poeticall commonwealth', *New Atlantis*, utopias were texts in dialogue with one another, written as part of a recognized mode of discourse. A recent discussion of Francis Bacon's *New Atlantis* places it at the opposite end of English humanism from More's *Utopia*, both in terms of its date and in its approach to the conception of the reformed society, whether

---

[1] Robert Burton, *The Anatomy of Melancholy*, ed. by Thomas Faulkner, Nicolas K. Kiessling and Rhonda L. Blair, intro. by J.B. Bamborough, 6 vols (Oxford: Clarendon Press, 1989), I, 85. The reference to 'a new Atlantis' was inserted into the 1628 edition of the text and is not present in the 1621 version, as noted by Paul Salzman, 'Narrative contexts for Bacon's *New Atlantis*,' in *Francis Bacon's NEW ATLANTIS: New interdisciplinary essays*, ed. by Bronwen Price (Manchester: Manchester University Press, 2002), pp. 28–47 (pp. 29–30).

[2] Arthur Gorges, *The Wisedome of the Ancients, written in Latine by the Right Honourable Sir Francis Bacon Knight, Baron of Verulam, and Lord Chancelor of England. Done into English by Sir Arthur Gorges Knight* (London, 1619), A2r, A2v.

[3] *The Wisedome of the Ancients*, A2v.

commonwealth or kingdom.⁴ The nature of the relationship between *New Atlantis* and *Utopia*, and the distance between the two texts, is encapsulated in the brief reference which *New Atlantis* makes to the earlier utopian fiction. The Jewish merchant Joabin, explaining to the narrator some of the social customs of Bensalem, the isolated island which becomes home to the narrator and his companions after a shipwreck, mentions *Utopia*: 'I haue read in a Booke of one of your Men, of a Faigned Common-wealth, wher the Married Couple are permitted, before they Contract, to see one another Naked.' This is a practice of which the people of Bensalem disapprove, Joabin explains; instead they have instituted pools near every town in which the friends of the prospective couple may observe them while naked, which is perceived as being a 'more ciuill Way' of achieving the same end.⁵

This brief reference has been discussed by scholars interested in exploring the relationship between the two best-known examples of Renaissance English utopian writing, but more remains to be said on this moment of conversation between the two texts.⁶ Firstly, this allusion to 'one of your Men' constitutes a rare moment at which the national or cultural identity of the narrator and his companions is described. Elsewhere the narrator does not make clear his own nationality or provenance; it is commonly presumed that the travellers are English, on the basis that the text is written in this language, although it has also been argued that they are Spanish.⁷ This attribution by Joabin of *Utopia* to 'one of your Men' could support the argument that the narrator, like Thomas More, is an Englishman; in any case, it emphasizes the shared identity of its own narrator and More. They share a cultural status in that neither is from Bensalem, but rather belongs to a different part of the world in which Bensalem is not known. But they are also connected by the fact that each has narrated a relation of a distant, unknown and seemingly ideal community, whether at first or second hand. *New Atlantis* demonstrates an appreciation of the similarity between the two texts which points to the growing awareness of utopias as constituting something approaching a genre of writing.

This reference to *Utopia* in *New Atlantis* not only acknowledges that utopias share common characteristics, but also highlights certain aspects of the way in which they are read. Joabin's description of *Utopia* not by name but as a 'Faigned Common-wealth' is significant as a reflection on the nature of the text of *New*

---

⁴ Phil Withington, *The Politics of Commonwealth: Citizens and Freemen in Early Modern England* (Cambridge: Cambridge University Press, 2005), p. 55.

⁵ Francis Bacon, *New Atlantis. A Worke unfinished*, in *Sylva Sylvarum: Or a Naturall Historie*, ed. by William Rawley (London: John Haviland for William Lee, 1627), d4v. All further references to *New Atlantis* will be to this edition and will be given in the text in parentheses.

⁶ See, for example, Jerry Weinberger, 'On the miracles in Bacon's *New Atlantis*', in *Francis Bacon's NEW ATLANTIS: New interdisciplinary essays*, pp. 106–28 (p. 109).

⁷ Denise Albanese presumes the travellers are Spanish; see *New Science, New World* (Durham: Duke University Press, 1996), p. 99. See also Claire Jowitt, '"Books will speak plain"? Colonialism, politics and Jewishness in Francis Bacon's *New Atlantis*', in *Francis Bacon's NEW ATLANTIS: New interdisciplinary essays*, pp. 129–55 (p. 132).

Atlantis itself. Bacon's reader is obviously aware that *New Atlantis* is, like *Utopia*, an imaginary relation of an unreal location. Thus, by indirectly calling to his reader's attention the similarity between his text and More's, Bacon implicitly recognizes that *New Atlantis* may also be read as a 'Faigned Common-wealth'. Joabin's reference presumes the imaginary nature of utopian writing and, in consequence, underlines the fictional status of *New Atlantis*. But at the same time, within the text itself, this reference to *Utopia* seeks to differentiate between More's text and the narrator's own relation. *Utopia* is a book which may be read, interpreted and rejected by characters within Bacon's narrative, and Joabin's reference to a 'Faigned Common-wealth' can also be read as a direct contrast to Bensalem, which is, as far as Joabin and the narrator are concerned, real; in this sense, *New Atlantis* asserts that *Utopia* is fictional while ostensibly maintaining the illusion of its own reality. By suggesting that the text is 'Faigned' while seeming to support the fact that it is true, Bacon calls attention to the question of truthfulness and authority in travel writing in a manner that recalls Lucian's *Vera Historia*, discussed in Chapter 1 as an influence on More's *Utopia*. In this critique of travel literature Lucian both mocks the writers of unbelievable travel narratives (and their gullible readers) and emphasizes the difficulty of relying on narrative authority in such writing. The preface to *Vera Historia* ends with a mocking warning to the credulous reader and an assertion of his difference from earlier travel writers:

> I shall be a more honest liar than my predecessors, for I am telling you frankly, here and now, that I have no intention whatever of telling the truth. [...] I am writing about things entirely outside my own experience or anyone else's, things that have no reality whatever and never could have. So mind you do not believe a word I say.[8]

Within the text itself, however, the narrator repeatedly affirms the veracity of what he saw based on the evidence of his own eyes: 'that is what it was like on the Moon. If you do not believe me, go and see for yourself' (262). David H. Larmour has argued that this splitting of the authorial persona results in a paradox in which 'for the "I" of the prologue, everything that follows is a lie; for the narrator of the story, however, everything is true'.[9] In a similar manner, Joabin's reference to *Utopia* in *New Atlantis* at once emphasizes the latter text's fictional status and ostensibly differentiates between the two fictional works in a way that superficially asserts the reliability of *New Atlantis*.[10]

---

[8] *Lucian: Satirical Sketches*, trans. by Paul Turner (Harmondsworth: Penguin, 1961), p. 250.

[9] David H.J. Larmour, 'Sex with Moonmen and Vinewomen: The Reader as Explorer in Lucian's *Vera Historia*', *Intertexts*, 1:2 (1997), 131–46 (133).

[10] Pete Langman notes a similar effect caused by *New Atlantis*'s oblique reference to Plato's description of the 'Great Atlantis' of *Timaeus* and *Critias*, in which the superior reliability of Bacon's text as a source of information is implicitly asserted. See Andrew Peter Langman, '"Beyond, both the Old World, and the New": Authority and Knowledge in the works of Francis Bacon, with special reference to the *New Atlantis*', unpublished PhD thesis, University of Sussex, 2007, pp. 264–5.

The splitting of the authorial persona and the simultaneous assertion of reliability and falseness are common features of the dialogue form, and their presence in *New Atlantis* demonstrates one way in which utopias continued to share features with the dialogue even when not employing that form directly. Bacon's utopian text, like *Christianopolis*, takes the form of an imaginary travel narrative rather than a dialogue; by the early seventeenth century it is the travel narrative which is the appropriate form for relating experiences of foreign societies.[11] Nonetheless, *New Atlantis* makes use of various elements of dialogue, most obviously through its representation of conversation, and these remnants of dialogue play an important role both in the description of Bensalem and in the workings of Salomon's House, the laboratory and college at its centre. This chapter will demonstrate that *New Atlantis* incorporates elements of dialogue in its representation of Bensalem and Salomon's House, and it will suggest that these elements, which include the use of spoken conversation and the role of conversation in the practice and dissemination of natural philosophy, reflect an engagement with notions of dialogue that demonstrates its continued importance to utopian literature, even when the dialogue form is not in use. Utopian writing began to move away from the dialogue form in the early seventeenth century, as the previous chapter demonstrated, but *New Atlantis* shows that the concept of dialogue continued to be integral to the utopian mode of discourse.

Conversation in Bensalem

The imaginary travel narrative of *New Atlantis* is preceded by a letter to the reader from Bacon's editor, William Rawley, which, in describing Bacon's intentions for the text and his desire that it be appended to *Sylva Sylvarum*, draws attention to its fictional nature as a '*Fable*'. Roughly two-thirds of the following narrative recount the narrator's arrival at and experiences of Bensalem, and the final third comprises a speech made by the Father of Salomon's House in private conversation with the narrator, in which he describes the workings and experiments of this institution. The notion of dialogue is present in the text through frequent reported conversation; as soon as the mariners touch dry land, they seem to be in continual discussion with at first one official and then another. The narrator reports conversations with the official who greets the mariners on their arrival (twice), his attendant, a notary, the governor of the Strangers' House (three times), Joabin the Jewish merchant (several times) and the Father of Salomon's House; the effect of these multiple exchanges in a relatively short text is that the narrator seems to be perpetually in dialogue. This effect is heightened by the frequent use of conversational markers, such as 'they called,' 'we answered', 'we said', 'he, smiling said', '(*he said*)', '[he] asked us', '[he] said familiarly', and so on (A3v, A4r, A5r, *et passim*). Conversation is the means by which the narrator learns about both Bensalem and Salomon's House.

---

[11] For the relationship between *New Atlantis* and contemporary travel, see Claire Jowitt, '"Books will speak plain"?'

The reporting of conversation in *New Atlantis*, like the report of direct encounter in a travel narrative, serves to lend the text verisimilitude, as a seemingly accurate version of actual events. The representation of dialogue in the text, however, is frequently fractured or constrained, as the narrator's interlocutors are often called away or otherwise end conversations prematurely; Amy Boesky has described the text as a 'collection of broken or incomplete prose kinds', and lists dialogue as one of these 'kinds'.[12] Joabin, for example, is '*commanded away in haste*' by a messenger during one conversation, and is unable to attend the narrator at another due to 'some charge the City hath laid upon me for the entertaining of this great Person' (B5r, B5v); the governor is likewise called away by a messenger in the middle of a conversation (A6v). These fractured conversations often occur at moments crucial to the mariners making sense of this foreign society; the governor is interrupted, for example, during his explanation of the miraculous revelation of Christianity to Bensalem. The effect of these aspects of the text's use of dialogue, then, is to signal the text's lack of completeness. Not only is *New Atlantis* a 'Worke unfinished', as noted on its title page, but it contains intriguing lacunae which are in part a feature of its use of reported dialogue.[13]

One of the functions of dialogue in *New Atlantis* is thus to complicate a straightforward reading of Bensalem. As in *Utopia*, dialogue ironizes seemingly simple encounters; the conversation between the narrator and Joabin regarding the practices surrounding marriage in Bensalem exemplifies this function. This discussion begins with the narrator mentioning to Joabin that, of all the 'Discourses' he has heard, he has been particularly interested by a 'Relation' from one of the company regarding the practice of the Feast of the Family, 'a most Naturall, Pious, & Reuerend Custome' which celebrates the fecundity of 'any man that shall live to see thirty persons descended of his body alive together' (B3r). This custom, which the narrator hears of in a conversation with one of his fellow mariners, greatly impresses him, because 'I had never heard of a Solemnity wherein Nature did so much preside' (B4v). Joabin commends his approval of this practice, and then goes on to discourse on the marital and sexual habits of the Bensalemites, prefacing his speech with the reminder of its conversational nature: '*heare mee now, and I will tell you what I know*' (B4v). Joabin's knowledge is itself presented

---

[12] Amy Boesky, 'Bacon's *New Atlantis* and the laboratory of prose', in *The Project of Prose in Early Modern Europe and the New World*, ed. by Elizabeth Fowler and Roland Greene (Cambridge: Cambridge University Press, 1997), pp. 138–53 (p. 143).

[13] Bacon's editor, William Rawley, who saw *New Atlantis* and *Sylva Sylvarum* into print in 1627 following Bacon's death, described the text as 'unfinished' on its title page, and noted that 'The rest was not perfected' at the end. Rawley suggested in his letter to the reader that Bacon was prevented from completing *New Atlantis* by his work on his natural histories, as Pete Langman notes in '"Beyond, both the Old World, and the New"', p. 68. Although it is important to remember that *New Atlantis* was not completed by Bacon, it remains the case that to focus on its unfinished nature 'belies the literary complexity of the work and the intricacy of its web of cross-reference to Bacon's oeuvre as a whole', as Sarah Hutton comments in her essay 'Persuasions to Science: Baconian Rhetoric and the *New Atlantis*', in *Francis Bacon's NEW ATLANTIS: New interdisciplinary essays*, pp. 48–59 (p. 49).

through the prism of reported speech; he often prefaces a statement about the Bensalemites' customs with 'they say', '*they say further*', and so on, as though there were another layer in the conversation which the narrator cannot access.

Similarly, the narrator only hears about the Feast of the Family via another conversation; that is, at second hand, rather than through direct experience. Joabin speaks of what he describes as the chastity and cleanness of Bensalem: 'You shall understand, that there is not under the Heavens, so chaste a Nation as this of *Bensalem*, nor so free from all pollution and foulness; it is the Virgin of the World' (B4v). In this society, Joabin explains, there are no brothels or prostitutes, no '*dissolute Houses*', in fact no opportunities at all for sexual sinning to take place. Bensalemites maintain '*faithfull and inuiolate*' friendships without any hint of 'Masculine Love', forbid polygamy and view reverence of the self (which is dependent on chastity) as second only to religion as the 'chiefest Bridle of all Vices' (B5r). Joabin presents the Bensalemites as believing that human nature is so open to depravity that it will take any opportunity to fall into sin, 'Unlawful Lust being like a Furnace, that if you stop the Flames altogether, it will quench but if you give it any vent, it will rage' (B4v–B5r). On the surface, Bensalemites are presented as being supremely chaste, but their view of human nature appears to suggest that people are actually incapable of not sinning if given even the slightest opportunity; even the existence of one 'dissolute House' would give rise to a 'rage' and conflagration of sin. Joabin's presentation of the Bensalemites as virtuous is further complicated by the fact that he stops talking mid-conversation, and needs to be prompted to continue: the narrator reports that 'the good *Jew* paused a little', so that the narrator is obliged to keep the conversation going, 'farr more willing to heare him speake on, than to speake my selfe; yet thinking it decent, that vpon his pause of Speech, I should not be altogether silent' (B5r). Joabin appears at this moment to be an unwilling conversant, bowing his head as he begins to describe Bensalem's '*many wise and excellent Lawes touching Marriage*'. It is at this point that Joabin mentions the Utopian practice of allowing couples to be viewed naked before they contract; immediately afterwards, the conversation is cut short by the arrival of the messenger. This conversation thus ends by calling to mind the fictionality of Bensalem and *New Atlantis*, and curtailing the dissemination of information.

Moments at which the reporting of conversation in Bensalem become interesting thus serve to confound a simplistic reading of the text, such as that provided by much twentieth-century scholarship, which read Bensalem as Bacon's own ideal society.[14] Some scholars, in opposition to the view that Bensalem

---

[14] For Bensalem as Bacon's ideal see James Spedding, 'Preface to *The New Atlantis*', in *The Collected Works of Francis Bacon*, ed. by James Spedding, Robert Leslie Ellis and Douglas Denon Heath, 7 vols (London: Longmans, 1857-9), III, 122. See also Moody E. Prior, 'Bacon's Man of Science', in *Essential Articles for the Study of Francis Bacon*, ed. by Brian Vickers (London: Sidgwick & Jackson, 1972), pp. 140–63; Harvey Wheeler, 'Francis Bacon's *New Atlantis*: The "Mould" of a Lawfinding Commonwealth', in *Francis Bacon's Legacy of Texts*, ed. by William A. Sessions (New York: AMS Press, 1990), pp. 291–310; David C. Innes, 'Bacon's *New Atlantis*: The Christian Hope and The Modern Hope', *Interpretation*, 22:1 (1994), 3–37.

presents an uncomplicated ideal of social organization, have highlighted negative aspects of life in this society.[15] In spite of this, there is much about Bensalem that seems idealized and consonant with the traditional view of the utopia as a better place, and in particular an improved version of the author's own society. When the land of Bensalem itself first appears to the travellers, it seems nothing short of miraculous, revealing itself in response to their prayers (A3r). During their stay, the travellers reiterate that this newfound land is a divine manifestation, even heaven-like: 'wee were come into a Land of Angells, which did appear to vs dayly, and preuent vs with Comforts, which we thought not of, much lesse expected' (B3r). The physical experience of being in Bensalem is for the travellers a comfortable one, with 'right good Viands [...] better then any *Collegiate* Diett, that I haue knowne in *Europe*' and 'wonderfull pleasing and Refreshing Drink'; comfortable lodgings; and effective medicine, so that those among the travellers who are ill improve by the hour, 'They mended so kindely, and so fast' (B1v, B2r). The people of Bensalem themselves are found to be good-natured and generous, 'At whose hands we found such Humanity, and such a Freedome and desire, to take Strangers, as it were, into their Bosome'. The experience of encountering these people and learning about their customs is enough 'to make vs forget all that was deare to vs, in our owne Countries', so that many of the travellers are minded to ask the governor if they may stay permanently. The narrator, for one, is convinced that 'if ther be a Mirror in the World, worthy to hold Mens Eyes, it is that Countrey' (D1r).

Bensalem is surely closer to representing a fantasy or ideal society for Bacon than Utopia is for More. It is important, however, not to lose sight of the ways in which the text highlights the remoteness of Bensalem from the narrator's own society, and indeed the society of Bacon himself. Bensalem represents for Bacon a situation that is desirable and technically possible, but which is kept so distant from immediate reality by a variety of factors that its achievement is problematic. David Colclough describes Bensalem as representing Bacon's imagination of the possible shape of things to come, serving as 'a model of the use of knowledge and reading for any society [...] rather than a model of a new, perfect society'. As Colclough points out, it is misguided to read *New Atlantis* as a utopia in the Morean mould.[16] *New Atlantis* represents a change in the use of the utopian mode of discourse: Bacon's focus is the achievement of the ideal system for supporting the advancement of learning, not the ideal society. His use of dialogue is not playful, like More's; neither is it concerned with social and moral improvement, like the 'Reformation fictions' discussed in Chapter 2. Primarily, the text constitutes

---

[15] Most notably, feminist readings have highlighted the exploitative nature of Salomon's House and Bensalem. See Carolyn Merchant, *The Death of Nature: Women, Ecology, and the Scientific Revolution* (London: Wildwood House, 1982), pp. 180–90; Susan Bruce, 'Virgins of the World and Feasts of the Family: Sex and the Social Order in Two Renaissance Utopias', in *English Renaissance Prose: History, Language and Politics*, ed. by Neil Rhodes (Tempe: Medieval and Renaissance Texts and Studies, 1997), pp. 125–46.

[16] David Colclough, 'Ethics and politics in the *New Atlantis*', in *Francis Bacon's NEW ATLANTIS: New interdisciplinary essays*, pp. 60–81 (p. 70, p. 62).

a celebration of the possibilities of natural philosophy for the improvement of society; it is also a testament to the extent of what is not yet known or has not yet been achieved in Bacon's own society. The aspects of dialogue present in the text, as discussed above, are crucial in creating the impression that Bensalem is at once a desirable state that Bacon wishes to see achieved and currently unachievable.

The focus of Bacon's text, and the aspect which clearly most interested him in terms of potential for change, is the central institute which the society of Bensalem supports, Salomon's House or the College of the Six Days' Works. Salomon's House, the state-administered research institute that is the '*very Eye*' and the '*Lanthorne*' of Bensalem, has been claimed as a progenitor of the most important scientific organization of seventeenth-century England, the Royal Society (B3v, C4r).[17] Although Bacon did not see its foundation in his lifetime, it is widely accepted that he influenced the institutionalization of natural philosophy in seventeenth-century England.[18] It is evident from Bacon's own writings that he wanted to reorganize and institutionalize natural knowledge and philosophy in a manner suggestive of both Salomon's House and the Royal Society, and the former institution has been read as a direct model for the latter. As has been well documented, much of Bacon's writing was geared towards establishing a new organizational structure of natural philosophy.[19] In the *Advancement of Learning*, for example, he placed great importance on the institutional framework, the 'Foundations, and Buyldings, Endowments with Reuenewes, Endowments with Franchizes and Priuiledges, Institutions and Ordinances for gouernment' necessary for progress, and it is just such an institutional framework that is imagined in *New Atlantis*.[20] Similarly, in *Valerius Terminus* Bacon suggests that there should be 'an

---

[17] The idea of Salomon's House as an influence on the founding of the Royal Society is well established. See E.N. da C. Andrade, 'Science in the Seventeenth Century', *Proceedings of the Royal Institution of Great Britain*, 30 (1938), 209–40 (226); Douglas McKie, 'The Origins and Foundation of the Royal Society', *Notes and Records of the Royal Society of London*, 15 (1960), 1–37 (9); Brian Vickers, *Francis Bacon and Renaissance Prose* (Cambridge: Cambridge University Press, 1968), p. 49; Paolo Rossi, *Francis Bacon: From Magic to Science*, trans. by Sacha Rabinovitch (London: Routledge & Kegan Paul, 1968), p. xiii; Antonia McLean, *Humanism and the Rise of Science in Tudor England* (London: Heinemann, 1972), p. 233. For the connection between Salomon's House and the Royal Society see Michael Hunter, *Science and Society in Restoration England* (Cambridge: Cambridge University Press, 1981), Chapters 1 and 2, and Michael Hunter, *Establishing the New Science: The Experience of the Early Royal Society* (Woodbridge: Boydell, 1989), p. 6.

[18] See, for example, A. Rupert Hall and Marie Boas Hall, 'The Intellectual Origins of the Royal Society, London and Oxford', *Notes and Records of the Royal Society of London*, 23:2 (1968), 157–68.

[19] John E. Leary, Jr., *Francis Bacon and the Politics of Science* (Ames: Iowa State University Press, 1994), pp. 247–8; Rose-Mary Sargent, 'Bacon as an advocate for cooperative scientific research', in *The Cambridge Companion to Bacon*, ed. by Markku Peltonen (Cambridge: Cambridge University Press, 1996), pp. 146–71 (p. 146).

[20] Francis Bacon, *The Aduancement of Learning* (Book 2, 2A2r), ed. by Michael Kiernan (Oxford: Clarendon Press, 2000), p. 56.

administration of knowledge in some such order and policy as the king of Spain in regard of his great dominion useth the state', with various individual councils being organized together under one central 'council of State or last resort'.[21] As a consequence, modern commentators have been quick to identify Salomon's House as Bacon's ideal institution of scientific research, a form of propaganda for his own projects.[22]

The centrality of Salomon's House to Bacon's text means that to read the social setting of Bensalem as the focus of Bacon's utopia is to misjudge the text. In fact, *New Atlantis* has comparatively little to say about social or political change: it is not a programme for social reform. If it were, we might expect it to detail the religious, economic and political differences between Bensalem and contemporary England, in an effort to show where positive changes might be made. However, many such areas are ignored: there is almost no information at all on how the society functions politically, how its church is organized, its education system and so on.[23] The aim of *New Atlantis* is not to motivate social reform on a wide scale but to explore the kinds of development that might be necessary to support an institution like Salomon's House. Hence the society Bacon creates in Bensalem is neither simply an ideal one nor a straightforward and direct model for his own; rather it reflects the social conditions that Bacon imagined would be needed if the practice of natural philosophy were to be institutionalized and supported by the state.

By placing the focus of the utopia not on society at large but on a centralized institution, Bacon contributes to the development of the utopian mode of discourse in two important ways. Firstly, like Andreae and Campanella, he brings the institution to the centre of utopian thought. Secondly, and also in accordance with contemporary authors of utopias, Bacon continues the development of the utopia from a rhetorical and playful mode of writing, as it was for More, into a means of seriously envisioning societal change. Bensalem is not an ideal society, but Bacon uses the utopian form to imagine an environment different from his own in specific ways, as a means of exploring the effects of social change, and this was the way in which the utopian mode was to develop in the later seventeenth century. By the 1640s, the utopia had become a serious means of projecting social

---

[21] *Valerius Terminus*, in *Works*, ed. by Spedding, Ellis and Heath, III, 231.

[22] For Salomon's House as Bacon's ideal research community see, for example, John M. Steadman, '"Beyond Hercules": Bacon and the Scientist as hero,' *Studies in the Literary Imagination*, 4:1 (1971), 3–47 (43); J. Peter Zetterberg, 'Echoes of Nature in Salomon's House', *Journal of the History of Ideas*, 43:2 (1982), 179–93; John Channing Briggs, 'Bacon's Science and Religion', in *The Cambridge Companion to Bacon*, pp. 172–99 (p. 192). More recently Christopher Kendrick has argued that 'Bacon's obsession was to refashion intellectual production, and no one doubts that *The New Atlantis* (1626) came into existence as propaganda for the refashioning', in 'The Imperial Laboratory: Discovering Forms in *The New Atlantis*', *English Literary History*, 70:4 (2003), 1021–42 (1021).

[23] On the absence of politics in *New Atlantis* and the lack of reference to basic matters, such as its geography and administration, see David Colclough, 'Ethics and politics in the *New Atlantis*', pp. 61–2.

change in order to promote improvement in that direction; this was an advance that was partly rooted in the developments made by *New Atlantis*. This chapter will go on to examine the ways in which the concept of dialogue contributes to the perceived superiority of Bensalem over Europe, the presentation of scientific activity in Salomon's House and the underlying anxiety about the production and dissemination of knowledge.

Natural Philosophy and Religion in Bensalem and Salomon's House

Salomon's House is described as an order or society, which is the '*Noblest Foundation, (as wee thinke,) that euer was vpon the Earth; And the Lanthorne of this Kingdome*'. '[D]edicated to the Study of the Works, and Creatures of GOD', it is also known as the 'Colledge of the sixe Daies Workes', instituted by King Solamona in order that its Fellows might gain knowledge of the outside world, 'And especially of the Sciences, Arts, Manufactures, and Inuentions of all the World' via its 'Merchants of Light' (C4r, C4v). The mariners are informed of the existence of Salomon's House by the governor, but they are given little further information about it until the narrator is favoured with a private audience with one of its senior members, one of the Fathers of Salomon's House. All knowledge of Salomon's House is communicated to the narrator by speech; Joabin informs him that the Father has heard of the mariners' presence in Bensalem, and is prepared to speak to one of them in '*private Conference*'. The day and time for this conference are appointed by the Father, who receives the mariners with full ceremony:

> We found him in a faire Chamber, richly hanged, and carpetted vnder Foote, without any Degrees to the State. He was sett vpon a Low Throne richly adorned, and a rich Cloath of State ouer his Head, of blew Sattin Embroidered. He was alone, saue that he had two Pages of Honour, on either Hand one, finely attired in White. His Vnder Garments were the like that we saw him weare in the Chariott; but in stead of his Gowne, he had on him a Mantle with a Cape, of the same fine Black, fastned about him. When we came in, as we were taught, we bowed Lowe at our first Entrance; And when we were come neare his Chaire, he stood vp, holding forth his Hand vngloued, and in Posture of Blessing; And we euery one of vs stooped downe, and kissed the Hemme of his Tippett. (E1v)

The conference between the two men takes place in a manner reminiscent of an audience with a monarch; or perhaps, given that the Father blesses the narrator and calls him '*my Sonne*', the context of religious encounter is more appropriate. After all, the purpose of the conversation is to communicate truth; it constitutes a revelation which the Father blesses at the end of his speech and '*to Publish it; for the Good of other Nations; For wee here are in* GODS *Bosome*' (G2r). The formality of the occasion is appropriate to the seriousness of the Father's speech, which will '*impart vnto thee, for the Loue of* GOD *and Men, a Relation of the true State of* Salomons House' (E2r).

That the Father's stated purpose is the communication of truth is part of his speech's exertion of rhetorical control. The way in which he demonstrates authority – through rhetorical prowess and physical display – calls to mind the use of rhetoric and physical performance in contemporary travel writings in their efforts to testify to the truths of their experiences.[24] As a whole, the Father's speech endeavours to convince the narrator (and, by implication, the reader) of the wonderful achievements of Salomon's House (and, by extension, the desirability of their existence in the real world). The Father begins by explaining the 'order' of his oration, which will cover four main topics:

> First I will set forth vnto you the End of our Foundation. Secondly, the Preparations and Instruments we have for our Workes. Thirdly, the seuerall Employments and Functions wherto our Fellowes are assigned. And fourthly, the Ordinances and Rites which we obserue. (E2r)

His speech not only serves to inform the narrator of the workings of Salomon's House, however; its secondary function is to demonstrate the superiority of the Bensalemites over the Europeans.[25] This is achieved through the direct comparison between the two groups' state of knowledge and possession of technology, in which the Father continually emphasizes that, thanks to their superior grasp of natural knowledge and dominion over nature, the Bensalemites possess many skills and objects that are beyond the Europeans' reach: 'which you haue not' and 'more then you haue' are frequent refrains. The Father's speech is thus meant to inform or teach, but teaching is not its only mode of persuasion; it also seeks to move its auditor or reader to desire the possession of the wonders of Salomon's House. The Father's rhetorical control and the serious and formal nature of this conversation, as well as its size in proportion to the rest of the text, reflect the weight Bacon places on the importance of the establishment and protection of natural philosophy.[26] In order to understand this more fully, it will be helpful briefly to consider the broader place of natural philosophy and its relationship to religion in Bacon's thought and in *New Atlantis* specifically.

Although *New Atlantis* describes the Bensalemites' experience of Christian revelation (in another curtailed conversation), it gives little information about the actual workings of religion and its relationship to the state in Bensalem. It is likely that the dominance of the conversation about Salomon's House in the text is caused in part by the fact that, according to Bacon's editor, William Rawley, *New Atlantis* is 'A Worke unfinished' and was intended to include 'a *Frame* of *Lawes*, or the

---

[24] See Jonathan P.A. Sell, *Rhetoric and Wonder in English Travel Writing, 1560–1613* (Farnham: Ashgate, 2006), Chapter 5.

[25] On this see Langman, '"Beyond, both the Old World, and the New"', pp. 276–8.

[26] Pete Langman notes that of the 15,385 words of *New Atlantis*, the 3,572 words of the section on Salomon's House (e2r–g2r) take up seventeen pages; the larger font size of this section increases its apparent proportion to 36 percent of the total number of pages, compared to 23 percent of the total word count. See Langman, '"Beyond, both the Old World, and the New"', pp. 69–70, n. 122.

best State or *Mould* of a *Common-wealth*', but was prevented from completion by Bacon's distraction by his work on his natural history.[27] Had such details been incorporated, it is possible that the present focus on the activities of Salomon's House would have diminished, but it seems likely, given the weight given to this institution in the text as it stands, that it would have remained central. Similarly, it is possible to attribute the neglect of description of the church and religious practices of New Atlantis to its incomplete nature. The comparative neglect of such issues does not necessarily prove, therefore, that Bacon was less interested in such issues than More or Andreae, who both devote more time to the explanation of religion in the utopian society. Nonetheless, it does suggest that Bacon's concern in *New Atlantis* was the description of a state-supported scientific community, rather than a whole society. While *New Atlantis* has sometimes been read in support of the notion that Bacon himself was a 'non-believer', one scholar has argued that the lack of attention to the religious dimension of the text is symptomatic of a traditional neglect of Bacon's religious thought.[28] Indeed, questions of religion are central to *New Atlantis*, given that natural philosophy is not for Bacon a purely secular activity, but has a fundamentally spiritual and religious purpose.

As is typical in seventeenth-century thought, the spheres of scientific and religious activity generally overlap in Bacon's writings, and he commonly seeks to describe one sphere in the terms of the other. In *Cogitata et Visa* (1607), for example, Bacon discusses the way in which discoveries are made in religion and natural philosophy, arguing that both must be proved through their works: '*Et quod in religione verissime requiritur, ut fidem quis ex operibus monstret; idem in naturali philosophia competere, ut scientia similiter ex operibus monstretur.*'[29] Bacon also held that the book of Nature is the key to understanding the book of God's written word and that men should 'endeauour an endlesse progresse or proficience in both'.[30] In his view, the rise of experimental science was directly sanctioned by God, and would not lead men away from divine truth: 'it is an assured truth, and a conclusion of experience, that a little or superficiall knowledge of Philosophie may encline the minde of Man to Atheisme, but a further proceeding therein doth bring the mind backe againe to Religion'.[31] The divine

---

[27] *Francis Bacon: The Major Works*, ed. by Brian Vickers (Oxford: Oxford University Press, 1996; revised 2002), p. 785. Bacon was, of course, also prevented from finishing *New Atlantis* by his unexpected death after a short illness.

[28] Jerry Weinberger, 'Francis Bacon and the Unity of Knowledge: Reason and Revelation', in *Francis Bacon and the Refiguring of Early Modern Thought*, ed. by Julie Robin Solomon and Catherine Gimelli Martin (Farnham: Ashgate, 2005), pp. 109–27 (p. 111); Travis DeCook, 'The Ark and Immediate Revelation in Francis Bacon's *New Atlantis*', *Studies in Philology*, 105 (2008), 103–22 (107).

[29] *Cogitata et Visa*, in *Works*, ed. by Spedding, Ellis and Heath, III, 612. In English: 'And what is required in the truest religion, is that faith which is shown from works; this is in accordance with natural philosophy, that knowledge is similarly shown from works.'

[30] *Aduancement of Learning*, ed. by Kiernan (Book 1, B4r), p. 9.

[31] *Aduancement of Learning*, (Book 1, B3v–B4r), pp. 8–9.

sanction for the pursuit of natural philosophy is also suggested by his celebrated use of the image of the ship and the quotation from Daniel in the frontispiece to *Instauratio magna* (1620): '*multi pertransibunt et augebitur scientia*'.[32] Bacon frequently wrote that the practice of natural philosophy would provide the means of restoring man's dominion over nature, enabling him to re-attain a complete level of knowledge akin to that of Adam, and thus for him natural philosophy had a religious motivation; the 'true ends of knowledge' constituted 'a restitution and reinvesting (in great part) of man to the sovereignty and power (for whensoever he shall be able to call the creatures by their true names he shall again command them) which he had in his first state of creation'.[33] Moreover, Bacon understood natural philosophy as a potential inducement to religious faith: 'if we take the matter rightly, natural philosophy after the Word of God is the best medicine for superstition and most highly recommended food for faith'.[34] Consequently, he was adamant that the inquisition of nature must not be restricted, and that religious controversies must not hinder natural philosophy, as he warns in the Preface to his *Great Instauration*: it is an error to think that 'any aspect of the inquiry into nature is forbidden as if by decree.'[35]

Natural philosophy and religious belief have an inevitably complex relationship in Bacon's imaginary society. For the purposes of this chapter, I wish to show that the function of religion in Bensalem is to support the investigation of the natural world, while natural philosophy in turn has achieved a dominion over nature which makes the Bensalemites' state vastly superior to that of Bacon's contemporaries. One of the first things the travellers learn about Bensalem is that it is a Christian society; before any conversation takes place, a scroll is delivered to the travellers' boat, bearing the symbols of the cherubim's wings and the cross.[36] The first verbal communication that takes place is the Bensalemite official's question, '*Are yee Christians?*', to which the travellers are confident to reply in the affirmative, having

---

[32] Daniel 12:4. In English, 'Many shall pass to and fro and knowledge shall be increased.' On the use of this verse in the early seventeenth century, see David Harris Sacks, 'Rebuilding Solomon's Temple: Richard Hakluyt's Great Instauration', in *New Worlds Reflected: Travel and Utopia in the Early Modern Period*, ed. by Chloë Houston (Farnham: Ashgate, 2010), pp. 17–55.

[33] *Valerius Terminus*, in *Works*, ed. by Spedding, Ellis and Heath, III, 222. On Bacon's belief that learning could undo the consequences of the fall, see J.C. Davis, *Utopia and the Ideal Society: A Study of English Utopian Writing, 1516–1700* (Cambridge: Cambridge University Press, 1981; repr. 1983), p. 125.

[34] *Novum Organum* (89), in *The* Instauratio Magna *Part II: Novum Organum and Associated Texts*, ed. and trans. by Graham Rees with Maria Wakely (Oxford: Clarendon Press, 2004), p. 143.

[35] 'Preface' to the *Great Instauration*, in *The* Instauratio Magna *Part II: Novum Organum and Associated Texts* (A6r), p. 23.

[36] J.C. Davis points out that their common Christian faith is the most important feature of the relations between New Atlantis and the outside world, and in particular the European visitors. See Davis, *Utopia and the Ideal Society*, p. 109.

been reassured by the cross on the scroll (A4v). Subsequently the mariners' first question to the governor of the Strangers' House regards Bensalem's Christianity; they want to know how the nation was converted and by whom. The governor explains that by a miracle which took place twenty years after Christ's birth, the Bensalemites had delivered to them an ark containing a Bible and a letter from Saint Bartholomew, written so that everyone could read it in his own language (B4r).

The story of the revelation made to the people of Bensalem is helpful in establishing their unusual spiritual status. Firstly, the governor mentions that the Bible received by the Bensalemites contained '*all the* Canonicall Bookes *of the* Old *and* New Testament, *according as you haue them* [...]; *and the* Apocalypse *it selfe, And some other* Bookes *of the* New Testament, *which were not at that time written, were neuertheless in the* Booke' (B4r). Bacon goes to considerable lengths to emphasize the complete status of this Bible. As Brian Vickers notes in his commentary upon the text, hardly any of the books of the New Testament had been written at the presumed time of this revelation to the Bensalemites, but this was not in fact known at the time at which Bacon was writing.[37] Hence Bacon's emphasis on the completeness of the Bible received from the ark demonstrates his insistence that the Bensalemites have full knowledge of the word of God, and are not in any way disadvantaged by the unusual manner in which this knowledge is delivered to them; on the contrary, they are in a position to recover the total knowledge of the world contained in the New Testament. Secondly, the act of revelation includes an assurance to the Bensalemites, not only of the '*Good Will*' of God and Jesus, but that on the '*same day*' that they receive the ark '*is come vnto them Saluation and Peace*' (B4v). This assurance of salvation would appear to place the Bensalemites in a unique position according to seventeenth-century Protestant theology; they have received assurance not of the prospect of entering heaven after death, but of the certainty of salvation itself. According to Calvinist theology, the act of being saved can refer to a past, present or future action. All three together are needed for the full process of salvation, and the knowledge that an individual has been saved signifies that the others will follow. The important question, then, is whether or not the individual has been saved. For the Bensalemites, this question has been collectively answered at the moment of revelation: '*the same day, is come vnto them Saluation*' (B4v). At the moment at which the Bensalemites gain knowledge of Christ and of the world through revelation and the reception of the Bible, they also receive assurance of their salvation.

Following this description of the revelation, the governor is called away by a messenger, and the conversation is interrupted. Subsequently, little attention is paid to the practical aspects of religion in Bensalem. However, there are two aspects of the religious life that are of particular significance. The first is that there appears to be no differentiation between different sects or confessions of Christianity. The Bensalemites' question is 'Are yee Christians?', not 'Are yee Protestants?' or 'Are yee Catholics?' The Bensalemites themselves seem to worship Christ in one unified manner. The second point of interest is the degree of religious tolerance

---

[37] *Francis Bacon: The Major Works*, p. 792.

that the Bensalemites exhibit to non-Christian groups. When Christian revelation reaches Bensalem, there are present 'Hebrewes, Persians, *and* Indians, *besides the Natiues*', and the narrator's friend Joabin, who informs him about various social practices, is Jewish: 'for they haue some few Stirps of *Iewes* yet remaining among them, whom they leaue to their owne Religion' (B4v). It would be facile to argue that Bacon was directly promoting either of these strategies for practice in England. Although there is limited evidence elsewhere in his writings to suggest that he may have been broadly in favour of both religious unification and religious tolerance, it would be too simplistic to read *New Atlantis* as a direct endorsement of either.[38] Rather, we must look at what is achieved by Bensalem's single form of Christianity and religious toleration.

As far as we are aware, there are no religious controversies in Bensalem. There have been no holy wars; indeed, the text has recently been read as 'a fantasy of the end of [...] religious controversy'.[39] The unity and tolerance practised by the Bensalemites is a vital part of their stability. If this stability has a direct function, it is to smooth the surroundings of Salomon's House. With no interference from religion, natural philosophy can be freely explored; there are no religious sanctions or arguments to threaten it. Indeed, the Fellows themselves have taken on roles we might otherwise expect to be accorded to religious leaders; as well as being a civic leader, the Father appears to have a religious role, as suggested by his title. In the midst of the procession, in front of the Father's chariot, walk two men, one carrying a crosier and one a pastoral staff, 'like a Sheep-hooke; neither of them of Metall, but the Crosier of Balme-wood, the Pastoral staffe of Cedar'. These two staffs, the former traditionally carried by the archbishop and the latter by the bishop, clearly accord the Father religious as well as social status. As he is carried through the crowds, 'he held up his bare Hand, as he went, as blessing the People, but in Silence', and it is because he wishes to offer the travellers his blessing that they are invited into his presence (E1r, E1v). The degree of religious status given to the natural philosophers within Bensalem even appears to be vindicated

---

[38] For example, in his essay 'Of Unity in Religion' from the 1625 collection, Bacon enumerates the benefits of a unified and tolerant church, though he does not suggest that a unification of all factions in the Christian church is possible or desirable. See 'Of Unity in Religion', in *The Essayes or Counsels, Civill and Morall*, ed. by Michael Kiernan (Oxford: Clarendon Press, 2000).

[39] DeCook, 'The Ark and Immediate Revelation in Francis Bacon's *New Atlantis*', 122. It is possible to read the lack of religious controversy in Bensalem as a feature of its unique status at a point in time when the final revelation of all knowledge is taking place. The Bensalemites' complete Bible, and their knowledge of the world, suggest that they are located in the 'end time' referred to in Daniel 12, when Daniel is told that the book shall be unsealed, a time that may be identified with the coming of the Messiah. The whole of *New Atlantis* may itself be read as an apocalypse, or revelation of divine secrets in nature, as David Colclough suggests in his essay 'Ethics and politics in the *New Atlantis*', in *Francis Bacon's NEW ATLANTIS: New interdisciplinary essays*, p. 71, but the narrative itself also seems to be set at a time of apocalypse, when the full revelation of knowledge is in the process of taking place.

by an external force: when the miracle of revelation is given to Bensalem, it is a fellow of Salomon's House who prays for guidance and officially acknowledges the miracle, and who is then the only person able to approach its site.

Thus the purpose of religion in Bensalem, in its unity and stability, is to support natural philosophy; natural philosophy, as we might expect from Bacon's writings elsewhere on its potential for human improvement, also has a religious purpose. The practice of natural philosophy in Bensalem has enabled its inhabitants to achieve a kind of dominion over nature of which the European travellers could only dream. The technologies of Salomon's House are capable of their own wonders: they can, for example, improve human sight and hearing; achieve flight; light fires that will never go out; and imitate and control other living creatures (F3v). Although the Bensalemites have not gone so far as to have discovered the secret of eternal life, they have developed their own 'Water of Paradise', which is not only good for the health but also prolongs human life (E3v). In his description of the wonderful powers of Salomon's House, the Father constantly reiterates their superiority to anything the travellers have known. The spoken nature of the conversation between the narrator and the Father is important here, because it facilitates the Father's repeated emphasis on the Bensalemites' superiority via rhetorical opposition: 'Wee haue also diuerse Mechanicall. Arts, which you haue not', 'Wee haue [...] a Number of Fossiles, and Imperfect Mineralls, which you haue not', 'Wee haue Harmonies which you haue not', and so on. In combination with his emphasis on the fact that the Bensalemites have already achieved spiritual salvation and the guarantee of divine grace, their knowledge and control of the natural environment places the people of Bensalem in a position which is far superior to that of the European travellers who encounter them.[40] If Salomon's House is a model for how a scientific society might operate in the future, the Bensalemites' supremacy in matters of natural knowledge over their European counterparts represents the potential superiority of the future over the present.[41]

It is worth noting that acts of conversation play a role at each of these moments in which either the religion or the activity of natural philosophy of Bensalem or Salomon's House are described. Conversation, as suggested above, is of importance to the Father's relation to the narrator, not only in the persuasive nature of the Father's rhetoric, but in conveying the honour accorded to the narrator in hearing the relation, and the gravity of such an occasion. The serious and formal nature of the speech in which Salomon's House is described is both part of a rhetorical display of power and superiority on behalf of the Father and part of an attempt by Bacon to demonstrate the awe and respect with which such activities deserve to be treated. At other important moments, too, such as the question about the mariners' religious status and the description of the miraculous revelation, the spoken word

---

[40] See Langman, '"Beyond, both the Old World, and the New"', p. 277.

[41] On Bacon's belief that 'Bensalem in the future, now', see A.P. Langman, 'The Future Now: Chance, Time and Natural Divination in the Thought of Francis Bacon', in *The Uses of the Future in Early Modern Europe*, ed. by Andrea Brady and Emily Butterworth (London: Routledge, 2010), pp. 142–55 (p. 155).

is used. Notably, a written text is used for the very first communication between the Bensalemites and their visitors, when the latter are given 'a little Scroule of Parchment' warning them not to land and to agree to leave the area within sixteen days unless allowed a longer stay (A3v). Pete Langman has argued that this latter scroll represents the 'privileging of written information on the island', not least because it obliges the travellers to communicate their own requests in writing, rather than do so orally, 'presumably a way of preventing misunderstandings as well as providing written records which may be kept in Bensalem's voluminous archives'.[42] But the preference for written rather than oral communication here may also be related to the Bensalemites' fear that the travellers may constitute a source of infection. Once they have been properly assessed and quarantined, all further communication between the two groups is spoken. Other written texts do exist within Bensalem; notably, as mentioned above, the act of revelation itself takes place partly through a text, and the text of *New Atlantis* itself is representative of a movement from oral communication towards print. Nonetheless, it is spoken conversation, rather than the written text, that is privileged in Bensalem, and this applies also to the workings of Salomon's House.

Conversation in Salomon's House

The Father's speech describes in detail the different inventions and experiments carried out by the Fellows of that college, emphasizing the usefulness of this activity to the wider community. The section describing the experiments undertaken with sound exemplifies this; the Father explains that they are able to replicate, alter and amplify sounds and create echoes, and have developed instruments that improve the hearing, as well as convey sounds across long distances by means of 'Trunks *and* Pipes'. Oral communication in Bensalem can thus presumably take place across greater distances than would have been possible in contemporary Europe. Such devices would have been useful in communicating with Bensalem's hermits, who live upon 'High Towers; The Highest about halfe a Mile in Height; And some of them likewise set vpon High Mountaines' (E2v). From these long-lived hermits, the Father says, the Fellows 'learne many things', things presumably communicated to the Fellows on their occasional visits, when the hermits are also instructed what to observe. This is one example of the reliance of the Fellowship of Salomon's House upon oral communication for the dissemination of information.

A further instance of this reliance is to be found in the activities of the 'Merchants of Light', twelve Fellows who sail around the world gathering information and imparting it to Bensalem. Part of their function is to bring back 'the Bookes, and Abstracts, and Patternes of Experiments of all other Parts'; it is also to enter into the Fellowship's 'Consultations' regarding what information should be published, and what should not. Travel here functions as a kind of one-sided conversation, in which Bensalem learns from the rest of the world while concealing its own identity

---

[42] Langman, '"Beyond, both the Old World, and the New"', p. 261.

and knowledge. Similarly, the Fellows' communication with the rest of Bensalem regarding their findings appears to rely at least in part on verbal communication:

> Lastly, wee haue Circuites or Visits, of diuers Principall Cities of the Kingdome; wher, as it commeth to passe, we doe publish such New Profitable Inuentions, as wee thinke good. And wee doe also declare Naturall Diuinations of Diseases, Plagues, Swarmes of Hurtfull. Creatures, Scarcety, Tempests, Earthquakes, Great Inundations, Cometts, Temperature of the Yeare, and diuerse other Things; And wee giue Counsell thereupon, what the People shall doe, for the reuention and Remedy of them.

The Father says that they 'publish' new inventions, but there is no suggestion that this involves print publication; 'publish' might easily mean to report or declare openly, rather than to put into print, and the additions of 'declare' and 'giue Counsell' suggest an oral communication rather than a written one.[43] It is through spoken language, then, that the wonders of Salomon's House are collected and are communicated to the inhabitants of Bensalem, as well as to the narrator. Indeed, the activities of Salomon's House are about to move from spoken discourse into print for the first time with the publication of the narrator's story.

In representing natural philosophy as both taking place through and being disseminated by conversation, Bacon anticipated a culture that was to develop in the practice of natural philosophy in the seventeenth century. Studies of the history of science in this period have demonstrated that the notion of conversation operated as a model for experimental practice and that conversation and discussion were themselves important elements of scientific activity. A number of cultural studies of scientific practice in Europe have suggested that, in Steven Shapin's words, strands of such activity can be seen 'as a courtly version of civil conversation'.[44] Shapin himself has shown how the concept of conversation was to become a model for scientific investigation and has argued that conversation formed a means of 'illuminating the nature of scientific practice'.[45] In their introduction to a collection of essays on science, literature and rhetoric in the period, Juliet Cummins and David Burchell draw attention to the frontispiece to Galileo's *Dialogo sopra i due massimi sistemi del mondo* (*Dialogue on the Two Principal Systems of the World*, 1632), which shows three men in animated conversation and is suggestive of the ways in which the creation of scientific knowledge was seen to rely not

---

[43] OED, third edition, September 2007; online version June 2012 [http://www.oed.com/view/Entry/154072, accessed 10.8.2012].

[44] Shapin cites the studies of Jay Tribby, 'Cooking (with) Clio and Cleo: Eloquence and Experiment in Seventeenth-Century Florence', *Journal of the History of Ideas*, 52 (1991), 417–39; Mario Biagoli, *Galileo, Courtier: The Practice of Science in the Culture of Absolutism* (Chicago: University of Chicago Press, 1993); Paula Findlen, 'The Limits of Civility and the Ends of Science' (unpublished paper); Steven Shapin, *A Social History of Truth: Civility and Science in Seventeenth-Century England* (Chicago: University of Chicago Press, 1994), p. 120, p. 121.

[45] Shapin, *A Social History of Truth*, p. 120, p. 351.

only on social networks, but on the act of conversation.[46] Galileo's dialogue is an example of how the dialogue form was to remain of central importance to scientific writing in the seventeenth century, even as that form declined in imaginative literature.[47] Cummins and Burchell's book demonstrates the close relationship between literary and scientific discourses in the Renaissance period; it also establishes the ways in which the social aspects of scientific production, including conversation, were central to the practices and conventions of the Royal Society. Meeting and discussion were, of course, a vital part of the workings of that society from its inception, forming part of its basis in collaboration and open debate.[48] This collaborative model arguably has its roots in the Baconian programme, exemplified in the network of natural philosophers described in Salomon's House. Thus Bacon's model of natural philosophy relying upon verbal communication for its creation and dissemination typified the developing relationship between conversation and scientific activity during the seventeenth century.

Conversation is central to the practice and communication of natural philosophy in *New Atlantis*, but it is a problematic element within the text. The conversation between the Father and the narrator is one-sided and monologic rather than discursive. As Amy Boesky and Nina Chordas have both noted, the potential for conversation between the travellers and their hosts elsewhere in the text is closed off, because the mariners are told that there is no need for them to share information about their home in return for the information they are learning about Bensalem; the officials of Bensalem know everything about Europe already, thanks to their intelligence networks. Thus, in Chordas's words, dialogue becomes 'superfluous'; similarly, in the conversation between the narrator and the Father, the Father's voice dominates.[49] In Salomon's House, conversation is generally kept under careful control, as it is in Bensalem at large, and there is much secrecy around both the practice of natural philosophy and conversation. When the governor first talks to the travellers about Salomon's House, he stresses its secretive nature and hints tantalizingly at the things he is not allowed to say. As Bensalem is a '*Land vnknowne*', so must its agents deal secretively with the outside world:

> Now for me to tell you, how the Vulgar sort of Marriners are contained from being discouered at Land; And how they that must be put on shore for any time, colour themselues vnder the Names of other Nations; And to what places these

---

[46] *Science, Literature and Rhetoric in Early Modern England*, ed. by Juliet Cummins and David Burchell (Farnham: Ashgate, 2007), 'Introduction', p. 2.

[47] Richard Serjeantson has argued that the form 'came into its own' in natural philosophy in the seventeenth century; see R.W. Serjeantson, 'Proof and Persuasion', in *The Cambridge History of Science, Volume 3: Early Modern Science*, ed. by Katherine Park and Lorraine Daston (Cambridge: Cambridge University Press, 2006), p. 166.

[48] Ann Blair, 'Natural Philosophy', in *The Cambridge History of Science, Volume 3: Early Modern Science*, p. 404.

[49] Nina Chordas, *Forms in Early Modern Utopia: The Ethnography of Perfection* (Farnham: Ashgate, 2010), p. 120; Amy Boesky, 'Bacon's New Atlantis and the laboratory of prose', p. 148.

Voyages haue beene designed; And what places of Rendez-Vous are appointed for the new Missions; And the like Circumstances of the Practique; I may not doe it; Neither is it much to your desire. (C4v)

The interest of Salomon's House as described by the Father is '*the Knowledge of Causes, and Secrett Motions of Things*'. When they have found out these secrets, it is up to the Fathers to decide what knowledge should be kept public and what can be disseminated, to which end they '*take all an* Oath *of* Secrecy' (E2r, G1r). It is appropriate, then, that the Father's purpose in returning to Bensalem is secret, and that only one of the travellers may hear his oration on Salomon's House in '*priuate Conference*' (E1v). The institution is shown to be secretive not only in its dealings with the rest of the world but with the society of which it is a part.

The superior and hidden nature of natural knowledge in Bensalem demonstrates how closely power, knowledge and secrecy are intertwined in this society. Just as the practitioners of Salomon's House have power over the natural world, so they exhibit power in civic life, with the Father's procession through Bensalem tantamount to the progress of a monarch or religious leader. The practitioners also have an authority over their European counterparts, in that they are able to observe foreign cultures without themselves being observed. In 1,900 years, only thirteen of the visitors to Bensalem appear to have left the island. Citizens of Bensalem are themselves prevented from travelling abroad, and thus spreading information about their country (C3v). But the Fellows of Salomon's House are perpetually travelling to foreign lands, collecting information and knowledge and pretending to belong to other nations, thus keeping their own identity and knowledge secret. Hence the only trade Bensalemites hold with other nations is for '*GODS first Creature, which was* Light', or knowledge, and this is not a reciprocal form of trade, for the nations with whom the Fellows do business are not given anything in return (C4v). Bensalem is a limitless sponge for knowledge, absorbing and holding information but never releasing it. The private, secret nature of knowledge acquisition and practice in Bensalem is a vital component in the establishment of the power of Salomon's House. At the moment at which the text is narrated, the Bensalemites seem to be on the cusp of changing the degree of secrecy in which they shroud their culture and knowledge, as the Father of Salomon's House authorizes the narrator '*to Publish* [this relation] *for the Good of other Nations*' (G2r).

The Private and Public Dimensions of Knowledge

The relationship between natural philosophy and secrecy is explored in depth in William Eamon's study of medieval and Renaissance books of secrets. Eamon discusses the changing nature of the books of secrets during this period:

> In the sixteenth century [...] the term was still densely packed with its ancient and medieval connotations: the association with esoteric wisdom, the domain

of occult or forbidden knowledge, the artisan's cunning, the moral injunction to protect secrets from the *vulgus*, and the political power that attended knowledge of secrets.[50]

The significance of this term was to alter during the coming decades so that by the eighteenth century, 'secrets' referred only to techniques. This understanding of secrecy in the sixteenth century provides a fitting summary of the nature of natural knowledge and the practice of natural philosophy in *New Atlantis*. In Bensalem the practice of natural philosophy is certainly occult and forbidden to certain sections of the community; the practitioners of Salomon's House alone possess the skill and cunning of the artisan; and there is a clear compulsion to keep natural knowledge away from the threats posed to it by society at large, or the *vulgus*. Finally, natural knowledge in Bensalem appears tantamount to political might; it is the Fellows of Salomon's House who wield power in their society. The similarity of the connotations attributed to the term 'secrets' in the sixteenth century, and the way in which Bacon describes natural knowledge in *New Atlantis* in the early seventeenth century, highlights the fact that Bacon portrayed natural philosophy as a secretive and elitist activity, and that the process of opening the treasure of scientific secrets was still in its infancy.

That Bacon should choose to idealize a system of natural knowledge in which its institutionalization has resulted in its establishment as a private activity, and in which scientific practices are themselves kept secret, may seem paradoxical, given Bacon's insistence that natural philosophy should be a public activity and later Baconians' promulgation of the ideal of public dissemination of works. As he writes in the *Advancement of Learning*:

> The Sciences themselues which haue had better intelligence and confederacie with the imagination of man, than with his reason, are three in number; Astrologoe, Naturall Magike, and *Alcumy*: of which Sciences neuerthelesse the ends or pretences are noble. [...] But the deriuations and prosecutions to these ends, both in the theories, and in the practises, are full of Errour and vanitie; which the great Professors themselues haue sought to vaile ouer and conceale by enigmaticall writings, and referring themselues to auricular traditions, and such other deuises, to saue the credite of Impostures.[51]

Mysterious secrecy in itself, if it is to cover up mistakes, for example, is clearly not the aim. Eamon, who argues that Bacon's conception of the secrets of nature ultimately instigated the idea of science as public knowledge, puts Bacon's argument thus: 'Since science had to be grounded upon a new foundation of reliable factual information, Bacon argued, it needed the ordinary talents of many investigators rather than the uncommon genius of a few.'[52] It would not

---

[50] William Eamon, *Science and the Secrets of Nature: Books of Secrets in Medieval and Early Modern Culture* (Princeton: Princeton University Press, 1996), p. 5.

[51] *Aduancement of Learning* (Book 1, F3v), p. 27.

[52] Eamon, *Science and the Secrets of Nature*, p. 300, p. 319.

do for individual practitioners to hide their discoveries away, as this would lead to the downfall of the combined endeavour. Eamon goes on to describe how this Baconian spirit of openness influenced a later generation of thinkers, including those who formed the Royal Society of London, an organization for which he, amongst others, sees Salomon's House as an influence.[53] The secrecy of science in *New Atlantis* would appear to go against this ideal of openness and mutual enterprise, but in fact, although natural knowledge in Bensalem is closed off from the public at large, it still relies upon a considerable body of practitioners within Salomon's House. The Father of Salomon's House explains the various office-holders within the institution, naming thirty-six different officials: twelve Merchants of Light, three Depredators, three Mystery-men, three Pioners or Miners, three Compilers, three Dowry-men or Benefactors, three Lamps, three Inoculators and three Interpreters of Nature. In addition to this, Salomon's House contains 'Nouices and Apprentices, that the Succession of the former Employed Men doe not faile; Besides, a great Number of Seruants and Attendants, Men and Women' (G1r). The structure of Salomon's House is reminiscent of Bacon's ideal in the *Aduancement of Learning*, in which there is 'a fraternitie in learning and illumination', and knowledge is possessed by the group rather than the individual.[54]

Although Salomon's House is clearly a sizeable institution, natural knowledge and hence the exercise of power remains the preserve of a privileged elite, who are bound by oath only to reveal to the state that which they all agree may be disseminated. But Bacon's spirit of openness did not necessarily mean that he hoped for universal access to knowledge as a result of reforms to natural philosophy. What Bacon favours in Salomon's House is group collaboration, rather than public dissemination. Stephen Gaukroger argues that Bacon saw 'knowledge as being something which might serve the monarch, in some ways on a par with territorial conquest'.[55] Again we observe the potential parallel between the gaining of knowledge and physical travel, with its concomitant processes of discovery and exploration. In evidence, Gaukroger quotes from the second book of the *Aduancement of Learning*, where Bacon writes:

> And this proficience in navigation and discoveries may plant also an expectation of the further proficience and augmentation of all sciences; because it may seem they are ordained by God to be coevals, that is, to meet in one age. For so the prophet Daniel speaking of the latter times foretelleth ['many pass to and fro, and knowledge shall be multiplied'], as if the openness and through passage of the world and the increase of knowledge were appointed to be in the same ages.[56]

---

[53] Eamon, *Science and the Secrets of Nature*, p. 291.

[54] *Aduancement of Learning* (Book 2, 2B1v), p. 60.

[55] Stephen Gaukroger, *Francis Bacon and the Transformation of Early-Modern Philosophy* (Cambridge: Cambridge University Press, 2001), p. 9.

[56] Stephen Gaukroger, *Francis Bacon and the Transformation of Early Modern Philosophy*, quoting from *Advancement of Learning*, in *Works*, ed. Spedding, Ellis and Heath, III, 340 (addition in brackets is Gaukroger's).

Thus Bacon envisaged that the reform of natural knowledge would serve the purposes of the nation, and that access to such knowledge would be limited. In Bacon's plan for reform, natural philosophy will be '*opera basilica*' or 'works for a king', not open indiscriminately.[57] In his assessment of *New Atlantis*, Eamon notes that Bensalem's scientists place the advancement of knowledge above even the interests of the state, but in fact, in Bensalem the advancement of knowledge is synonymous with the interests of the state.[58] The state appears to have no other interests or function than to revolve around its source of light, its 'eye' or 'lanthorn'. So although natural philosophy in Bensalem takes place in private, behind closed doors, it is still being undertaken by the few in the interests of all.

The private and controlled nature of natural philosophy in *New Atlantis* is all the more evident when contrasted with the ways in which science and thinking about science were to develop in the later seventeenth century. By the 1660s and the institution of the Royal Society, the practice of natural philosophy was both more public and more political. The model of collaborative activity suggested by Salomon's House was to be embraced by the earliest members of the Royal Society; but the secrecy and control exerted by Bacon's Fellows of Salomon's House were no longer appropriate. A literary continuation of *New Atlantis*, printed in 1660, reflects the changing relationship between the private and public dimensions of knowledge and the move towards a more open and collaborative model of scientific activity. This is reflected both in its portrayal of natural philosophy and in its attitude to conversation and the role of natural philosophy in society.

New Atlantis Begun by the Lord Verulam, Viscount St. Albans: and Continued by R.H. Esquire. Wherein is set forth A Platform of Monarchical Government with A Pleasant intermixture of divers rare Inventions, And wholsom Customs, fit to be introduced Into all kingdoms, states, and common-wealths differs in many ways from the Baconian fable which inspired it. R.H., following William Rawley's suggestion that Bacon intended to furnish his utopia with a set of laws and government in order to complete it, undertakes this task himself.[59] The text opens with a letter of dedication to Charles II, who is presented as England's hope for a return to religious as well as political correctness:

---

[57] For Bacon on natural philosophy as '*opera basilica*', see *Advancement of Learning* (Book 2, 2B2v), p. 61.

[58] Eamon, *Science and the Secrets of Nature*, p. 324.

[59] For Rawley's assessment of Bacon's intentions, see notes to *New Atlantis*, 785. The authorship of this text is a matter of some dispute. Most influential has been the suggestion that Robert Hooke wrote it: see Edmund Freeman, 'A Proposal for an English Academy in 1660', *Modern Language Review*, 19 (1924), 291–300 (297); Geoffrey Keynes, *A Bibliography of Dr. Robert Hooke* (Oxford: Clarendon Press, 1960), pp. 2–4. More recently, however, William Poole has argued that Hooke is an unlikely candidate, as the putative 'Hookeian' elements of *New Atlantis Continued* are exclusive neither to Hooke nor to the continuation itself; William Poole, 'Who Wrote the 1660 Continuation of *The New Atlantis*?', unpublished article, p. 2. Poole suggests that an alternative candidate might be the younger Robert Honywood, son of Sir Robert Honywood, the politician and Hartlibian agriculturalist and pupil of his father's friend Henry Oldenburg; Poole, p. 4.

the brightness of your Majesty so happily now returned, we hope will scatter these mists; and not only restore our Laws to their pristine vigour, by restoring them to us and all of us to our own; but make Religion, as well as Justice, shine again in every corner of your Kingdoms.

New Atlantis Continued is the author's contribution towards the achievement of 'this so much desired happiness'.[60] Unlike *New Atlantis*, therefore, and in common with the Royal Society, which was being established at the same time, the continuation is written with a specific political audience and purpose. The author feels himself to be writing at a time when the constitution of England is changing, and when it is appropriate to make suggestions to influence the nature of these changes. Following an explanatory preface, he offers an epitome of *New Atlantis* as written by Bacon before continuing the tale in the narrator's voice. There are several illuminating differences between the original text and *New Atlantis Continued* that demonstrate how the later text advocated the open, public practice of natural philosophy and directed its attention more closely to actual social reform and change. Firstly, and inevitably considering the author's avowed political purpose, the continuation is more concerned than *New Atlantis* with the practical workings of the society it describes: its government, church, education system and laws. The narrator is told about the customary organization of these chief social structures, from the marriage habits of the priests and the names of the churches and cathedrals to the administration of the universities. The excellent organization of this Bensalem appears to have resulted in a *Utopia*-like goodness in its people:

> We have a loyal and peaceful Populacie, and no less virtuous, rich, wise, and valiant. Who being aemulous of honour and virtue, vie with each other in the service of the State. [...] We have no poor, no Beggars, or idle Vagrants: every Tradesman and Artificer being obliged to teach his children his own trade, besides teaching them to read, to shoot flying, and to swim. (26–7)

Unsurprisingly, given its monarchist agenda, King Solomona rules R.H.'s Bensalem almost independently, with only the advice of his Council. The narrator asks his interlocutor how the king manages to do this without calling his people together in some sort of Parliament. It is easily possible, the official replies, because 'the people of *Bensalem* have it as a received Maxim among them, *That their* Solomona *neither can nor will do them any injury, they being the members of that body whereof he is the head*'. For this reason, 'they leave the manage of all public affairs to him and his wise Council, wholly submitting their lives and fortunes, whilst they follow their private vocations quietly, to his protection' (20, 20–21). The king is not only the political head of state but also the ultimate head of the church, and is even believed to have the gift of healing, 'as some of your *European*

---

[60] R. H., *New Atlantis Begun by the Lord Verulam, Viscount St. Albans: and Continued by R.H. Esquire. Wherein is set forth A Platform of Monarchical Government with A Pleasant intermixture of divers rare Inventions, And wholsom Customs, fit to be introduced Into all kingdoms, states, and common-wealths* (London, 1660), A3v. All further references will be to this edition and will be given in the text.

Kings have, particularly those of *England* from *Edw.* the Confessours time, and those of *France*' (97). Following this enlargement on Bensalemite customs and institutions, the narrator witnesses the admission of a new Fellow to Salomon's House. Verdugo, who has invented a kind of incombustible paper, is blessed by the Father of the institution, given a large financial reward and praised for his contribution to the sum of Bensalem's knowledge (62–3). R.H.'s description of his procession, including his rich clothing, mimics the pleasure in exotic ritual that Bacon exhibits in *New Atlantis*. But there is a crucial dissimilarity between the kinds of ritual described in the two texts that leads us to the second significant difference between them. In *New Atlantis*, the rituals that are described are chiefly social, such as the Feast of the Family. In the continuation, the prolonged ceremony of the admission of the new Fellow is an example of the public and ostentatious nature of the scientific community and its use of natural knowledge. In R.H.'s Bensalem, the rituals of the scientific community take place in the open. The Father of Salomon's House not only proceeds through the town so that the populace may see him, but addresses them publicly. The move to a more public functioning of natural philosophy in *New Atlantis Continued* is reflective of a contemporary shift in the practice of natural philosophy.

In the early 1660s, experimental philosophy was beginning to have an increasingly public and political function. Experimental apparatus such as Robert Boyle's celebrated air-pump was used in the 1660s to demonstrate the wonders of the new science to interested parties and patrons, such as Charles II.[61] Science could function as public display, both wonderful and edifying. The Royal Society itself was an explicitly public organization, designed to institutionalize science as other public organizations did their professional activities. Thus Nathaniel Fairfax described the Society to Henry Oldenburg: 'a body form'd to that end [the advancement of useful philosophy] as much as the Universityes ar for scholars, the Inns of Court for Lawyers, Cityes & Townes for Merchants & Craftsmen'.[62] Just as Bacon drew inspiration from contemporary institutions such as Gresham College, so Fairfax saw the Society as being related to contemporary public establishments. Indeed, the public nature of the Royal Society contributed to its innovation, and its founders sought to uphold this public function. The Society was granted its charter of incorporation by Charles II in 1662. As William Viscount Brouncker, President of the Royal Society, wrote to the Earl of Ormonde in the same year, the 'very deserving' interest of 'private persons' must be subordinated to 'the public concern of a society, whose designs, if protected and assisted by authority, may so much conduce to the greatness and honour of their prince, the real good of his dominions, and the universal benefit of mankind.'[63] In Brouncker's aims we can see the influence of Bacon's desires for a publicly instituted science as '*opera basilica*'.

---

[61] See Steven Shapin and Simon Schaffer, *Leviathan and the Air-Pump: Hobbes, Boyle, and the Experimental Life* (Princeton: Princeton University Press, 1985), pp. 30–31.

[62] Letter dated 28 September 1667, quoted in Michael Hunter, *Establishing the New Science*, p. 3. Quotation in parentheses is Hunter's.

[63] Quoted in Thomas Birch, *The History of the Royal Society of London*, 4 vols (London, 1756–57), I, 168.

The Royal Society's emphasis on observation and the utility of experiment was enshrined in its aims from the very beginning.[64] Members of the public who visited would be witnesses to the discoveries of experimental philosophy as they took place.[65] This emphasis on the public observation of science is reflected in *New Atlantis Continued*. When the narrator visits Salomon's House, he is not only told about the discoveries made by the natural philosophers working there, but shown physical proof. First among these wonders is a miraculous stone (a magnet), which allows long-distance communication:

> he immediately reached forth of a little Ark, wherein many rarities were placed, a Loadstone far bigger than that which holds up *Mahomets* tomb in *Mecha*. This is the truly precious stone, of such divine use (said he) that by its charitable direction it not only ciments the divided World into one body politic, maintaining trade and society with the remotest parts and Nations, but is in many other things of rare use and service. [...] Two needles of equal size being touched together at the same time with this Stone, and severally set on two tables with the Alphabet written circularly about them; two friends, thus prepared and agreeing on the time, may correspond at never so great a distance. For by turning the needle in one Alphabet, the other in the distant table will by a secret Sympathy turne it self after the like manner. (67–8)

The scientist goes on to describe how this discovery was made and to what use it has been put. Gone is the degree of mystery and secrecy with which the treasures of Salomon's House were originally shrouded in *New Atlantis*; in the continuation, the narrator is permitted to see and touch the materials used for the scientists' experiments, such as the selenoscope and microscope, 'wherein the eyes, legs, mouth, hair, and eggs of a Cheesmite, as well as the bloud running in the veins of a Lowce, was easily to be discerned' (68). Thus the narrator himself becomes a practitioner, involved in the experimental use of instruments. And unlike the medical cures of Bacon's Bensalem, the treatments of this society are not only efficacious but described in full, so that when the narrator is told about a '*Sympatheticall* powder' which cures wounds, he is instructed on how the powder is found, and how to turn it into the healing balm (69).[66]

The idea that secrecy might be of use, or necessary, to the scientific community is entirely absent in *New Atlantis Continued*. Instead, natural knowledge is openly and publicly owned and rewarded, and any practitioner who is discovered to be secretive about his work, keeping beneficial results to himself, is punished as unnatural:

---

[64] See Marie Boas Hall, *Promoting Experimental Learning: Experiment and the Royal Society 1660–1727* (Cambridge: Cambridge University Press, 1991), p. 9.

[65] See Marie Boas Hall, *Robert Boyle and Seventeenth-Century Chemistry* (Cambridge: Cambridge University Press, 1958), p. 185.

[66] For a contemporary 'sympatheticall powder', see Kenelm Digby, *A Late Discourse Made in a Solemne Assembly of Nobles and Learned Men at Montpellier in France [...] Touching the Cure of Wounds by the Powder of Sympathy*, trans. by R. White (London, 1658).

> We study the public good so much, that whereas we reward those that discover, so he is in some measure punished that conceals and hides a benefit which may pleasure his countrey: For they that do no good when they can, as well as they that do mischief are here accounted debtors alike, and are looked upon as unnatural children to their Common parent their Countrey. (54)

In R.H.'s Bensalem, the power of scientific discovery remains in the hands of the practitioners, but its benefits are fully open to all, seemingly without restraint. *New Atlantis Continued* is thus a valuable text in demonstrating the degree to which attitudes to science in seventeenth-century England were to change during the years after Bacon's death, so that the concept of a state-supported scientific institution became a practical reality rather than a pipe dream.

In keeping with this move to openness, the narrator's experience of verbal discussion in this Bensalem also reflects a lesser degree of control and secrecy. In conversation with the Father of Salomon's House in Bacon's *New Atlantis*, the narrator is a silent participant who listens while the Father orates. In conversation with the equivalent official in *New Atlantis Continued*, the 'Alcadorem', R.H.'s narrator is encouraged to take an active part in the conversation. After describing the system of punishment, the Alcadorem pauses, 'supposing me ready to offer some reply, or start some new questions'; perceiving the narrator's 'silence, or rather wonderstrucken backwardnesse to offer any renewing discourse', he encourages him to contribute to the discussion: 'if you have any desire to know more of our Laws and customs [...] it lyes on your part to offer the question.' 'Encouraged with this friendly invitation', the narrator summons the boldness to ask a series of questions about life in this society, which the Alcadorem answers (17, 18). In his conversation with the narrator, whom he repeatedly calls a 'Friend', this official describes the practices of Salomon's House and the laws and customs of the whole society in great detail. As in *New Atlantis*, these conversations are sometimes cut short by the arrival of a messenger; in the continuation, however, the reason for such truncation is made known (the official is needed to take part in the process of justice), and the promise of future conversation is both made and kept. At the end of the conversation about the laws and customs of this society, the Alcadorem offers the narrator a 'view of their *Codes* and *Presidents*, if at any time I pleased to come to the Seminary of *Law-Students* to be farther instructed in their laws and form of Government' (53). Apologizing for cutting short their discussion, he offers further conversation '*to morrow or any day next week*' at the narrator's convenience (53–4). Similarly, after their discussion about Salomon's House, the Alcadorem is called away on business, but makes ready promises of further discussion:

> Herein he shewed a great willingness to inform me farther, but to prevent me of that happiness, an *Alguazillan* summoned him away to do speedy Justice. This must not at all be neglected; therefore *my Friend* (said he) *haue me excused* at this time; when I am at leisure you shall command me farther. (74)

The rhetorical display and control of the Father of Salomon's House in *New Atlantis* is replaced with dialogue and renewed discussion, in a change that reflects the move made in *New Atlantis Continued* from closed to open communication.

New Atlantis: Conclusions

In recent years a number of scholars have highlighted the dangers of reading *New Atlantis* in a vacuum. The text's use of contemporary travel writing and natural philosophy as sources for the travellers' experiences and the formation of Salomon's House demonstrates the degree to which *New Atlantis* is in conversation with other forms of literature.[67] In particular, recent reassessment of the relationship between *New Atlantis* and the text with which it was always published in the seventeenth century, *Sylva Sylvarum*, has shown that this utopian fable needs to be read alongside others of Bacon's works. David Colclough has used the analogy of the journey to describe this relationship in his explanation of why *Sylva Sylvarum* is 'a necessary port of call on the way to *New Atlantis*'; one might also employ the metaphor of conversation, and say that there is a dialogue between these texts which informs our understanding of what Bacon was saying in *New Atlantis*.[68] *New Atlantis* does not offer the response to other 'best state of the commonwealth' exercises that might seem to have been implied by its utopian form and its reference to the 'Faigned Common-wealth' of Bacon's compatriot; rather, it enters a broader textual conversation on the purposes of natural philosophy and what it can do for society, and in doing so, establishes the utopian mode of discourse as a means of describing a desired future state, rather than an unachievable ideal.

The concept of dialogue is valuable to our reading of *New Atlantis* in a variety of ways. Conversation is a means of communicating information in *New Atlantis*; fractured or problematic conversations can also be a means of closing down or complicating the dissemination of information. Conversation is central to the production and dissemination of natural knowledge in Salomon's House and to the process of publicizing Bensalem; as such, it needs to be controlled in the interest of protecting natural philosophy. *New Atlantis* is thus a useful marker in the movement from private to public knowledge and in the institutionalization of scientific activity in the seventeenth century. As a utopia, despite its use of multiple conversations and various voices, it is ultimately monologic in tone: Bacon is interested in portraying the necessary set of conditions for the achievement of the proper support of natural philosophy, not in opening discussion as to the nature

---

[67] On this see Rosalie L. Colie, 'Some paradoxes in the language of things', in *Reason and the Imagination: Studies in the History of Ideas 1600–1800*, ed. by J.A. Mazzeo (New York: Columbia University Press, 1962), pp. 93–128 (pp. 94–5); J. Peter Zetterberg, 'Echoes of Nature in Salomon's House', p. 189; Salzman, 'Narrative contexts for Bacon's New Atlantis'.

[68] David Colclough, '"The Materialls for the Building": Reuniting Francis Bacon's *Sylva Sylvarum* and *New Atlantis*', *Intellectual History Review*, 20:2 (2010), 181–200 (182).

of the ideal society. Nonetheless, the use of dialogue in the text demonstrates its continued importance to the utopian mode, even when the dialogue form had been overtaken by its successor as the dominant utopian form: the travel narrative. Aspects of dialogue remained interesting to writers of utopias because dialogue was itself a fundamental aspect of the utopian tradition. As the next chapter will show, the dialogue form became increasingly less important to utopia during the mid-seventeenth century, in part because it suggested a distance between utopia and reality that the authors of utopias wished to deny.

Chapter 5
'Counsel and Endevors': Millennium and Reform in the 1640s

Introduction: The Utopian Moment and the Rejection of the Utopian Form

The mid-seventeenth century has come to be characterized by its utopianism; as David Norbrook has commented, 'the very act of situating this period historically [...] also entails bringing out its utopian dimension'.[1] As this chapter will demonstrate, the 1640s saw a proliferation of utopian thought in forms other than that of the conventional utopia, and a simultaneous turning away from the conventional utopian forms of dialogue and travel narrative. Much of this utopianism was directly influenced by Bacon and by European utopian writing; it was also influenced by the political developments of the 1640s and the growth of millenarianism, which focused attention on the question of the ideal society. As political conditions and millennial enthusiasm converged to make the perfect earthly community appear to be within reach, the utopia formed a central means of both imagining and promoting its achievement. The final two chapters of this book will contend that this unique religious and political context changed the form of the utopian discourse, as the utopia developed in two opposite though related ways. One strand of utopian literature became more imaginative, as demonstrated by Samuel Gott's *Nova Solyma*, printed in 1648. Later Renaissance utopias, such as Margaret Cavendish's *The Blazing-World* (1666), were to draw on this developing tradition of utopian narrative fiction, representing the beginning of the development of the utopian novel, which achieved prominence in the nineteenth and twentieth centuries.

At the same time, the concept of the utopia became distinctly less imaginative in the hands of reformers who wanted to make use of it in order to promote social reformation. This second strand of utopian writing is reflected in the increasingly widespread use of utopian ideas, for example in the group of thinkers and reformers surrounding the polymath and intelligencer Samuel Hartlib. This group was made up of various individuals who met or corresponded with Hartlib to discuss their ideas about natural philosophy, pedagogy and divinity, and to consider schemes for practical improvements in these and other fields.[2] For these reformers,

---

[1] David Norbrook, *Writing the English Republic: Poetry, Rhetoric and Politics, 1627–1660* (Cambridge: Cambridge University Press, 1999), p. 19.

[2] For an introduction to the Hartlib circle, see *Samuel Hartlib and the Universal Reformation: Studies in Intellectual Communication*, ed. by Mark Greengrass, Michael Leslie and Timothy Raylor (Cambridge: Cambridge University Press, 1994); Antonella Cagnolati, *Il Circolo di Hartlib: riforme educative e diffusione del sapere (Inghilterra 1630–1660)* (Bologna: CLUEB, 2001).

conversation was an activity to be undertaken – and the utopian society a prospect to be achieved – in the here and now, in order to hasten the beginning of Christ's reign, rather than in fiction. The writings of the Hartlib circle demonstrate the expansion of utopian thought beyond the conventional form; that is, the movement away from an explicitly fictional narrative involving a journey and encounter with an imagined society. This rejection of the traditional form of the utopia was also to dominate utopian writing beyond the 1640s. In the immediate future, the rhetoric of the Levellers and other such groups owed a debt to the development of the utopia during this crucial period. As the period in which these two strands of utopian thought separated from each other and began to dominate utopian literature, the mid-seventeenth century constitutes a utopian point in time during which the achievement of the ideal human society genuinely appeared possible.

This chapter will trace the development of the second of these two strands of utopian literature in the middle years of the seventeenth century. After looking at the ways in which the political and religious fervour of the 1640s created an environment in which the ideal society seemed an imminent prospect, it will demonstrate how these conditions facilitated the proliferation of the utopia. Crucial to this proliferation is the fact that writing in a particular form ceased to be of central importance to utopian writing, and explicitly fictional forms – such as the dialogue – were generally avoided by writers of utopias. The very aspects of dialogue which had made it interesting to the authors of sixteenth-century utopias, such as its capacity for playfulness and irony, led to its rejection in the seventeenth century. The concept of conversation was important to the members of the Hartlib circle, who saw themselves as a group of interlocutors whose discussions via letters and pamphlets, as well as in person, could bring about the social changes they wished to see. In so doing they were influenced by previous circles of friends with shared intellectual interests, including the 'republic of letters', which was their precedent.[3] Like other seventeenth-century networks of collegial scholars who 'created a shared intellectual identity', the Hartlib circle, driven by a desire to share and disseminate learning, used the idea of conversation through writing as a means to achieve their ideals.[4] As such debates took place, literary forms of debate became obsolete and utopia diffused into other forms. Gabriel Plattes's *Macaria* (1641) is a unique example of a utopian dialogue from this period. Although it is little more than a suggested blueprint for political reformation, *Macaria*'s use of the dialogue form demonstrates, ironically, an attempt to distance utopian literature from travel writing and to claim the possibility of achieving the ideal society in the author's own time and place. The utopian literature of this period must be understood as the product of a historical period during which the realization of utopia became viable. Despite the enthusiasm of the texts considered here, however, this utopian period would soon pass. Though the utopia continued to change as a mode of writing

---

[3] See Philip Withington, *Society in Early Modern England: The Vernacular Origins of Some Powerful Ideas* (Cambridge: Polity Press, 2010), p. 118.

[4] Carol Pal, *Republic of Women: Rethinking the Republic of Letters in the Seventeenth Century* (Cambridge: Cambridge University Press, 2012), p. 10.

throughout the seventeenth century and beyond, it would not recapture the unique and genuine optimism of this critical point in its development.

The 1640s: Millennium and Reform

As has long been recognized, the 1640s, dominated by an awareness that the old order was changing, witnessed 'unsettling, dramatic processes of political, religious, and social revolution'.[5] By 1640 it had been eleven years since Parliament had been in session, and the new Parliament was seen as a potential agent of change, heralding 'a great wave of expectation'.[6] Samuel Hartlib, writing on the subject of England's Reformation in 1647, identified the 'Long' Parliament as one of the main reasons why England could hope for the achievement of reform, because 'God hath put into the hands of this Parliament sufficiently all the Meanes and Advantages that may enable them to discharge their duty in order to this engagement'.[7] As reformers turned to Parliament in expectation, the church strengthened the feeling that significant change was coming. In the sermons delivered before this Parliament, preachers' calls for reform were characterized by their belief that Christ's reign on earth was imminent.[8] William Sedgwick, preaching a fast day sermon in June 1642, drew on the imagery of the apocalypse to illustrate this, arguing that the 'Tabernacle of God, is comming downe to dwell with men [...] God will at last *establish, and make Jerusalem a praise in the earth*'; a year later Henry Wilkinson reported the 'generall talk' on the subject of Christ's 'comming to take possession of his Throne'.[9] In addition, the outbreak of civil wars from 1642 demonstrated the commitment of the warring factions to their respective views of the best form of management of the country. The sought-after reforms were long awaited, and seen as part of a longer process of reformation; opponents of Charles in the 1640s saw their chance to achieve the godly reformation that they and their predecessors had wanted since at least the 1580s.[10] The religious and political developments of

---

[5] David Loewenstein, *Representing Revolution in Milton and His Contemporaries: Religion, Politics, and Polemics in Radical Puritanism* (Cambridge: Cambridge University Press, 2001), p. 1.

[6] Paul Christianson, *Reformers and Babylon: English Apocalyptic Visions from the Reformation to the Eve of the Civil War* (Toronto: University of Toronto Press, 1978), p. 204. See also B.S. Capp, *The Fifth Monarchy Men: A Study in Seventeenth-Century English Millenarianism* (Oxford: Oxford University Press, 1972), pp. 54–5.

[7] Samuel Hartlib, *Considerations Tending To the Happy Accomplishment of Englands Reformation in Church and State* (London, 1647), p. 2.

[8] John F. Wilson, *Pulpit in Parliament: Puritanism during the English Civil Wars, 1640–1648* (Princeton: Princeton University Press, 1969), p. 195.

[9] William Sedgwick, *Zions Deliverance And Her Friends Duty: Or the Grounds of Expecting, and Meanes of Procuring Jerusalems Restauration* (London, 1642), pp. 53–4; Henry Wilkinson, *Babylons Ruine, Jerusalems Rising* (London, 1643), p. 21, both quoted in Wilson, *Pulpit in Parliament*, p. 210, p. 211.

[10] Barry Coward, *The Stuart Age: England, 1605–1714*, 2nd edn (London: Longman, 1994), pp. 188–9.

the mid-seventeenth century thus witnessed the realization of a new atmosphere in which longed-for change and reform could and did take place. As the MP and army colonel Thomas Rainsborough was to imply in the Putney Debates of 1647, the dethronement of the king meant more than just the removal of a monarch, and could lead to far wider social change. Indeed, with the king could disappear the foundations of society as he knew it: 'I do very much care whether a king or no king, lords or no lords, property or no property; and I think, if we do not all take care, we shall all have none of these very shortly.'[11] The unique political circumstances of this period thus shaped conditions in which reformist thinking and the prospect of a better society became a valid topic for political debate.

An essential context for understanding the development of utopian thought in this period is the widespread rise of religious zeal that expressed itself in millenarianism, the belief that Christ's thousand-year reign on earth was shortly to begin.[12] If the utopian location is the ideal environment in which to live the good life, then millenarians believed that it was soon to be realized. As one of their number described it, the events leading to the end of the world had been set in train:

> *God* is beginning the powring forth of the fifth Viall, namely, upon the Throne of the *Beast*, upon *Babylon*; this is the worke that is in hand: as soone as ever this is done, that *Antichrist* is downe, *Babylon* fallen, then comes in *Jesus Christ* reigning gloriously.[13]

Apocalyptic prophecies foretold that the dawn of Christ's rule would bring justice and perfection to the world and establish a form of heaven on earth; earthly monarchies would be destroyed and the Catholic Church would fall.[14]

---

[11] 'The Putney Debates (the second day, 29 October 1647) in the Clarke Manuscripts', in *The Levellers in the English Revolution*, ed. by G.E. Aylmer (London: Thames and Hudson, 1975), pp. 97–130 (p. 102).

[12] On this see Sarah Hutton, 'The Appropriation of Joseph Mede: Millenarianism in the 1640s', in *Millenarianism and Messianism in Early Modern European Culture: Volume III: The Millenarian Turn: Millenarian Contexts of Science, Politics, and Everyday Anglo-American Life in the Seventeenth and Eighteenth Centuries*, ed. by James E. Force and Richard H. Popkin (Dordrecht: Kluwer, 2001), pp. 1–13. For the links between millenarianism and radical politics, see Michael Walzer, *The Revolution of the Saints: A Study in the Origins of Radical Politics* (London: Weidenfeld and Nicolson, 1966); Christopher Hill, *The Antichrist in Seventeenth-Century England*, revised edn (London: Verso, 1990), Chapter 3, and '"Till the Conversion of the Jews"', in *Millenarianism and Messianism in English Literature and Thought, 1650–1800*, ed. by Richard H. Popkin (Leiden: Brill, 1988), pp. 12–36. For the history of millenarian thinking from the first to the seventeenth century, see Robert Gordon Clouse, *The Influence of John Henry Alsted on English Millenarian Thought in the Seventeenth Century*, unpublished PhD thesis, State University of Iowa, 1963.

[13] Thomas Goodwin, *A Glimpse of Sions Glory* (London, 1641), p. 2.

[14] See, for example, John Archer, *The Personall Reigne of Christ Upon Earth* (London, 1641 and 1642), and Robert Maton, *Israels Redemption* (London, 1642). For the background to mid-seventeenth century millenarianism, see Capp, *The Fifth Monarchy Men*, pp. 23–49.

The anticipation of Christ's reign has been shown to be an extensively and deeply held belief during this period, constituting a widespread and significant movement in England, as apocalyptic thought served to motivate action on the social and political stage.[15] Superficially, it might seem logical to presume that millenarian beliefs would obviate the need for social reform. If the ideal state (in the form of Christ's rule) were approaching, there would appear to be no desperate need to improve society as it stands, the millennium achieving all social reform at a stroke. In fact, the opposite was felt to be true. An influential text on the millenarianism of this period was Joseph Mede's *Clavis Apocalyptica*, first published in Latin in 1627 and reprinted in 1632. Translated into English by Richard Moore, it was printed as *The Key of Revelation* in 1643 and as *Clavis Apocalyptica: Or, a Prophetical Key* in 1651.[16] This translation publicized the belief that Christ's rule was imminent. Not only Christian communities, but also Jewish ones were aware that the millennium was coming; hence, 'wee might rationally conclude, that the Lord is hastening to finish his work in righteousness'.[17]

But although the advent of the millennium was inevitable, the Christian reader was not expected to await it idly. Rather, the coming of Christ's rule could be helped on its way through human actions, and not just the actions of kings and rulers, but those of normal people. Mede writes that:

> Our dutie in subordination to the waie of God is cleerly this; that we should with all readiness of minde applie ourselvs to entertein all spiritual motions, tending to mutual and universal edification: not onely by praiers [...]; but by counsel and endevors, [...] one single act of correspondence at an adventure, will do more to make his designe effectual, than a whole years contrived and setled intelligence, and agencie of manie Statesmen for politick designments.[18]

The communication of ideas was part of the important action that would anticipate the coming of Christ's rule; the discussions held by the Hartlib circle and others were themselves seen as part of these necessary endeavours. It was not discussion for its own sake that was important, but useful communication; action that went no further than words was distrusted by Dury, at least, who railed against those who preferred speech to activity. 'It is not in pratling & talking, but in doing, that men should approoue themselues servants of Christ', he had once written to Hartlib, 'Therefore intreat such in my name in the feare of God either to doe what is required of them, that is to giue reall counsell how this worke should bee prosecuted: or

---

[15] Capp, p. 20. See also Peter Toon, *Puritans, the Millennium and the Future of Israel: Puritan Eschatology 1600 to 1660* (Cambridge: Clarke, 1970); William Lamont, *Godly Rule: Politics and Religion, 1603–1660* (London: Macmillan, 1969); Katharine R. Firth, *The Apocalyptic Tradition in Reformation Britain 1530–1645* (Oxford: Oxford University Press, 1979), Chapter 7.

[16] For the publication of *Clavis Apocalyptica* and its influence on the 1640s, see Hutton, 'The Appropriation of Joseph Mede: Millenarianism in the 1640s'.

[17] Joseph Mede, *Clavis Apocalyptica: Or, A Prophetical Key* (London, 1651), p. 6.

[18] *Clavis Apocalyptica*, p. 8.

else to bee silent'. His mistrust of 'idle talkers' reflects a suspicion that too much discussion would prevent the actual work of reformation from being undertaken, and his preference for 'doing' over 'talking' reflects the move of utopianism from literary forms such as the dialogue into non-imaginative writing.[19]

The need for immediate action is also put forward in the writings of Samuel Hartlib. Hartlib's *A Further Discoverie of the Office of Addresse*, written circa 1648, begins with an introduction 'Concerning Christian Perfection, What the vtmost Degree therof is & How wee must come to it'. Hartlib, too, is clear that the millennium is near: 'For wee believe that his Kingdome will be set up & that all such as are faithfull unto him for the Advancement thereof; shall bee accepted'. Before this can happen, however, earthly reforms must be completed:

> Wee expect also, that before this Kingdome of His Mediatorship between God and the Elect bee ended, & given up unto the Father; the Restitution of all this shall be wrought in the Churches & by the Church in the World & therefore wee desire to sow our seed upon all waters, whiles wee have opportunity.[20]

The fact that the last days of the world were looming meant that politics no longer needed to be thought of as a repetitive cycle, but could be described in terms of permanent historical change.[21] From a letter to Hartlib from his colleague Moses Wall dated 18 June 1652, it is clear that the 1640s were for Hartlib and his associates the crucial decade. Looking back, Wall remembered that 'We looked that annus 1650 shold haue produced somwhat towards [the Jews'] conversion'. Though disappointed by its non-appearance, Wall reminds himself that the coming millennium will happen in the fullness of time and through divine action: 'a Nation shall be born in a day, when Gods time is come; & it shall be gods work, & not mans.'[22] For Hartlib, however, as for Joseph Mede, the proximity of Christ's rule did not obviate the need for reformers to be active in their mission:

> And because wee judge the time to be neere at hand, Wee prepare ourselves; wee trimme our lampes, wee are willing to goe forth & desirous to meet the bridegroome, that wee may by our attendance upon him with our lightes in our handes; increase the manifestation of his Glorie, Not that wee conceive our endeavours to bee of any worth in themselves.[23]

The humble tone of the final clause of this quotation exhibits the belief of Hartlib and others that their attempts at reform were a small part of a divine project which

---

[19] [John Dury?] to [Samuel Hartlib?], 24 October [1636?], Hartlib Papers (hereafter HP) 9/1/41A.

[20] Hartlib, *A Further Discoverie of the Office of Addresse* (1647), HP 47/10/2B.

[21] David Wootton, 'Leveller democracy and the Puritan Revolution', in *The Cambridge History of Political Thought, 1450–1700* (Cambridge: Cambridge University Press, 1991), pp. 412–42 (p. 422).

[22] Moses Wall to Samuel Hartlib (18 June 1652), HP 34/4/1A.

[23] Hartlib, *A Further Discoverie of the Office of Addresse*, HP 50H, 47/10/2B–47/10/3A.

they could neither fully know nor understand, but in which they nevertheless had an important role to play. The relationship between human and divine will is crucial here; Hartlib believes that reform must be effected by the active human fulfilment of divine will, but he is careful to maintain that reformers' efforts are entirely subject to that will. This balance between human and divine will is reiterated by John Dury, writing to Hartlib in 1636: 'Wee must leave every One to Gods direction. For hee hath his owne way with all Mens Spirits, yet to vse the Meanes that are to draw them to the best effects is expedient.'[24]

Thus Hartlib suggests that human attempts at reform can only be understood as taking place within the scope of divine providence, and that it is a duty, as the time of Christ's rule approaches, for such efforts to be made. In this way, it is possible to progress towards a perfect state: 'there is a graduall proceeding therein from one to the other in the way of perfection'.[25] Dury had earlier expressed a similar sentiment in his letter: 'The Lord direct vs and assist vs. Let us bee busy whiles wee haue time. The dayes are evil therfore the time must bee the more redeemed.'[26] These writings reflect the reformers' conviction that they were working at a special time and were operating within the control of God's desires, but that their own actions could be part of the fulfilment of those desires. There is a new understanding of the special nature of the contemporary moment and its importance in historical development. This assurance that they had an essential role to play in hastening the millennium is reflected elsewhere in Hartlib's works:

> The onely ground of all Our Standing and prosperity is this, even Our Publike Interest in Christs Universall and Communicative Kingdom; [...] by this Interest we are bound to raise Our Resolutions to some Duties of a larger extent then those are, which the solemn League and Covenant doth require of Us. [...] the whole Happiness and the Glory of this State will depend upon the Wisdome and the piety of this great Duty.[27]

Apocalyptic beliefs thus created a cycle of optimism and reform: the fact that society was improving was an indicator of the imminent millennium, and the fact that the millennium was coming meant that there was a need to improve the present society in order to prepare for it; this was God's will. As Thomas Goodwin had written in *Sions Glory*:

> It is the work of the day to cry downe *Babylon*, that it may fall more and more, and it is the worke of the day to give *God* no rest, till he sets up *Ierusalem* as the praise of the whole World [...] This is the work of this Exercise; to shew unto you, how upon the destruction of *Babylon Christ shall reigne gloriously*, and how we are to further it.[28]

---

[24] John Dury to Samuel Hartlib (1636), HP 9/1/48B.
[25] *A Further Discoverie of the Office of Addresse*, HP 47/10/12B.
[26] John Dury to Samuel Hartlib (1636), HP 9/1/35A.
[27] Hartlib, *Considerations Tending To the Happy Accomplishment of Englands Reformation in Church and State*, p. 10.
[28] Goodwin, *A Glimpse of Sions Glory*, p. 2.

For Hartlib and his colleagues, an important part of this activity was the establishment of utopian societies for reform, such as Hartlib's spiritual and international fraternity, the Societas Reformatorum et Correspondency.[29] The English millenarian and minister John Stoughton, whose works Hartlib edited, interpreted Bacon's *Instauratio magna*, the pansophic aims of Jan Amos Comenius and Dury's efforts at reform as verifiable signs that the millennium was approaching.[30] This pervasive belief in the coming of Christ's rule produced a fervour and enthusiasm for reform which, combined with the social developments of the times, created unique conditions in which change seemed not only desirable but inevitable. In these circumstances, it was imperative for those who sought reform to instigate it, and for this reason would-be reformers printed a wide range of material, in particular political pamphlets and sermons, aimed at promoting change.

The writings considered in this chapter and the next were produced as part of a widely held belief that those who sought reform were agents of divine Providence, furthering God's wishes for human society. Thomas de Eschallers de la More, for example, in *The English Catholike Christian, or, The Saints Utopia*, which was published in 1649 but largely written during the civil war years, perceived his calls for reform as the proper expressions of his responsibilities as a Christian:

> as I am a member of the body of Christ my supream Head; Christian duty binds me, not onely to pray for Kings, and all that are in authority: but to labour with my hands, and assay all lawful means possible, for the building up and repairing of the breaches, which all our sins have made in that mystical Temple, the Church of God.

De la More's calls to King Charles to undertake the necessary reforms are also couched in terms of religious duty and fervour, as he urges Charles to 'set your heart and your soul to seeke the Lord your God: arise therefore, and build ye the Sanctuary of the Lord God [...] repair ye the breaches, and build up the waste places in the Church and State'.[31] In a sermon made before the Long Parliament in

---

[29] For Samuel Hartlib and his efforts at social reform and utopian activities, see Donald R. Dickson, *The Tessera of Antilia: Utopian Brotherhoods & Secret Societies in the Early Seventeenth Century* (Leiden: Brill, 1998), pp. 145–72. For the Hartlib circle more generally, see G.H. Turnbull, *Hartlib, Dury and Comenius: Gleanings from Hartlib's Papers* (London: Hodder & Stoughton, 1947); Nell Eurich, *Science in Utopia: A Mighty Design* (Cambridge, MA: Harvard University Press, 1967), pp. 147–55; and Hugh Trevor-Roper, 'Three Foreigners: the Philosophers of the Puritan Revolution', in *Religion, the Reformation and Social Change*, 3rd edn (London: Secker & Warburg, 1984), pp. 237–93.

[30] See Dagmar Čapková, 'Comenius and his ideals: escape from the labyrinth', in *Samuel Hartlib and Universal Reformation*, pp. 75–91 (p. 84); Trevor-Roper, 'Three Foreigners', pp. 258–9.

[31] Thomas de Eschallers de la More, *The English Catholike Christian, or The Saints Utopia* (London, 1649), dedicatory letter to Charles I (written 1646), A2v–A3r, a1r–a1v.

November 1645, John Dury also attempted to promote action by appealing to the conscience of his auditors. In a speech reminiscent of Hartlib's fervour for the new Parliament, Dury claimed that no other ruling body was nearer to God's desires. The legislators before him were in a unique position to carry out the reforms that their divine ruler intended:

> In all the world there is not a Magistracy so eminently entrusted with such a charge, over a people so neerly united unto God as you and the Parliament of *Scotland* are [...] God hath since the beginning of the Reformation of his Church from Popery and Antichristian superstition intended to bring his vessels out of *Babylon* into *Sion*.[32]

Like others, Dury saw this Parliament as having a special role to play in the fulfilment of practical reforms, which represented nothing less than the spiritual emancipation of the nation; England was to become the focal point for millenarian reformers, who saw it as having a vital function in the events of the final days.

It is clear, therefore, that reformers such as John Dury desired change on a broad scale, and not only in terms of their belief that the end of the world was near. For Dury, as for Hartlib, the need for practical improvement was by no means restricted to England. Much of Dury's life was devoted to travelling and working in Europe, trying to carry out ecclesiastical reform across the Continent. Dury, who was closely involved with Hartlib's Societas Reformatorum et Correspondency, insisted in his 1631 *The Purpose and Platform of my Journey into Germany* that the achievement of peace in the church relied upon international reformation and agreement:

> By the Gracious assistance of God I intend, in passing through the cheife places of Prussia and Germany, to lay a ground, and settle a way of Correspondency betwixt us and the reformed Divines of Germany: that wee and they may be able to communicate in all spirituall things, but chiefly in our Counsells and meditations, for the advancement of Peace in the Churches; & for the building up of one another, in the power & truth of Godlines.

He referred to his attempts to 'further the Works of Christian peace and ecclesiasticall unity' as his 'cheefe and main purpose'.[33] The utopian efforts of Dury, Hartlib and others were rooted in the wider European reform movement and in the international communication of ideas. Samuel Hartlib, having himself been born in Elbing (now Elblag) in Polish Prussia, and having travelled between Elbing and England in the 1620s, enjoyed correspondence with intellectuals across Europe, particularly in Germany and the Low Countries. He was renowned as 'the Great Intelligencer of Europe'; his schemes and those of his associates were

---

[32] John Dury, *Israels Call Ovt of Babylon Unto Jerusalem* (London, 1646), p. 24.

[33] John Dury, *The Purpose and Platform of my Journey into Germany*, BL MS Sloane 654, fol. 247r.

restricted to England neither in inspiration nor in practice.[34] The Hartlib circle drew directly on the works of the leaders of the Further Reformation in Europe, such as Alsted and Andreae via Comenius, the Czech pastor and pedagogue.[35]

Comenius's writings chimed with Hartlib's interest in education and human perfectibility. Comenius himself believed that his didactic principles were revolutionary, 'capable of changing by slow degrees the aspect of civilisation'.[36] Reform of the current situation depended on the establishment of a system based on order.[37] Such a perfect system, Comenius argued, would function like clockwork:

> It will be as pleasant to see education carried out on my plan as to look at an automatic machine of this kind, and the process will be as free from failure as are these mechanical contrivances, when skilfully made. [...] Let us therefore endeavour, in the name of the Almighty, to organise schools in such a way that in these points they may bear the greatest resemblance to a clock.[38]

In his plans for educational reform, Comenius proposed an idealized system of institutions through which knowledge could be organized and disseminated in a mechanical fashion. His plans for new and reformed institutions clearly influenced the Hartlibians. Hartlib himself published some of Comenius's writings in England, and persuaded the great pedagogue to pay a visit to England in 1641.[39] As one who secularized the methods and systems of Protestant scholars such as Alsted and Keckermann, Dury and Hartlib looked to Comenius for help with their own programmes of reform.[40]

The reforming efforts of the Hartlib circle can thus be properly understood only as part of the wider drive for improvement in Europe. But despite this pan-European basis and interest, reformers concentrated their attention on specific

---

[34] See Greengrass, Leslie, and Raylor, eds, *Samuel Hartlib and Universal Reformation*, 'Introduction', pp. 1–25. For Hartlib as 'the Great Intelligencer of Europe', which he was titled by the first governor of Connecticut, John Winthrop, Jr., see Charles Webster, ed., *Samuel Hartlib and the Advancement of Learning* (Cambridge: Cambridge University Press, 1970), p. 2.

[35] See Dickson, *The Tessera of Antilia*, p. 145, and Michael Srigley, 'Thomas Vaughan, the Hartlib Circle and the Rosicrucians', *Scintilla*, 6 (2002), 31–54 (42).

[36] Jan Amos Comenius, *The Great Didactic of John Amos Comenius*, trans. by M. W. Keatinge, 2 vols (London: Adam and Charles Black, 1910), 'Introduction', I, 13.

[37] *The Great Didactic*, II, 93; *J. A. Comenii: Magna Didactica*, ed. by Fridericus Carolus Hultgren (Lipsiae: Sumptibus Siegesmund & Volkening, 1894), p. 80.

[38] *The Great Didactic*, II, 97, in Latin: 'Nec minus expedite procedent omnia, quam expedite horologium pondere suo recte libratum procedit. Tamque suaviter et jucunde, quam suavis est et jucunda automati ejusmodi speculatio. Tanta denique certitudine, quanta ullum tale artificiosum instrumentum haberi potest', *Magna didactica*, p. 83.

[39] Dickson, *The Tessera of Antilia*, p. 167.

[40] Stephen Clucas, 'Samuel Hartlib's *Ephemerides*, 1635–59, and the Pursuit of Scientific and Philosophical Manuscripts: the Religious Ethos of an Intelligencer', *The Seventeenth Century*, 6:1 (1991), 33–55 (35).

and apparently achievable changes at the local and national levels. Political writers of the 1640s focused closely on the particular changes needed to make concrete improvements, for example, in education, mining and agriculture. For these reformers, the arrival of perfection in human history was at hand, but their millenarian beliefs encouraged them to focus on the need for quantifiable improvements in the present. Millennialism thus centred on the creation of a utopian environment and made the achievement of that environment seem possible, partly through human efforts (though understood as subject to divine providence). The literature considered in this chapter shows the reformers' belief that change was possible and that their own works, including their writings, could contribute to it. This assertion that the text itself can help to bring about the creation of the ideal society it imagines is central to the development of utopianism of the mid-seventeenth century, and is a recurrent feature of the Renaissance utopia. Bacon's narrator in *New Atlantis*, for example, is enjoined by the Father of Salomon's House to go forth and publish his narrative in order to publicize the achievements of the society; Hythloday's enthusiasm for the society of Utopia has been read as a call to Tudor England to seek to emulate it.[41] For a text to claim for itself a role in the process of improving society, so that its own creation is part of the journey towards utopia, is an important part of the utopian tradition.

The Utopian Institution: *Macaria* and the City of God

The changes called for by the reformers of the 1640s and beyond can be seen as utopian in their consideration of how to live well on earth, and their imagining of a better place and a better way of life. More specifically, they are linked to the utopian tradition in terms of their projections of perfected institutions, such as Dury's reformed school and reformed library and Hartlib's planned 'Office of Address', which in some respects recall Andreae's ideal college and Protestant brotherhoods. Hartlib's Office of Address was planned as an institutional network which would have several branches and cover a range of functions, such as 'patent office, employment agency, commodities exchange, spiritual counselling centre and public library'.[42] The Office would provide a means of institutionalizing the activity already undertaken by Hartlib as a correspondent with a wide network of contacts across Europe, functioning as a point of communication for many correspondents or a 'communications center for the collection and dissemination of information of all sorts'.[43] Also referred to as the 'the Agency for Universal Learning' or the 'College' in Hartlib's correspondence, it demonstrates Hartlib's desire to institutionalize his

---

[41] See for example Russell A. Ames, *Citizen Thomas More and His Utopia* (Princeton: Princeton University Press, 1949), p. 13.

[42] Kevin Dunn, 'Milton among the monopolists: *Areopagitica*, intellectual property and the Hartlib circle', in *Samuel Hartlib and Universal Reformation*, pp. 177–92 (pp. 179–80).

[43] Betty Jo Teeter Dobbs, *The Foundations of Newton's Alchemy, or "The Hunting of the Greene Lyon"* (Cambridge: Cambridge University Press, 1975), p. 62.

communications network in a manner that would be socially useful.[44] Hartlib later wrote the preface to another text which promoted the establishment of an ideal institute of education and knowledge, Dury's *The Reformed School* (1650). Dury conceived of an idealized school which would provide the education necessary for turning out useful citizens. In this pamphlet, he detailed the arrangements for a boarding school for approximately fifty or sixty boys, who would attend from around the age of eight for eleven years. He discussed the practical organization of the school in considerable detail, describing the building, equipment and staffing needs, as well as a regimented timetable, with no hour left unoccupied. In Dury's plans, the structure of the daily programme, the particulars of the curriculum and the organization of the schoolhouse all have a role to play in 'the building up of the Citie of God in our generation', which is the ultimate task of the reformed school.[45]

Godly civic institutions have played a role in each of the utopias considered in this book; as Dury's plans demonstrate, they are described in increasing levels of detail. Not only do Renaissance utopias centre on ideal institutions, but they were also being written at the same time that civic establishments were developing and becoming increasingly institutionalized. Clearly, a link can be observed between the development of the institution and the progression of the utopian mode of discourse. Indeed, this might be placed within a wider context and understood in more general terms as a reflection of the development during the Renaissance period of a belief that good institutions would be capable of producing good people. Perhaps as a consequence of this belief in the improvability of humanity and the centrality of the institution in that improvement, it is in the form of the centralized social establishment that utopian writers found the best means of achieving reform. Like earlier utopian authors, these writers concentrated their ideas for reform on idealized institutions, and the unifying central feature of these establishments is their promotion of godliness. For the Protestant in the middle of the seventeenth century, the idea of godliness was tied up with concepts of utility and practicality, the themes we have seen emerging from the utopias of early seventeenth-century Europe. Utopian writing both imagined and addressed itself to godly civic institutions.

The publication of Gabriel Plattes's *Macaria* in 1641 exemplifies this process, seeming to have been calculated to coincide with the second session of the Long Parliament, which opened on 20 October.[46] The text's Traveller, who relates his experience of the idealized land of Macaria in conversation with the Schollar, makes his hoped-for audience and purpose clear: 'I hear that they [Parliament] are generally bent to make a good reformation [...] and if any experience which I have

---

[44] Dunn, 'Milton among the monopolists', p. 180; Norbrook, *Writing the English Republic*, p. 122.

[45] John Dury, *The Supplement to the Reformed School* (London, 1650) ed. by H.M. Knox (Liverpool: Liverpool University Press, 1958), p. 11.

[46] Charles Webster, *Utopian Planning and the Puritan Revolution: Gabriel Plattes, Samuel Hartlib, and* Macaria (Oxford: Wellcome Unit for the History of Medicine, 1979), p. 5.

learned in my long travels, may stand them in stead, I would willingly impart it for the publick good.'[47] *Macaria* accordingly centres its projection of an idealized society on an improved Parliament. The society is a form of welfare state, in which resources are distributed to the entire nation rather than concentrated in London.[48] It is founded on a centralized system of education and local services, funded by a five percent inheritance tax. Instead of the Houses of Parliament, the Macarians are controlled by 'a Great Councell like to the Parliament in England', which conveniently sits once a year for a short space of time. To ensure the smooth running of this council and all its functions, it is supported by 'five under Councels' which administer Husbandry, Fishing, Trade by Land and Sea and new Plantations, and by the 'Colledge of experience', which conducts medical research and rewards those who benefit the common good.[49] Like many other utopian writings considered in this chapter, *Macaria* centres its imagined ideal community on reformed versions of existing institutions. The Great Councell and the Colledge of experience are perfected forms of English systems of government and education; their emulation is desired in order to 'make England to bee like to *Macaria*'.[50]

Although the text describes an imagined society and includes features of the conventional utopia, it dispenses with many of the traditional utopian conventions, most notably the journey and the narrator's encounters with the inhabitants of the new country. *Macaria* is a brief and direct social treatise, and has been described as 'a thinly veiled statement of the social and economic policies of experts advising the parliamentarian party'.[51] Plattes does not concern himself with inventive detail or excessive information; rather, he focuses on how the central institution in England, Parliament, can be made to resemble the central institution in Macaria, the Great Councell. Importantly, the author of *Macaria* addresses himself to changes that he thinks it would be possible to effect. Just as Bacon was able to imagine his idealized institution, Salomon's House, due to the existence of new establishments of learning, such as Gresham College, so Plattes's educational institute, the Colledge of experience, has shared features both with existing institutions like Gresham and with projected ones, such as Hartlib's Office of Address.[52] Plattes's utopia is at once optimistic about the potential for change and practical in imagining how that change might be brought about.

The one element of the utopian form that Plattes chooses to retain is the dialogue. The conversation between the Traveller and the Scholar takes place as they walk to and in 'Moore fields'; their deliberate avoidance of 'this noise,

---

[47] Gabriel Plattes, *A Description of the Famous Kingdome of Macaria; Shewing its Excellent Government* (London, 1641), p. 2. All further references to this text will be to this edition and will be given in the footnotes.

[48] See Trevor-Roper, 'Three Foreigners', p. 269.

[49] *Macaria*, p. 3, p. 5.

[50] *Macaria*, p. 15.

[51] Webster, *Utopian Planning and the Puritan Revolution*, p. 23.

[52] Similarly, Hartlib imagined using existent institutions such as Chelsea College in his plans for educational reform. See Turnbull, *Hartlib, Dury and Comenius*, p. 48.

and throng of people' of the city mimics the dialogue's frequent use of a pastoral setting.[53] The didactic associations of the dialogue form are clearly part of its appeal to Plattes; the Traveller's purpose in speaking to the Schollar is to convince him of the possibility that a country should exist in which 'the people doe live in great plenty, prosperitie, health, peace, and happinesse, and have not halfe so much trouble as they have in these European Countreyes'.[54] The doubting Schollar's function in the conversation is to prompt the disclosure of information via a series of questions and to model the reader's presumed conviction of the worthiness of attempting the emulation of Macaria, as he exclaims, for example: 'I am imparadised in my minde, in thinking that England may bee made happy, with such expedition and facility'.[55] He also serves to remind the reader of the renowned untrustworthiness of travellers' tales. Travellers, he says,

> must take heed of two things principally in your relations; first, that you say nothing that is generally deemed impossible. Secondly, that your relation hath no contradiction in it, or else all men will think that you make use of the Travellers priviledge, to wit, to lie by authority.[56]

By setting his dialogue in the immediate vicinity of London, and by referring in it to members of his acquaintance, such as one particular 'Gentleman that is greatly addicted to try experiments', Plattes seeks to distance his utopia from the fictional elements of travel writing.[57] That he chooses to do so via the dialogue form demonstrates an attempt to divorce both utopian literature and the dialogue from the mendacious associations of travel writing and thus to emphasize his central premise, that the ideal society can be realized here and now. *Macaria* is a rare example of a utopian dialogue in which the fictional elements of the form and its associations with travel are entirely downplayed in favour of claims to direct truth and usefulness.

While *Macaria* is concerned with the reform of a real and existing establishment, utopian thinkers also turned to fictional institutions in their efforts to promote civic reform in their own society. English utopian political writing of the 1640s in part endeavoured to make real (largely due to the belief that they soon would be real) the perfected institutions and societies of earlier Protestant utopian fiction. The utopian writing of this period focused, as earlier utopian writing had, on the institutions society needed in order to become more perfect: it was through the ideal institution that reform could be managed simultaneously on an individual and social scale. The crucial difference was that imagining the ideal institution, and in consequence the ideal society, was no longer felt to be a matter for fiction. In the political context of the mid-seventeenth century, inadequate institutions were themselves felt to be at fault in contributing to social problems. Many such

---

[53] *Macaria*, p. 2.
[54] *Macaria*, p. 11.
[55] *Macaria*, p. 14.
[56] *Macaria*, p. 3.
[57] *Macaria*, p. 14.

establishments were to be altered or removed during the revolutionary years, such as the Star Chamber, the Court of High Commission and the Councils of Wales and the North.[58] Such institutional breakdown may, in part, have provided an impetus to imagine the superior operations that might be erected in their place.

While the dialogue form was not common, the metaphor of the voyage was sometimes useful to authors of reformist writings. An anonymous pamphlet published in 1649 and entitled *The Teacher of the English School* uses a reference to a biblical voyage to reinforce the notion that the changes he proposes are both timely and divinely inspired:

> Now compare the defective and little profit which in time past hath been gotten by english scholeing, with this teaching, absolutely more perfect and more profitable; they that finde, feel and see the invaluabel benefits of it, will think themselves as happie as they who were brought out of the *obscurities* of *Egypt*, into the *light* of the land of *Goshen*.[59]

As with Goodwin's *Sions Glory*, the analogy of the journey is useful in describing the prospect of reform. The voyage metaphor is, of course, central to the utopia, but the comparison here is to a biblical journey, rather than one from the narrator's own society to the utopian location. Similarly, in a sermon preached before Parliament in 1645, Dury made clear his belief that 'it is Gods intention the thing should be done'[60] and, like Goodwin and the anonymous author of *The Teacher of the English School*, expressed his understanding of the gradual but continual nature of the reforms underway through the analogy of the journey. This time the passage is from Babylon to Jerusalem:

> although we are thus involved and intangled under the powers of this Babylonian captivity, [...] neverthelesse the way is open for us to march away from thence, and come to the spirituall Jerusalem.[61]

This voyage is something which must be undertaken by the church as an institution: 'now you must either fall utterly, and draw with you into ruine the other reformed Churches; or else secure them and your selves by the building up of Zion.'[62] At the same time, however, it is understood as being a spiritual process, a work which each person must undertake on an individual basis: 'the great and main work of a Christian in this life is, to march away, and make a safe retreat from Babylon, to come to Jerusalem.'[63]

---

[58] On this see Loewenstein, *Representing Revolution in Milton and His Contemporaries*, pp. 7–8.

[59] [n.a.], *The Teacher of the English School Soliciting For the Common-Wealth of Learning. Written by one that wisheth verie heartily well towards a more easie and profitable education of English Youth* (London, 1649), p. 327.

[60] John Dury, *Israels Call*, p. 44.

[61] *Israels Call*, p. 43.

[62] *Israels Call*, A2v.

[63] *Israels Call*, p. 33. Dury repeats this sentence almost identically on p. 45.

The metaphor of the journey was also employed by John Dury's wife, Dorothy, in a letter to Lady Ranelagh (born Katherine Boyle and sister of Robert), written in 1645 and sent to her as an enclosure in a letter from Dury, who was then in Rotterdam, to Hartlib in London. Dorothy Dury described having previously discussed with Lady Ranelagh 'my thoughts concerning the shaping the whole course of my life in all circumstance as one who is in a journey'. On this journey, Dorothy noted, it was better not to be encumbered by much baggage, and to leave behind everything that was not necessary to it. Not only did unnecessary burdens interfere with a 'straight passage', but they increased the risk of 'not setting all our mind vpon the constant pursuite of holding a conversation with God himself to which wee are called through our Vnion with his sonne'.[64] The ongoing conversation between the individual and God to which Dorothy refers was part of the spiritual journey necessary to come out of Babylon into Jerusalem.

In Dury's calls for alteration on a spiritual and institutional level, we observe the balance familiar in utopian writing between the need for reform on an individual basis and that on a social basis. In Dury's sermon, Babylon represents confusion and disorder, both of the spirit and of the state, while the vision of peace that is Jerusalem is similarly understood both symbolically, as a spiritual haven, and literally, as a well-ordered society. Dury explains the difference between Babylon and Jerusalem as being that of 'two wayes of government'. The best form of government has both a practical and a spiritual purpose:

> The mystery then of *Babylon* doth consist chiefly in this; That it is the method or way of Government which naturall reason doth suggest unto worldly men, to secure themselves from danger, to get themselves a name upon Earth, and to subdue others unto their power, after their own will. But the mystery of *Jerusalem* is the way of government which the Word of God doth prescribe unto spirituall men, to assure them of Gods favour, to get their names written in Heaven [...] not intending to bring any under their power, but all to the obedience of the will of God in Christ.[65]

The two methods of government, Dury explains, reflect both 'immediatly upon the souls of men' and 'upon their bodies and bodily state'. Hence, while Jerusalem or the City of God is conceived in spiritual terms, realistic and practical reforms can be begun to bring it about, both ecclesiastically and politically: 'look to the house of God to settle it in good order; and then look to the further settlement of the civill state'. Dury goes on in this sermon to detail some such necessary developments in the field of education. Attention to such a sermon demonstrates firstly that the areas of church and state were perceived as closely related; reform had to take place throughout society. It also reveals, however, that improvements were imagined in specific and detailed ways, for example in the 'Schooles of the Prophets', 'the Universities' and 'all the inferiour common Schooles', because 'the

---

[64] Dorothy Dury to Lady Ranelagh (copy), sent 7 July 1645, HP 3/2/138A.
[65] *Israels Call*, pp. 35–6.

corruption of all states and qualities of people doth arise from the neglect of these Schooles'.[66] Dury's use of the Augustinian concept of the City of God exemplifies the change in the use of utopia in the period considered by this book. In Chapter 1, I argued that an Augustinian reading of *Utopia* demonstrated More's belief in the impossibility of achieving the City of God on earth; for the seventeenth-century reformers, I contend that the City of God was an immediate prospect that would have historical reality.

Dury did more than call for institutional improvements to be undertaken; he soon published writings detailing exactly how they might be implemented. Texts such as *The Reformed School* (thought to date from 1650), *A Supplement to the Reformed School* and *The Reformed Librarie-Keeper* (both also 1650) directly tackled the problems of institutional reform. Hartlib's preface to *The Reformed School* expresses the widely held belief that the restructuring of education was fundamental to all hopes of improvement: 'For, all things being rightly weighed, we shall perceive that this endeavour alone, or nothing, will be able to work a reformation in this our age.'[67] In Dury's text, as we have seen in other utopian writings, it is the utility of education that is felt to be paramount: 'nothing is to be counted a matter of true learning amongst men, which is not directly servicable to mankind.'[68] Dury speaks in general terms of the 'Babylonian generation wherein we live', but here he is able to pay much closer attention to the practicalities of the necessary improvements, detailing the desired scholastic timetable, times for rising and sleeping, daily prayers and so on. The effecting of such changes has a grand purpose, 'the building up of the Citie of God in our generation', but it must also be begun in smaller ways, such as the structure of the daily programme, the particulars of the curriculum and the organization of the schoolhouse.[69] For Dury, the City of God is not only a spiritual ideal, but one that can be fostered at once. It is in the reworking of these details, minor though they may seem, that the wider purposes of reformation may be begun. This highlights the tendency of the political utopian writing of this period to imagine reforms taking place within the structures of contemporary society.

Calls for improvement in sermons of the period such as those of Dury reflect the wider attention that was being paid to the need for institutional reform. The pamphlet exchange that was to take place between John Webster and Seth Ward (and his colleagues) in 1653 and 1654 demonstrates how ubiquitous demands for change had become by the early 1650s. Webster's *Academiarum Examen* called upon those who cared for the universities of Oxford and Cambridge to join his demands for their rectification. Webster emphasized that his criticisms related to the degenerate practices these establishments fostered, not the universities themselves:

---

[66] *Israels Call*, p. 41, p. 47, pp. 48–9.

[67] John Dury, *The Reformed School*, ed. by H.M. Knox (Liverpool: Liverpool University Press, 1958), p. 19.

[68] *The Reformed School*, p. 38. See also p. 26 and p. 48.

[69] Dury, *The Supplement to the Reformed School*, p. 11.

> I intend not to asperse the persons of any, nor to traduce nor calmunate the *Academies* themselves, but only the corruptions that time and negligence hath introduced there, but simply to attempt (according to my best understanding) some reformation, not eradication of their customes, and learning.[70]

Ward's reply, *Vindiciae Academiarum*, which was printed in Oxford, found considerable fault with Webster's criticisms, but nonetheless recognized the need for reformation in principle, 'the reforming of Publick Schooles' being 'suitable to my owne frequent wishes' and 'with reason to be hoped for in this inquisitive age'.[71] It was not only educational institutions that were made an object of the impetus for change. The anonymous *One More Blow at Babylon*, for example, published in 1650, called upon the Parliament to revolutionize '*the corrupt Magistracy and Ministry of this Nation*', seeing their present corruption as '*the only Obstruction to a through* [sic] *Reformation in matters Sacred and Civil*'.[72] Nine years earlier, another anonymous pamphlet had called for further reformation of the clergy in order to achieve a simpler form of church management, harking back to the ideal of the apostolic system.[73] This earlier pamphlet was one of those aimed at the new Parliament of 1641, although, perhaps due to the controversial nature of its desire for the removal of bishops and synods, it was printed in Amsterdam. These texts, although they may differ in their perceptions of how institutional reform is to be achieved, evince a common understanding that the time for such reform is ripe.

During the 1640s and beyond, attempted modifications of social institutions such as the university and the church were not only the subject of political pamphlets, but were actively being carried out by parliamentary reformers. Throughout the 1640s, Royalist clergy were removed from their benefices by parliamentarians, whether for misbehaviour, teaching 'scandalous' doctrine or general bad practice.[74] While there is an element of anti-Royalist or anti-Laudian sentiment in the purpose of these reforms, there was a wide divergence in the forms and nature of the criticism levied against such clergy, who were certainly not all Royalists or Laudians. It is clear that their removal was viewed by the parliamentary side as constituting part of a necessary reformation of the ministry and the church. As historians have reflected, church reforms alone were insufficient, 'for whilst the universities continued unreformed, their work was but half done'.[75] During the first half of

---

[70] John Webster, *Academiarum Examen, or the Examination of Academies* (London, 1653), B3 ('The Epistle to the Reader').

[71] [Seth Ward], *Vindiciae Academiarum* (Oxford, 1654), p. 1.

[72] [n.a.], *One More Blow at Babylon* (London, 1650), av–a2.

[73] [n.a.], *A Copie of two writings sent to the Parliament. The one intituled Motions for reforming the Church of England in the present Parliament* (Amsterdam, 1641).

[74] See I.M. Green, 'The Persecution of "Scandalous" and "Malignant" Parish Clergy during the English Civil War', *The English Historical Review*, 94 (1979), 507–31 (510–51).

[75] John Walker, *The Sufferings of the Clergy during the Great Rebellion* (Oxford: Henry and Parker, 1862), p. 191. As may be gathered from Walker's title, he perceives the attempted reforms of the ministry in an unfavourable light, as 'ruining and destroying the local clergy' (p. 191).

the decade, attempts were made by the new Parliament to begin the restitution of the universities. At Cambridge, for example, all 'scandalous' or 'ill-affected' heads, fellows and members of colleges, ministers and schoolmasters were to be examined, and put out of their places if action was deemed necessary, and in May 1641, the Vice-Chancellor himself, Richard Holdsworth, was arrested.[76] Such attempts at the control or removal of recalcitrant clerics and academics reflect the determination of Parliament to undertake the active reorganization of institutions. It was in the prospect of institutional reform that Dury, Hartlib and others founded their plans for the ideal society.

Conclusions: Baconian Utopias

In basing their ideal societies around ideal institutions, the Hartlibians were again showing the influence of their utopian antecedent, Francis Bacon. It has long been recognized that Samuel Hartlib was profoundly influenced by Bacon in his attempts to promote the advancement of learning.[77] For Hartlib, the realization of the Baconian advancement of learning was vital for the 'true and fundamentall Reformation' of the state.[78] At the heart of Hartlib's sympathy with Bacon lay their shared belief that the reorganization of human knowledge could result in a return to a prelapsarian dominion over nature. More specifically, in his efforts to create a system of correspondence between like-minded reformers across Europe, we can see the attempted realization of Bacon's 'Noble and Generous Fraternity' producing 'correspondence by mutual intelligence'.[79] Samuel Hartlib and his colleagues were having the discussions that Bacon had imagined such a correspondence network would produce. Moreover, in attempting to build institutions that would undertake the advancement of learning, such as his Agency

---

[76] J.D. Twigg, 'The Parliamentary Visitation of the University of Cambridge, 1644–1645', *The English Historical Review*, 98 (1983), 513–28 (514).

[77] For the Baconianism of Hartlib and the Hartlib circle, see Trevor-Roper, 'Three Foreigners', p. 250, p. 258; Charles Webster, *The Great Instauration: Science, Medicine, and Reform, 1626–1660* (London: Duckworth, 1975) pp. 97–9, p. 113, p. 514, and *Samuel Hartlib and the Advancement of Learning*, p. 69, p. 70; Stephen Clucas, 'In Search of "The True Logick": methodological eclecticism among the "Baconian reformers"', in *Samuel Hartlib and Universal Reformation*, pp. 51–74 (pp. 51–2); Stephen Pumfrey, '"These 2 hundred years not the like published as Gellibrand has done de Magnete": the Hartlib circle and magnetic philosophy', in *Samuel Hartlib and Universal Reformation*, pp. 247–67 (p. 260); William T. Lynch, 'A Society of Baconians?: The Collective Development of Bacon's Method in the Royal Society of London,' in *Francis Bacon and the Refiguring of Early Modern Thought: Essays to Commemorate* The Advancement of Learning *(1605–2005)* (Farnham: Ashgate, 2005), pp. 173–202 (pp. 179–80).

[78] Samuel Hartlib, *Englands Thankfulnesse, or, An Humble Remembrance presented to the Committee for Religion in the High Court of Parliament* (London, 1642), p. 9.

[79] Francis Bacon, *De dignitate at augmentis scientiarum* (1623), in *Works*, I, 491, quoted in Webster, *Samuel Hartlib and the Advancement of Learning*, p. 3.

for Universal Learning or the Office of Address, Hartlib was directly influenced by the Baconian ideal, as manifested in Salomon's House.[80] Indeed, Hartlib specifically refers to Salomon's House in his thinking on the kinds of institutions he wishes to see created. In undated notes contained within the Hartlib Papers, Hartlib comments under the title 'Londons Vniversity': 'Arca Noa and House of Salomon or a Library of Representations.'[81] Both Noah's Ark and Salomon's House are used as exemplars of the organization and administration of empirical knowledge. Elsewhere he suggests for the projected university 'one of the Houses or Colledges as Verulam for breeding of states men for Politicks vide Verulam'.[82] The ideal university for London would be one that emulated the utopian research institution and laboratory in *New Atlantis*. Thus the image of Salomon's House was clearly in the forefront of Hartlib's mind when he came to thinking about the institutional reforms necessary for contemporary England.

Nor was Hartlib the only figure to think of Bacon's ideal institute as a model. In addition to its influence on the founding of the Royal Society, the Hartlib Papers record a reference in 1653 to 'Mr Bushels Mineral Overtures a sheets in 4to. where hee desires assistance that hee may erect Salomons-House described by the Lord Verulam.'[83] In a letter to Robert Boyle dated 8 May 1654, Hartlib wrote: 'Yesterday I was invited by the famous *Thomas Bushel* […] to *Lambeth-Marsh*, to see part of that foundation or building, which is designed for the execution of my lord *Verulam*'s *New Atlantis*'.[84] Bushell, 'Farmer of His Majesty's Mines in Wales', in fact went on to produce a practical abridgement of Bacon's *New Atlantis* in 1659.[85] For Bushell, the ideas of Salomon's House were a realistic and workable model for improving the mining of minerals. Bushell is clearly not reacting to *New Atlantis* only as a work of fiction; rather it is itself a treasure-house for practical reforms. Such evidence demonstrates that there is plainly a direct link from the projected utopian institutionalization of Francis Bacon to that of the 'Baconian reformers' of the Hartlib circle in the mid-seventeenth century. For the Hartlibians, Salomon's House provided an inspiration for the ideal institutions which they believed were a necessary factor in the achievement of social reform and the arrival of Christ's rule.

In attempting to realize the sort of idealized institution that Bacon had imagined in *New Atlantis*, Hartlib and his colleagues were using utopian literature as a blueprint. They presumed that utopias could be direct models for change, both in terms of how they read earlier utopian fiction and in terms of how they expected their own utopian literature to be read. In doing this, with the exception

---

[80] For this view, see, for example, Dickson, *The Tessera of Antilia*, p. 169.

[81] Undated Note on London University, HP 47/9/38A.

[82] Undated Notes on London University, HP 47/9/17A.

[83] *Ephemerides* (1653), 28/2/75B–28/2/76A. For the influence of Salomon's House on the inception of the Royal Society, see Chapter 4 of the present study.

[84] Robert Boyle, *The Works*, ed. by Thomas Birch, 6 vols, 3rd edn (Hildesheim: Georg Olms Verlagsbuchhandlung, 1965), VI, 88.

[85] Thomas Bushell, *Mr Bushell's Abridgement of the Lord Chancellor Verulam's philosophical theory in Mineral Prosecutions, etc* (London, 1659).

of *Macaria*, they rejected the traditional elements of the utopian form. If utopia were to become reality, then any formal aspects which pointed to its fictional status were not useful. In the utopian writings of the mid-seventeenth century, real conversations were taking place between reformers which, in their view, had the power to change the world. Fictional conversations, travel narratives and other aspects of literary form were, by and large, put to one side. Not all efforts at reform, of course, were utopian; but these reformers' writings play an important part in the history of Renaissance utopias, as they epitomize the sincere and fervent optimism about reform which characterized this period. Despite this rejection of the fictional aspects of the utopian form, the mid-seventeenth century was also to witness the publication of utopian literature that embraced the imaginative elements of the utopian tradition, as we shall see in the next chapter.

Chapter 6
'Instructive Discourses':
The Proliferation and Rejection of Utopia in the 1640s and Beyond

Introduction: 'imaginary whimseys' and Explorations in Utopia

As the previous chapter has shown, utopian writings continued to be produced in the mid-seventeenth century, although their forms became more diverse in the hands of reformers using the utopian mode of discourse to promote the improvement of society. This chapter will examine the development of the imaginative strand of utopianism, the forerunner of the utopian novel, through Samuel Gott's *Nova Solyma* (1648), a Latin prose romance which imagines an ideal society as a model for contemporary England. In demonstrating the points of communication between this imaginative utopia and contemporary utopian reformist literature, it will argue that these similarities themselves represent a form of dialogue between texts which was important to the ways in which the utopian mode was to develop; such utopias also reflect the ways in which the utopian form had changed by the end of the period considered by this book. By the mid-seventeenth century, utopian dialogues took place between rather than within texts, a fact which, as this chapter will argue, reflects their attempts to access a wider and more diverse public audience. It will begin by looking at a number of different utopias which reflect the range of ways in which the mode was used by the middle of the seventeenth century.

By this period, the traditional utopian form suffered from its association with unreality; references to the place or idea of utopia in early seventeenth-century English literature tend to be comic, as utopia is taken to mean a place that is non-existent, ridiculous or fantastic.[1] This explains the attitude towards utopia in Robert Burton's *The Anatomy of Melancholy*, first published in 1621, which described his '*Utopia* of mine owne', a seemingly ideal state. Here Burton speaks of the necessity for social reformation: 'We had need of some generall visiter

---

[1] For some typical references to utopia as comic or pointless, see, for example, the references to utopia in John Taylor, 'A brood of Cormorants', in *All the workes of Iohn Taylor the Water-Poet* (London, 1630), p. 13 (second series of pagination); Richard Brathwait, 'To the Pious Memory of Sir Richard Hutton Knight', in *Astraea's Teares. An Elegie Vpon the death of that Reverend, Learned and Honest Judge, Sir Richard Hutton Knight* (London, 1641), B4r; Richard Brathwait, *A Survey of History: Or, A Nursery for Gentry* (London, 1638), p. 240.

in our age, that should reforme what is amis.'² Like an institution in need of an overseer to regulate its behaviour, Burton views modern society as requiring many changes touching on all aspects of life, including religion, arts, sciences, education and morals. Such an overhaul, Burton explains, would outdo the labours of Hercules, and consequently his desires are 'vaine absurd, and ridiculous wishes not to be hoped: all must be as it is'. His conclusions reflect the prevailing association between utopianism and useless, blind optimism. In reality, humanity cannot be improved, so Burton can only imagine his own perfect community, not as an effort to implement the necessary reforms but rather to 'satisfie & please my selfe'. Written for his own self-indulgent pleasure, Burton's utopia will be 'a new *Atlantis*, a poeticall commonwealth of mine owne, in which I will freely domineere, build Citties, make Lawes, Statutes, as I list my selfe', but it will not have serious reform as its aim.³

Burton uses the utopian mode of discourse as an opportunity to satirize both his own world and the form of the utopia itself. He claims that it is highly unlikely, for example, that he will manage to find priests who live their lives in imitation of Christ, lawyers who love their neighbours as themselves, or philosophers who know themselves: he would if he could, but 'this is unpossible, I must get such as I may'.⁴ The utopia is exploited in order to make fun of its own conventions; in a mockery of the traditional ambiguity as to the utopia's precise location, Burton jokes that he will choose a site:

> whose latitude shall be 45 degrees (I respect not minutes) in the midst of the temperate Zone, or perhaps under the *Aequator*, that Paradise of the world [...] the longitude for some reasons I will conceale.⁵

Burton's use demonstrates that while he employs the utopian mode to criticize aspects of the status quo, he does not conceive it as a serious response to social ills. Burton never loses sight of the fact that he must deal with real people, who are 'partiall and passionate, mercilesse, covetous, corrupt, subject to love, hate, feare, favor, &c.'⁶ The creation of a utopia is an explicitly fictional process; imagining a better way of life is nothing more than a conjuring trick. While Burton's ideal

---

² Robert Burton, 'Democritus to the Reader', in *The Anatomy of Melancholy*, ed. by Thomas C. Faulkner, Nicolas K. Kiessling and Rhonda L. Blair, intro. by J.B. Bamborough, 6 vols (Oxford: Clarendon Press, 1989), I, 84. For the date of *The Anatomy*, see *The Anatomy of Melancholy*, I, xxxvii. Future references will be to this edition and will be given in footnotes in the form *The Anatomy of Melancholy*, I: 84. For more on Burton's use of utopia, see J. Max Patrick, 'Robert Burton's Utopianism', *Philological Quarterly*, 27 (1948), 345–58; J.C. Davis, *Utopia and the Ideal Society: A Study of English Utopian Writing 1516–1700* (Cambridge: Cambridge University Press, 1981; repr. 1983), Chapter 4.

³ *The Anatomy of Melancholy*, I: 85.
⁴ *The Anatomy of Melancholy*, I: 91.
⁵ *The Anatomy of Melancholy*, I: 86.
⁶ *The Anatomy of Melancholy*, I: 92.

society envisions how life might be better organized, its satirical tone undercuts any efforts to read it as a call for social reform along its own lines. A little over a century after the term was first coined by More, 'utopia' had already absorbed the meaning of something unrealistic or unfeasible. As a consequence, those who desired to reform society and its institutions had to tread carefully to avoid its negative connotations. In his *Academiarum Examen*, John Webster recognized that some might condemn his plans for the reformation of the universities by alleging that they were nothing better than utopian, and thus useless:

> Some may object and say, that this Treatise is but like Plato's *Republick*, *Sir Thomas Moor's Utopia*, or the Lord *Bacon*'s new *Athlantis*, fraught with nothing but *Heterodoxal* novelties, and imaginary whimseys, which are not to be imitated, but are meerly impracticable.[7]

Webster here recognizes possible distaste for the utopia, which contains idealistic schemes but lacks the actual ability to effect change. Nonetheless, and in spite of the fact that the treatise he is writing is by no means utopian in form, he seeks to defend utopianism against its critics:

> To this I answer, that phantastical heads may very well be filled with such roving thoughts, and conceited crotches, yet I would have them to know that in *Plato*'s *Commonwealth*, and *Sir Thomas Moor*'s *Utopia*, ar more excellent things contained than figments and impossibilities [...] and if these poor lines of mine contained but any treasure comparable to any of their rich mines, I should set an higher Character of esteem upon them, than now I ought, or they any way merit.[8]

Webster argues that it is not true to claim that utopias have no practical worth. *New Atlantis* is a useful case in point: Bacon's ideas in his utopia 'might be brought to some reasonable perfection, if the waies and means that he hath prescribed, were diligently observed and persued'.[9] The fact that Webster feels the need to protect his own reformist writings from the taint of utopianism reflects that, while some saw the utopia as a useful and valid form of political expression, others remained critical of the utopia's utility and validity. This critical stance offers another possible reason for why utopian thinkers might not have chosen to express their ideas in the conventional utopian form. In the mid-seventeenth century, the utopia proliferated beyond its own conventional form partly as a response to the ways in which earlier utopian writings were perceived. As the utopian discourse came to be used for different purposes (namely the achievement of specific social reforms), it began to adopt different forms. The dialogue, with its capacity for diversity and multiplicity, was less attractive in this context than narrative forms, better suited to expressing a single point of view.

---

[7] John Webster, *Academiarum Examen, or the Examination of Academies* (London, 1653), Bv ('The Epistle to the Reader').

[8] Webster, *Academiarum Examen*, Bv–B2r.

[9] Webster, *Academiarum Examen*, B2r.

For social reformers, the traditional utopian narrative, of journey, discovery and encounter, was an unnecessary distraction from their schemes for idealized societies and institutions. The borders between utopian and other modes of literature became increasingly fluid as utopia itself seemed closer to home. This kind of utopianism, manifested in the political and religious writing of the period, did not need to consider the ideal society as a remote, foreign realm. Quite the opposite; for millenarian reformers, the ideal society was imminent, and so the fictional conventions of utopia, the distance afforded by the long journey and the isolated location were neither necessary nor desirable. Indeed, utopian writers explicitly sought to imagine England as the ideal state. Despite this development of utopianism outside the conventional utopian form, however, more traditional utopias continued to be produced in the mid-seventeenth century, some deeply engaged with social reform and others less so. Amongst these can be counted early forms of science fiction which mimic the travel narrative, in the tradition of Joseph Hall's *Mundus Alter Et Idem* of 1605. Francis Godwin's *The Man in the Moone*, for example, printed in 1638 under the pseudonym of 'Domingo Gonsales', is presented like a genuine traveller's tale, part of which describes the narrator's voyage to the moon and back in a harness, drawn by a flock of large birds and an encounter with giant moon-people, who are of such 'excellent disposition' that their home seems 'a very Paradise'.[10] Godwin's utopian narrative manipulates a variety of genres – the picaresque, the travel narrative, the scientific treatise – in describing Gonsales's travels on the moon and elsewhere. The utopian elements of the text, as Sarah Hutton has noted, encourage the reader to compare the societies that Gonsales encounters.[11] The travel narrative form points to similarities and differences between life on the moon and life on earth, but the text takes little interest in reforming or altering the latter.

Another category from this period is the political utopia, like *Macaria*, in which the utopian form is merely a framework for political manifesto. For James Harrington, whose work *The Commonwealth of Oceana* was printed in 1656, the device of the imaginary ideal state is little more than a convenient mirror for the author's own society, which is fictionalized in the text but remains 'instantly recognizable'.[12] Harrington pictures an idealized society which represents an immediately achievable future England, with the aim of promoting the changes which he wished to see instituted. As his editor, J.G.A. Pocock, points out, Harrington himself referred to *Oceana* as a 'model' in the modern sense of the word.[13] Harrington employs the utopian mode in constructing an alternative

---

[10] [Francis Godwin], *The Man in the Moone, or a Discourse of a Voyage Thither, by Domingo Gonsales the Speedy Messenger* (London, 1638), p. 104, p. 85.

[11] Sarah Hutton, 'The Man in the Moone and the New Astonomy: Godwin, Gilbert, Kepler', *Études Épistémè*, 6 (2004), 3–13. See also William Poole, 'Kepler's *Somnium* and Francis Godwin's *The Man in the Moone*', in *New Worlds Reflected: Travel and Utopia in the Early Modern Period*, ed. by Chloë Houston (Farnham: Ashgate, 2010), pp. 57–69.

[12] James Harrington, *The Commonwealth of Oceana and A System of Politics*, ed. by J.G.A. Pocock (Cambridge: Cambridge University Press, 1992), p. xvii.

[13] Harrington, *The Commonwealth of Oceana and A System of Politics*, p. xvii.

society, in this case an idealized republican commonwealth, but has little interest in the more fictional aspects of the utopian form, such as the journey and personal encounters with foreign peoples and places. For Harrington, the utopian form was a means of modelling political reform and no more, but for others, such as Samuel Gott, it opened up possibilities for the construction of imaginary worlds.

The texts discussed in this chapter and the previous one demonstrate that the dialogue form with which utopianism was linked in the sixteenth century was entirely absent by the mid-seventeenth century, though the concept of dialogue, through the use of conversation as narrative device and metaphor, remained a feature of utopian literature. The next section of this chapter will consider Gott's *Nova Solyma*; despite the disparity in form between *Nova Solyma* and other utopian writings of the 1640s considered in Chapter 5, the texts share an interest in millenarianism and specifically in the prospect of England as the New Jerusalem, as well as in educational reform, which suggests a commonality and dialogue between certain utopian texts of this period.

Nova Solyma: England and the New Jerusalem

Nova Solyma by Samuel Gott was published in 1648. This lengthy Latin prose narrative, a forerunner of the utopia novel, demonstrates that the religious and political motivations manifested in the utopian texts discussed in the previous chapter are also to be found in more conventional utopias. *Nova Solyma* tells the story of two young Cambridge graduates, Eugenius and Politian, who evade their parents' control to visit Nova Solyma, or New Jerusalem, and become the guests of Joseph, a young citizen of that city. Unlike most other utopias, the text's narration is in the third person, and the narrator does not appear as a character in the tale. Little attention is paid to the students' journey; rather, the narrative is concerned with their experiences of this ideal city and their individual progression towards moral righteousness. Joseph's family, consisting of his father, Jacob, twin sisters, Anna and Joanna, and younger brothers, Auximus and Augentius, is established as the example of the ideal domestic life within the larger realm of the perfect city.

Indeed, *Nova Solyma* is the first utopia to be so intimately concerned with the domestic sphere and the personal nature of ideal living, a move which, along with its form and style of narration, signals its relevance to the history of the early utopian novel. The text not only reveals the construction of the ideal society, but deals with how each individual must approach the question of how to live well; the utopia is moving away from a direct concern with the mechanics of travel and discovery and towards the more domestic field of the ideal family. Joseph's family is renowned for its piety, learning and social standing. Through its example and the experience of living in New Jerusalem, Eugenius and Politian undertake a process of spiritual education which is cemented by their double wedding to Anna and Joanna, and by which the utopian city is linked to the protagonists' own. This interest in the domestic as well as in the individual nature of the ideal life, in addition to the stylistic elements of third-person narrative and the intricate, digressive plot, are the chief elements which demonstrate how *Nova Solyma* can be seen as a forerunner of the novel.[14] Gott is clearly more interested in sophisticated narrative devices and in the literary nature of the utopia than most of his contemporaries, and the text's digressions, all of which have a direct moral interpretation, feed into the main trajectory of the narrative, which is that the best path is that which is morally right.

Nova Solyma not only shows its inheritance of the utopian concerns of social reform and education, but also points the way to the development of the utopian mode of discourse beyond the Renaissance period. When the text was first translated into English in 1902 by Walter Begley, he believed it to be the work of John Milton, though it was soon after reattributed to Milton's contemporary at Cambridge, Samuel Gott.[15] Gott was a barrister, having graduated from Cambridge in 1632, and from 1645 to 1648 was the Member of Parliament for Winchelsea, Sussex. *Nova Solyma* seems to have been written in the first half of the 1640s, and was published in 1648.[16] Gott's theology, according to one critic of *Nova Solyma*, encompassed 'a broad Puritanism that emphasized individual religious experience and personal morality', which is arguably reflected in his utopian fiction.[17] Perhaps because a reliable modern edition is not yet available, this text has received comparatively little critical interest in studies of the utopian mode.[18] But in fact *Nova Solyma* has much in common with other utopian literature of the period, including that of the Hartlib circle, discussed in Chapter 5.[19]

---

[14] Amy Boesky sees *Nova Solyma*'s 'resoundingly bourgeois' qualities as the result of its reflection of the ethos of the emergent English middle classes. See Boesky, *Founding Fictions: Utopias in Early Modern England* (Athens: University of Georgia Press, 1996), p. 96.

[15] For the establishment of Gott's authorship, see Stephen K. Jones, 'The Authorship of *Nova Solyma*', *Library*, ser. 3, 1 (1907), 225–38.

[16] For biographical information on Samuel Gott, see Davis, *Utopia and the Ideal Society*, pp. 141–5; J. Max Patrick, 'Puritanism and Poetry: Samuel Gott', *University of Toronto Quarterly*, 8 (1938–39), 211–16; Jennifer Morrish, 'Virtue and Genre in Samuel Gott's *Nova Solyma*', *Humanistica Lovaniensia*, 52 (2003), 237–317 (248–51). For the date of *Nova Solyma*, see Davis, *Utopia and the Ideal Society*, p. 145.

[17] J. Max Patrick, '*Nova Solyma*: Samuel Gott's Puritan Utopia', *Studies in the Literary Imagination*, 10:2 (1977), 43–55 (47).

[18] The most wide-reaching studies of *Nova Solyma* are those of J.C. Davis in *Utopia and the Ideal Society* and Jennifer Morrish, who considers *Nova Solyma* as a neo-Latin romance in 'Virtue and Genre in Samuel Gott's *Nova Solyma*'. See also William Allen Nielsen, 'Nova Solyma: A Romance Attributed to John Milton', *Modern Philology*, 1:4 (1904), 525–46; Johann Valentin Andreae, *Christianopolis: An Ideal State of the Seventeenth Century*, trans. and intro. by F.E. Held (New York: Oxford University Press, 1916), pp. 75–99; Victor Dupont, *L'utopie et le Roman Utopique dans la Littérature Anglaise* (Toulouse: Didier, 1941), pp. 186–200; William Alfred Leslie Vincent, *The State and School Education, 1640–1660, in England and Wales* (London: SPCK, 1950), pp. 34–5, pp. 56–7; Boesky, *Founding Fictions*, pp. 96–100.

[19] On the probability that Gott was acquainted with the Hartlibians, see Davis, *Utopia and the Ideal Society*, p. 142.

The most obvious link is provided by the text's testimony to the millenarian convictions of the times through its imagination of what the holy city, Jerusalem, might be like following the conversion of the Jews, fifty years after the event. Influenced by the philosemitism of the period, and in common with other utopian writings, Gott's text imagines Jerusalem as an alternative England. The conversion of the Jews was a recurrent feature of the professions of millenarians, who believed that the Jews would accept Christ and convert to Christianity before the Day of Judgement. Such a belief found its biblical precedent in Saint Paul's promise that 'all Israel shall be saved' when 'the fullness of the Gentiles be come in'.[20] The writings of earlier seventeenth-century millenarians such as Thomas Brightman demonstrate the conviction that the conversion of the Jews was a historical fact only waiting to be achieved. Around the turn of the century, Brightman had predicted that the Day of Judgement would fall in 1650, by which time people of the Jewish faith would have transferred their allegiance to Christianity. Brightman's works were republished in the 1640s, and were influential on contemporary millenarian thought.[21] A later millenarian, Zachary Crofton, was one of those who located the end of the world some years afterwards: 'It was in 1656, the flood came on the old world, and lasted fourty daies: Ergo in that year 1656, fire must come on this world and last fourty years'. Crofton, however, was in agreement that before this time 'the Jews will sure be suddenly called, and Antichrist ruined'.[22]

The certainty that the Jews were integral to the processes of the Day of Judgement was common in England during this time. Such convictions were also disseminated through the writings of European millenarians like Alsted, and philosemitism became increasingly popular; adherents included members of the Hartlib circle.[23] Hartlib himself certainly looked forward to the Jews' conversion; in his notes on the prospective London University, Hartlib proposes that there should be 'One of the *House*s or Colledg's for Conversion of the Jew's', and interest in the subject of Jewish conversion seems to have reached a new height at around the inception of the Long Parliament.[24] This interest found its expression

---

[20] Romans 11:25–6.

[21] See Thomas Brightman, *The Revelation of St Iohn Illustrated*, 4th edn (London, 1644). For more on Brightman and the history of seventeenth-century philosemitism and its relation to millenarianism, see David S. Katz, *Philosemitism and the Readmission of the Jews to England, 1603–1655* (Oxford: Clarendon Press, 1982), Chapter 3, *et passim*.

[22] Zachary Crofton, *Bethshemesh Clouded* (London, 1653), pp. 3–4, quoted in Katz, *Philosemitism and the Readmission of the Jews to England*, p. 89.

[23] See Richard H. Popkin, 'Hartlib, Dury and the Jews', in *Samuel Hartlib and Universal Reformation*, ed. by Mark Greengrass, Michael Leslie and Timothy Raylor (Cambridge: Cambridge University Press, 1994), pp. 118–36. For a revisionist account of Christian philosemitism in the seventeenth century, see Eliane Glaser, *Judaism without Jews: Philosemitism and Christian Polemic in Early Modern England* (London: Palgrave Macmillan, 2007).

[24] Undated Notes on London University, HP 47/9/17B; Katz, *Philosemitism and the Readmission of the Jews to England*, pp. 89–90, pp. 97–8.

in a variety of texts contemporary to *Nova Solyma* that aimed to draw Jews and Christians together, with the purpose of eventual reconciliation. Henry Jessey's *The Glory and Salvation of Jehudah and Israel*, for example, printed in 1650, intended to achieve a reunion between Christians and Jews, on the basis that they were in agreement on the fundamentals of religion. As part of this effort, Jessey sought to prove to those of the Jewish faith that their own authorities were in fact in support of Christian views about the Messiah.[25]

As well as the basic fact that the Jews would be converted to Christianity, the reclaiming of territory was an important part of their destiny in the coming millennium, and it was widely believed by millenarians that the Jewish people would be restored to their homeland of Israel. Robert Maton wrote in *Israels Redemption* in 1642 that he hoped his book would demonstrate to the English 'the wonders of Gods mighty hand / When Jews come backe unto the Holy Land.' For Maton, the only correct interpretation of the prophets is that they must have intended the Jews to inhabit their own terrain.[26] The prevalent idea of the Jews reclaiming their land provides an interesting background for the study of Gott's *Nova Solyma*. Firstly, it is evident not only that Gott is engaging with the millenarian tradition in imagining a time in which people of the Jewish faith have become Christian, but that he is doing so within the context of their reclamation of the Holy Land and the instigation of a New Jerusalem. Secondly, close examination of the millenarian sources shows that it was not only Jerusalem or Israel that figured in imaginings of Jewish conversion. England, too, had a significant role to play in achieving the return to the Holy Land. The English desire to convert the Jewish people to Christianity can be understood as another example of the wish to make something occur which it was believed was imminent, thus actively anticipating the millennium; and it was England, many millenarians believed, that would lead the Jews to their salvation. John Eachard, for example, a minister in Suffolk, stated in his *Good Newes for all Christian Soldiers* of 1645 that he was 'perswaded that the *Jewes* shall receive their Christs Nativitie day from *England*, and from our blossoming Thorne, rather than from any other Church in Christendome'.[27] Not only could the English nation have a part to play in the Jews' calling, but it was believed that their restoration would have direct benefits for England. In the same year that Eachard published his *Good Newes*, William Gouge preached before Parliament a fast day sermon which closely assessed Paul's writings on the conversion of the Jews and refuted potential opposition, claiming that their calling would be 'as a resurrection from the dead'. This happy day was close at hand, Gouge confirmed, but before that

---

[25] See Ernestine G.E. van der Wall, 'A Philo-Semitic Millenarian on the Reconciliation of Jews and Christians: Henry Jessey and his "The Glory and Salvation of Jehudah and Israel" (1650)', in *Sceptics, Millenarians and Jews*, ed. by David S. Katz and Jonathan I. Israel (Leiden: Brill, 1990), pp. 161–84 (p. 168).

[26] Robert Maton, *Israels Redemption* (London, 1642), p. *vs.* title page. On the prospect of the restoration of the Jews to a homeland, see James Shapiro, *Shakespeare and the Jews* (New York: Columbia University Press, 1996), p. 178.

[27] John Eachard, *Good Newes for all Christian Soldiers* (London, 1645), B2r, quoted in Katz, *Philosemitism and the Readmission of the Jews to England*, p. 103.

time England could expect to see material improvements, the result of 'Gods doing better for us here in *England* then at our beginnings'.²⁸

This relationship between the restored Jerusalem and England was a notable feature of English millenarianism. In the minds of the English, their own homeland had long been established as the location for the action of the millennium. In the sixteenth century, John Foxe had encouraged the view that the English were an elect nation, an opinion later endorsed by Brightman and other seventeenth-century millenarians.²⁹ By the mid-seventeenth century, with millenarian hopes spreading to all levels of society, many felt that England, the first among God's nations, would be the instrument through which the godly revolution was to be disseminated throughout the world.³⁰ So post-millennium Israel would have for Gott's readers a natural association with contemporary England and its future reformation, and in *Nova Solyma*, appropriately, the New Jerusalem is offered as a model for England, with the Cambridge students making direct comparisons between their host society and the one they have left behind.³¹ In this way, Jerusalem becomes an alternative or other England, a suitable location for imagining the kinds of improvements that Gott might like to see in his own country.

That Gott was influenced by contemporary millenarianism in his presentation of the Jewish calling is underscored by the way in which he imagines the actual conversion process to have taken place. Jacob explains that it is fifty years since 'our long and widely scattered nation was restored to its present wonderful prosperity.'³² He refers to the long-held belief that people of the Jewish faith would

---

²⁸ William Gouge, *The Progresse of Divine Providence* (London, 1645), p. 33.

²⁹ See Avihu Zakai, 'Thomas Brightman and English Apocalyptic Tradition', in *Menasseh Ben Israel and His World*, ed. by Yosef Kaplan, Henry Méchoulan and Richard H. Popkin (Leiden: Brill, 1989), pp. 31–44 (p. 35). On England as the leader of elect nations, see Patrick Collinson, *The Birthpangs of Protestant England: Religious and Cultural Change in the Sixteenth and Seventeenth Centuries* (London: Macmillan, 1988), pp. 1–27.

³⁰ See B.S. Capp, *The Fifth Monarchy Men: A Study in Seventeenth-Century English Millenarianism* (Oxford: Oxford University Press, 1972), p. 45, p. 53. For more on the idea of England as a land designated for a special destiny, see Graham Parry, 'A troubled Arcadia', in *Literature and the English Civil War*, ed. by Thomas Healy and Jonathan Sawday (Cambridge: Cambridge University Press, 1990), pp. 38–55.

³¹ See, for example, Eugenius's approval of the Solymans' focus on the utility of education, which he has found to be lacking in his own experience. Samuel Gott, *Nova Solyma The Ideal City; or Jerusalem Regained*, ed. and trans. by Walter Begley, 2 vols (London: Murray, 1902), I, 242–3. All further references to the English text of *Nova Solyma* will be to this translation, with some noted amendments, and given in the form *Nova Solyma*, I: 242–3; see also Samuel Gott, *Novae Solymae Libri Sex* (London, 1648), Liber Tertius, p. 130.

³² *Nova Solyma*, I: 88. Whilst quotations from this text will largely be from the English version, the Latin text will be given in footnotes. In Latin: 'Annus jam proxime adest quinquagesimus, ex quo longe lateque disjecta Judaeorum gens in hanc tantam foelicitatem redintegrata est', Samuel Gott, *Novae Solymae Libri Sex* (London, 1648), Liber Primus, p. 8. All further references to the Latin text of *Nova Solyma* will be to this edition, and given in the form *Novae Solymae*, Liber Primus, p. 8. It is interesting to note that Begley's translation neglects to offer a direct translation of 'Judaeorum' in this sentence.

'return' to true belief: 'Certainly that condition of the Jewish race has always been an assurance that the ardent desire that Christians have so long conceived for our return was not an impossibility, and gave them firm faith in its fulfilment, long before there were any signs of it.'[33] Importantly, Jacob describes how the Jews' calling came through divine inspiration:

> But when indeed, by the sudden flash of divine light, that stubborn mental darkness was removed, and, prompted by a heavenly impulse, we acknowledged the true Messiah, and became His disciples with unwonted zeal, then it was that to us of that same race that had been sunk so long in the lowest depths of misery there came, as it were, life from the dead, and our exaltation to the highest by divine mercy.[34]

This act of conversion, with its emphasis on godly action, bears a striking resemblance to contemporary millenarian discussions of how it might be manifested. It was believed that the Jews would not necessarily be converted by the efforts of humanity, but that divine inspiration must play a role. In the words of Joseph Mede, writing in 1629: 'For my part, I incline to think that no such thing will provoke them; but that they shall be called by *Vision* and *Voice from Heaven*, as S. *Paul* was.'[35] Mede believed that the Jews would become 'the most Zealous and fervent of the Nations' once they were converted to Christianity.[36] The presentation of the inhabitants of Nova Solyma mirrors this understanding: 'And as formerly we alone of all tribes of the earth followed after righteousness in the perfect fear of God, so now also we strive for the pre-eminence'.[37]

Nova Solyma's interaction with contemporary millenarianism demonstrates that Gott's utopia was very much of its age in imagining the conversion of the Jews and their return to Jerusalem, and emphasizes the comparisons that might be drawn between the New Jerusalem and England. Gott offered his Nova Solyma as a portrait of an idealized England of the future, a model of a better way of life, associated with an established spiritual ideal. The divine inspiration of the city's conversion is matched by its patriarch's individual realization that Christianity

---

[33] *Nova Solyma*, I: 88. In Latin: 'Certe is status Judaeorum semper fidem fecit, illud ingens Christianorum votum, quod pro reditu nostro tam diu conceperant, perfici posse, & jam tum antequam perimpletur, impleri', *Novae Solymae*, Liber Primus, p. 8.

[34] *Nova Solyma*, I: 88–9. In Latin: 'Ut vero subita coruscatione divinae lucis ista pervicax animorum caecitas dilapsa est, & coelesti instinctu perciti Messiam agnovimus, atque ad ipsum acrioribus studiis conversi sumus: tum nos iidem in imo miseriarum fundo tam longa seculorum serie demersi, tanquam a mortuis resuscitati, in fastigium divinae benignitatis attollimur', *Novae Solymae*, Liber Primus, p. 8.

[35] Joseph Mede, Epistle XVII, in *The Works of The Pious and Profoundly-Learned Joseph Mede, B.D.* (London, 1677), p. 761.

[36] Joseph Mede, *Remaines On some Passages in The Revelation* (London, 1650), p. 39.

[37] *Nova Solyma*, I: 89. In Latin: 'Atque ut hic olim omnium populorum solus fuit, qui sectatus est veram virtutem cum perfecta pietate conjunctam, ita nunc quoque summus esse contendir', *Novae Solymae*, Liber Primus, p. 8.

must be the one true religion, motivated by a personal intellectual consideration of the issue.[38] This emphasizes that it is spiritual rectitude that is the most important feature of this society, a rightness that has been achieved at a group and an individual level through both divine intervention and personal thought.

The personal nature of religious experience in *Nova Solyma* may be likened to the text's use of conversation. In Gott's utopia, conversation taking place between friends and family is a prime method of moral instruction and spiritual improvement; domestic conversation is a means of individual reformation. As in earlier utopias, the reporting of direct conversation is used to facilitate description of the society, but also to educate; shown to be an edifying experience for the protagonists, conversation is meant to fulfil the same function for the reader. In this process the role of teacher is frequently taken by Jacob, who commonly engages his two young guests in 'discourse [...] for their benefit'.[39] So, for example, when Jacob has discussed with the two travellers the way in which he became convinced of the truth of the Christian religion, they are prompted to consider their own spiritual condition and their unworthiness of salvation.[40] The numerous conversations that take place between Eugenius, Politian and their hosts in Nova Solyma become a source of nourishment and inspiration for their spiritual transformation. 'I now begin really to live,' says Politian to Joseph in response to a query as to the state of his inner life, 'and to see all things in a new light. If now I were to hear your instructive discourses again, they would not merely satisfy a craving for knowledge, but would build me up in practice as well.'[41] One purpose of dialogue in *Nova Solyma* is to replicate the educational function of the dialogue form in order to help the individual achieve spiritual knowledge and rectitude.

While the emphasis would thus seem to be on the individual's potential for betterment, the social element of the ideal life is by no means neglected. Gott is particularly interested in the improvements made by Nova Solyma in terms of education. When Jacob first explains how the citizens of Nova Solyma have sought to improve themselves following their conversion, he refers to the role of the education of children in this process:

> as is fitting in every true republic, we take special care of the young, and in this the providence of God has not made our endeavours ineffectual, for it is well known that a more beautiful and talented progeny has grown up among us since our restoration.[42]

---

[38] *Nova Solyma*, I: 221–4; *Novae Solymae*, Liber Secundus, pp. 113–16.
[39] *Nova Solyma*, II: 149; *Novae Solymae*, Liber Sextus, p. 317.
[40] *Nova Solyma*, II: 167; *Novae Solymae*, Liber Sextus, p. 331.
[41] *Nova Solyma*, II: 184. In Latin: 'Ille se nunc quidem vitam incipere dicebat, et omnia quasi novis oculis intueri: quod si, inquit, nobiscum, uti prius disserere vacaret, jucundissimos tuos sermones, haud tantum ad sciendi voluptatem, quin ad usum sensumque demitterem', *Novae Solymae*, Liber Sextus, p. 346.
[42] *Nova Solyma*, I: 89. In Latin: 'Itaque (sicut in omni recta republica esse debet) puerorum curam praecipuam habemus: neque in hac re providentia Dei nostram destituit industriam: pulchriorem enim ac magis ingenuam sobolem nobis post reditum succrescere notissimum est', *Novae Solymae*, Liber Primus, pp. 8–9.

Through wise care of the young, the Nova Solymans have been able materially to improve the quality of their race. The function of education as it is later described is to create good and useful citizens. Again, moral rectitude is emphasized over worldly learning, and religious teaching is considered the most important: 'Our first and chief care is to induce the religious habit of mind, our next to inculcate the ethical duties, and our last care (which others make their first) is a liberal education, both literary and scientific.'[43] The educational priorities in Nova Solyma recall those of Andreae's Christianopolitans, as their priority is 'to worship God with a pure and devout mind'; next, 'to achieve the best and most chaste morality; and [...] to develop their intellectual faculties'.[44] Here can be observed the similarity between Gott's utopia and earlier utopian writing, in the simultaneous insistence upon the primacy of piety and the individual's relationship with God in human learning, and the social usefulness of a good system of education. The utopias of this period in general have much in common with the themes which dominated their continental European forebears, in particular regarding their emphasis on the organization of learning and its social purpose. Given the influence that figures of the Further Reformation, such as Andreae and Comenius, were to have on the circle of thinkers centred around Hartlib, it is hardly surprising that this should be the case. Members of the Hartlib circle had been educated by those who were closely associated with Keckermann and Alsted.[45] Comenius himself, who had been the pupil of Alsted in Herborn, came to London in the 1640s, where he found a receptive audience for his pansophic plans; he, Hartlib and Dury, the 'Three Foreigners', were all central European reformed refugees.[46] They absorbed the pedagogical innovations of reformed Europe and set about disseminating them in England. For Hartlib, the utopian texts of reformed Europe also had an important role to play in this process of reform. He notes in his *Ephemerides* that Andreae's *Christianopolis* is 'a more Christian Idaea of a new Commonwealth' which 'deserves to be translated'.[47] Furthermore, Hartlib's and Dury's plans for the reorganization of learning represented a direct attempt to realize Comenius's

---

[43] *Nova Solyma*, I: 239. In Latin: 'Prima & maxima pietatis est cura: proxima morum: ultima, quae apud alios unica esse solet, literarum atque liberalium artium', *Novae Solymae*, Liber Tertius, p. 126. Walter Begley's 'the religious habit of mind' translates the original Latin '*pietatis*'; 'piety' perhaps offers a simpler and more appropriate rendition.

[44] *Christianopolis*, p. 220. For Andreae's influence on Gott, see Andreae, *Christianopolis: An Ideal State of the Seventeenth Century*, p. 93.

[45] For example, John Dury's mentor, Johannes Mylius, was a friend and collaborator of Keckermann, as was Melchior Lauban, the teacher of Samuel Hartlib. See Howard Hotson, 'Philosophical Pedagogy in Reformed Central Europe between Ramus and Comenius: A Survey of the Continental Background of the "Three Foreigners"', in *Samuel Hartlib and Universal Reformation*, pp. 29–50, p. 45.

[46] Hotson, 'Philosophical Pedagogy in Reformed Central Europe between Ramus and Comenius: A Survey of the Continental Background of the "Three Foreigners"', in *Samuel Hartlib and Universal Reformation*, p. 45.

[47] Hartlib, *Ephemerides* (1653, Part 2), HP 28/2/57A.

theory in practice; Comenius's writings on universal education constituted a 'call' to which social reformers in England were quick to respond.[48]

The dual function of education, for the individual soul and for society at large, is a common one in political writings. Milton's *Of Education* (1644), addressed to Hartlib, states that at the heart of all education lies a spiritual purpose:

> The end, then, of learning is, to repair the ruins of our first parents by regaining to know God aright, and out of that knowledge to love him, to imitate him, to be like him, as we may the nearest, by possessing our souls of true virtue, which, being united to the heavenly grace of faith, makes up the highest perfection.[49]

The social function, however, remains vital to Milton's understanding of the importance of education: 'a complete and generous education' is one 'which fits a man to perform justly, skilfully and magnanimously all the offices, both private and public, of peace and war'.[50] Dury's *The Reformed School* also sees education as having important social and religious functions. On the one hand:

> The mutual assistance to be given in necessary consultation should respect three things: first, the matters of spiritual concernment in common; secondly, the matters of common outward concernment; and thirdly, the matters of particular concernment whether spiritual or bodily.[51]

The primacy of piety is once again established. On the other hand, for Dury, too, the social usefulness of education is paramount. As well as being prepared spiritually, the products of ideal schooling must be primed for the life that awaits them in the larger community:

> the things which are to be taught them and wherein they shall be exercised, are all the useful arts and sciences which may fit them for any employment in Church and Commonwealth.[52]

In keeping with this dual priority, Gott's picture of education in the New Jerusalem offers a practical emphasis on appropriate curricula, the need for military training, motivational techniques and so on. The Nova Solymans' system of education, though idealized, is seen as practicable and realistic in its aims and practices. While all are given the opportunity of learning, there is a concern to provide for each person the education necessary for his or her role in life; consequently the

---

[48] See Charles Webster, *The Great Instauration: Science, Medicine, and Reform, 1626–1660*, p. 114, p. 514.

[49] John Milton, *Of Education* (1644) in *Complete English Poems; Of Education; Areopagitica*, ed. by Gordon Campbell (London: Dent, 1990), p. 557.

[50] Milton, *Of Education*, p. 559.

[51] John Dury, *The Reformed School* (1650), ed. by H.M. Knox (Liverpool: Liverpool University Press, 1958), p. 24.

[52] *The Reformed School*, pp. 47–8.

working classes are not taught more than it is believed they need to know. Indeed, Gott's projected system is not one in which everyone is educated to the highest degree. Like the political utopian writings examined earlier, his ideas are designed to be realizable and practically useful, for the creation of workable institutions.

The picture Gott produces of education in this society is clearly intended to serve as a model for its English readers. With relevance to the focus on the social and spiritual utility of education, Eugenius comments that this system of education seems better than the one he has experienced, drawing an explicit parallel between the utopian ideal and English reality. Having learned about the educational system in Nova Solyma,

> Eugenius said he agreed on every point, and from his own experience ventured to say that all this warned us that we are placed here not to be bound down to mere book learning, or incessantly devoted to letters, but that the affairs of the State had a special call upon us, a point to which our present-day pedagogues pay no regard whatever. They educate us as if we were all to become in the future philosophers or hermits, as if we had nothing in common with the interests of the family or the State, when, as a matter of fact, we are joined thereto by the closest of ties.[53]

Through Eugenius's comparison, the reader is invited to draw conclusions about the superiority of the practices of this utopia, and to consider whether they might not fit contemporary England. Again, education takes place through discourse, as the young men debate the merits of the various alternatives. If the invitation to compare is not yet forceful enough, Gott highlights the way in which the Nova Solymans relish the opportunity to imitate other societies. Alphaeus, the headmaster of Joseph's alma mater, when leading the English tourists around his superlative institution, states that they are happy to borrow from foreign sources:

> Do not think, my sons, that we disdain to borrow anything that is really good, because it had its origin with nations alien to us. We believe every good gift cometh from the same source of Divine Light.[54]

Gott's text thus establishes itself as just such a fountain of divine light, which contemporaries may use as a model for imitation.

---

[53] *Nova Solyma*, I: 242–3. In Latin: 'Eugenius ad singula annuens, & experientiae suae sensu edoctus, sic tandem applicuit. Et hoc ipsum, inquit, nonnihil est, adesse qui moneat nos non esse libris devinciendos, neque literis semper mancipandos, sed rem civilem praecipue spectandam, cujus nostri paedagogi nullam omnino rationem habent: ac si omnes aut philosophi aut eremitae futuri simus; neque haberemus quicquam cum familia aut republica commune, quibus revera summis necessitudinibus obstringimur', *Novae Solymae*, Liber Tertius, p. 130.

[54] *Novae Solymae*, I: 245. In Latin: 'Haudquaquam, o juvenes, ullam artem, aut elegentiam, aut perfectionem corporis, vel ingenii spernimus, aut ab aliis accipere dedignamur; cum haec omnia fluere credamus ab eodem fonte divinae lucis', *Novae Solymae*, Liber Tertius, p. 131.

Thus while the text evidently presents areas of social reform in the imaginary society as exemplars to the society of the contemporary reader, it nonetheless returns to the centrality of the spiritual ideal. Jacob's conclusions on religion, for example, reprise the Augustinian theme that a man may rise up against his rulers in matters of faith, but, provided he is able to live by the right religion, he can do so under any government's laws.[55] A similar conclusion might be reached about More's *Utopia*. *Nova Solyma*, however, unlike *Utopia*, provides the ideal social context in which to try to live the ideal life. The statutes of the city, displayed on the city wall and observed by the travellers early in their stay, emphasize the static and unperturbed nature of the society:

> No ill-gotten plunder, the damning proof of violence and wrong, here disturbs the conscience-stricken mind in the midst of its pleasures.
>
> For this house had its foundation on just gains, and was built from no proceeds of fraud, and so will last through many ages, and shall see children's children without break or change.
>
> Drink paves not here an easy road to every crime, nor does the ignoble mind, a slave to its vices, shirk all true and earnest work.
>
> No gambling nor secret lawless love, no strife nor anger, no long-pent-up revenge crying out for blood can find a place here.
>
> Thus it is that no restless spirits of the dead return here to their old abode to wail and fret; neither do the fauns and satyrs raise here their mournful laughter, or batter their deserted homes with vengeful hoof.[56]

Such emotional calm and lack of vice or crime is reminiscent of More's Utopians and Hythloday's conclusion that theirs was a society that would endure forever without change. The Nova Solymans are untroubled by vice, and Gott explicitly emphasizes that they are free of pagan interference. In *Nova Solyma*, unlike *Utopia*, such satisfaction is offered without an ironic note. There is no trace of uncertainty in Gott's endorsement of Nova Solyma as an ideal way of life; unlike More, he sees in his fictional creation the model for spiritual perfection as well as worldly success. Gott's ideal society, like More's, is characterized by its static and unchanging nature. This is typified by the two elaborate ceremonies which begin and end the travellers' experience of the city, the second replaying the chief features of the first.[57] There is little room for irony, however, in Gott's assessment

---

[55] *Novae Solymae*, I: 245; *Novae Solymae*, Liber Secundus, p. 115.

[56] Nova Solyma, I: 83. In Latin: 'Non scelerum merces, ostentataeq; rapinae/ Insanas torquent media inter gaudia mentes/ Sed justis opibus, nullisq; innoxia surgit/ Criminibus fundata domus, quae plurima duret/ Secula, perpetuos domini visura nepotes./ Non hic ebrietas aditu scelus omne patenti/ Excipit; aut veros, vitiis operata, labores/ Mens ignava fugit; non foelix alea nulli:/ Non furtivus amor, rixaeq; iraeq; nocentes;/ Sera vel occultum latrat vindicta cruorem/ Ergo nec queruli manes sua tecta requirunt:/ Nec Satyri tristes tollunt, Fauniq; cachinnos,/ Et vacuas lacerant infestis unguibus aedes', Novae Solymae, Liber Primus, p. 5.

[57] *Nova Solyma*, I: 79–81, II: 223–8.

of the best way to live on earth; unlike More, he does not seek to interrogate the genre of ideal-state writing, but uses the model the genre provides to hammer home his own ideas of moral living, useful education and the expectation of a better life. Insofar as he makes use of elements of the dialogue form, Gott is interested exclusively in the educational potential of conversation, and not the more complex and ironic capacities of the form itself. The elements of dialogue upon which *Nova Solyma* draws, such as the reporting of conversation, do not disrupt the force of the narrative; on the contrary, they enhance it. Whereas More complicated the force of the narrative of Book 2 of *Utopia* by positioning the sustained description between the dialogue elements of the text, later utopias do not emulate this disruptive potential of dialogue. Gott's Nova Solymans have much in common with More's Utopians, but their treatment lacks the ambiguous, ironic touch; the utopia has come full circle, and now presents in all seriousness what was once offered as jest.

Beyond the 1640s: The Arrival of Utopia

In the utopian writing considered in this chapter, the disparity between the utopian location and the author's own society remains present. While real life is insufficiently perfect, it is impossible for the ideal society to exist. But this understanding that utopia is currently non-existent is qualified by the underlying belief that the ideal society can be achieved, and that its manifestation is only a matter of time. During the 1640s the use of the utopian mode of discourse as a useful response to the political situation dominated. The writings of Samuel Gott, the Hartlib circle and others fashioned a different conception of utopia, one based not on the idea that utopia does not exist, but instead on the belief that utopia does not *yet* exist. The distance between the real world and the ideal society, according to this understanding, is one of time alone.[58] The particular religious and political conditions of the mid-1600s created a unique environment for imagining the ideal community and responding to the question of how to live a good life; utopianism was a means of addressing the immediate issue of how social change, which seemed inevitable, was to be managed and encouraged. Optimistic thinkers no longer saw utopia as *ou-topos*, or no place; instead they sought to imagine ways in which the imaginary could be made real. In so doing, they turned utopia from a place defined by its unreality and imagined in exotic locations into one that could be located in England itself, or in an alternative England. In Renaissance English utopianism, the ideal society had always been in God's gift; it would be realized as heaven, or an ideal spiritual community, the City of God. Now, that ideal state remained within the realm of providence, but it seemed that divine will would deliver a tangible utopia in the near future, the inevitable arrival of perfection in human history.

---

[58] Ernst Bloch identified this temporal difference, which he termed the 'Not Yet', as an important feature of the utopia. See Bloch, *The Spirit of Utopia*, trans. by Anthony A. Nassar (Cambridge: Cambridge University Press, 2000), p. 177.

In this way the use of the utopian mode of discourse in the 1640s changed the nature of future utopianism. Following this period, utopianism could appear in any genre; the utopia proliferated, whereas before it had been bound within the traditional confines of the form. This proliferation was facilitated in part by the explosion of print activity that took place in the 1640s, as censorship was relaxed and an increasing number of people felt empowered to offer their own ideas on the nature of the reforms needed and the better society that might be created. The mid-seventeenth century saw the development of a wide variety of new kinds and genres of writing, including 'a great outpouring of radical ideas'.[59] Abiezer Coppe, for example, whose *A Fiery Flying Roll* rolled off the presses in 1650, demonstrated the belief that it is perfectly valid for the individual layman to become involved with changing society. The style and content of his writing, like much of that contained within the pamphlets of the 1640s, is hard to quantify in generic terms. Enthusiastic and evangelical, yet also practical and unpretentious, Coppe's prose style is undeniably 'unlike anything else in the seventeenth century'.[60] With a wide range of such unconventional texts appearing in print, generic conventions could be challenged and broken down; this development was made possible for the utopian mode of discourse by the unique political climate of the 1640s and the outpourings of different kinds of literature it produced.

The beginnings of this proliferation can be observed in a range of utopian writings in the middle of the seventeenth century; what was now central to utopianism was the potential reality of the reformed institutions which utopias imagined at the heart of the ideal society. Gresham College, Théophraste Renaudot's Bureau d'Adresse, Hartlib's Office of Address: such institutions either were real or seemed as if they could become so as soon as adequate space and funding were provided. It was in part because the ideal institution (always at the heart of any utopia) seemed achievable that the ideal society itself could be imagined as a real possibility. Recognizing the centrality of the institution to Renaissance utopianism is thus crucial in tracing the trajectory that the utopia was to take during the period. It is evident that for utopian thinkers of this period, the ideal institution became the focal point of all social reformation. In William Petty's *The Advice of W.P. to Mr. Samuel Hartlib*, Petty begins with his desire to be of real, practical help, demonstrating the familiar refrain that expressions of utopianism can themselves promote the creation of a better society. He writes that his ideas:

> can please only those few, that are Reall Friends to the Designe of Realities, not those who are tickled only with Rhetorical Prefaces, Transitions, & Epilogues, & charmed with fine Allusions and Metaphors.[61]

---

[59] Andrew Hopton, ed., *Abiezer Coppe: Selected Writings* (London: Aporia, 1987), p. 3.

[60] Christopher Hill, *The World Turned Upside Down: Radical Ideas During the English Revolution* (Harmondsworth: Penguin, 1978), p. 210.

[61] William Petty, *The Advice of W.P. to Mr. Samuel Hartlib* (London, 1647), A3v.

Petty thus refuses to align his imaginings of a better way of life with the tradition of fictional utopianism. Nonetheless he explicitly sees his projected social reforms as the continuation of the schemes of Bacon, 'the great Lord *Verulam*', whom he names at the beginning of his tract as the original proponent of the advancement of learning. Before the 'great Work' of the advancement of learning can continue, however, Petty argues that 'some Generall Rande Vouz' must be established, that is, 'We must recommend the Institution of an Office of common Addresse according to the projection of Master *Hartlib* (that painfull and great instrument of this Designe)'.[62] Petty thus imagines himself and Hartlib as undertaking the groundwork necessary for Bacon's projected reforms; they are Bacon's colleagues as well as his inheritors. The institution resulting from this groundwork is described in terms reminiscent of that ubiquitous model for the reform of knowledge, Salomon's House. Petty desires the creation of a 'Gymnasium Mechanicum or a Colledge of Trades-men' in which representatives of every trade might be brought together. Within this gymnasium would operate a kind of living encyclopaedia, the fusion of the Baconian institution and reformed encyclopaedism. The description of this institution is worth quoting at length, in order to demonstrate the breadth of its conception. It is to be:

> a Nosecomium Academicum according to the most exact and perfect Idea thereof a complete *Theatrum Botanicum,* stalls and Cages for all strange Beastes and Birds, with Ponds and Conservatories for all exotick Fishes, here all Animalls capable thereof should be made fit for some kind of labour and imployment, thaa [sic] they may as well be of use living as dead; here should be a Repositorie of all kind of Rarities Naturall and Artificiall pieces of Antiquity, Modells of all great and noble Engines, with Designes and Platformes of Gardens and Buildings. The most Artificiall Fountaines and Water-works, a Library of Select Bookes, an Astronomicall Observatory for celestiall Bodies and Meteor, large pieces of Ground for severall Experiments of Agriculture, Galleries of the rarest Paintings and Satues [sic], with the fairest Globes and Geographicall Maps of the best descriptions, and so farre as is possible, we would have this place to be the Epitome or Abstract of the whole world.[63]

Petty's Nosecomium Academicum is reminiscent of earlier utopian treatments of the subject of the reformation of knowledge, but he refuses to place it in an imaginary setting. Petty is precise in his conception of how this institution could really work, right down to the various salaries that must be paid to its staff, such as the steward, physician, surgeon and student.[64] In his perfect academy we can see the fruition of the central features of earlier seventeenth-century utopianism that have been traced in the present study: the physical collections of the museum, the library and the laboratory; the interest in knowledge organization; the concern for utility and practicality. Such an imagination of a perfected institution is evidently

---

[62] *The Advice of W.P. to Mr. Samuel Hartlib*, p. 1.
[63] *The Advice of W.P. to Mr. Samuel Hartlib*, p. 8.
[64] *The Advice of W.P. to Mr. Samuel Hartlib*, p. 11.

engaging with the utopian tradition; *The Renaissance Utopia* has argued that such imaginings themselves constitute utopias. Amongst the intellectual circle of Petty, Hartlib, Plattes and Dury, the influences of the utopian tradition, channelled through Bacon, Andreae and Comenius, combined with religious fervour and political opportunity to enable the formation of an environment in which the creation of the utopia became an immediate reality, the proper subject of the serious political treatise as well as imaginative fiction.

A practical and optimistic utopianism also informs the writings of those involved in the Leveller and Digger movements, which represent an important continuation of utopian thought during and beyond the 1640s. The resonances between religious and political thought in Leveller writings recall those of the Hartlib circle, and, like those considered in this and the last chapter, these writings called upon their readership to take action in order to bring about the desired state of religious and political freedom. John Lilburne's conception of citizenship, for example, characterized by his notion of the 'free-born Englishman', demanded action from the citizens, whom he expected to exercise and defend their rights in order to keep them;[65] Gerrard Winstanley developed a 'utopian institutionalism' which clearly bears a relation to the concerns and interests of the Hartlib circle.[66] For one thing, Winstanley shows a commitment to changing the status quo, which stems from his belief that the ideal society is attainable. Charles Webster has described both radical sects and the broader puritan culture of this period as infused with a utopian idealism, founded in widespread millenarianism and desire for the revival of learning:

> However bleak the immediate prospects, the saints could look forward to a period of reconciliation and utopian conditions on earth. [... The revival of learning] was seen as thoroughly consistent with the envisaged utopian paradise and indeed capable of providing the means whereby the utopian conditions would be realised.[67]

Indeed, as the following quotation from one of his sermons demonstrates, Winstanley was convinced that 'heaven', that is, the good life, should be available to all on earth just as it is in the afterlife. Priests, Winstanley argues,

> lay claim to Heaven after they are dead, and yet they require their Heaven in this World too, and grumble mightily against the People that will not give them a large temporal maintenance. And yet they tell the poor People, that they must be

---

[65] See Rachel Foxley, *The Levellers: Radical Political Thought in the English Revolution* (Manchester: Manchester University Press, 2013), p. 109, on Lilburne and the implied action demanded from his readership.

[66] For Winstanley's 'utopian institutionalism', see Timothy Kenyon, *Utopian Communism and Political Thought in Early Modern England* (London: Pinter, 1989), Chapter 6.

[67] Webster, *The Great Instauration*, p. 1.

content with their Poverty, and they shall have their Heaven hereafter. But why may we not have our Heaven here (that is, a comfortable livelihood in the Earth) And Heaven hereafter too, as well as you, *God is no respector of Persons?*[68]

The political aims of the 'True Levellers', such as their belief that that the poor should have the right to vote, that all laws should apply to all people, that monopolies should be abolished, and that all subjects should have freedom of conscience, reflected this spiritual idealism. They demanded that laws should be reworked so that they were good and not detrimental to the common well-being. The 1647 *Agreement of the People* sought to bypass Parliament and establish an agreement between all native citizens that subsequent parliaments could not alter.[69] A later *Agreement* spoke of the desired reformation as all-encompassing:

> Thus, as becometh a free People, thankfull unto God for this blessed opportunity, and desirous to make use thereof to his glory, in taking off every yoak, and removing every burthen, in delivering the captive, and setting the oppressed free; we have in all the particular Heads forementioned, done as we would be done unto, and as we trust in God will abolish all occasion of offence and discord, and produce the lasting Peace and Prosperity of this Common wealth.[70]

Despite the emphasis on a covenant between people which could bypass the institutions of Parliament, Winstanley, as Timothy Kenyon has noted, nonetheless demonstrated a preparedness to defer to institutions that he considered properly constituted, where such deferment was necessary.[71] And while his calls for reform sound like a desire to recreate the world anew, Winstanley also recognized the importance of social institutions in regulating the behaviour of the community, as his later works, such as *The Law of Freedom* (1652), demonstrate.[72] Thus, as Kenyon and J.C. Davis have shown, institutions were central to Winstanley's thinking, as he sought 'to use, rather than to discard, those existing authorities and powers which felt could be on the side of righteousness'.[73] The need for the reform of existing institutions, and more broadly the social relations on which society is based, leads Winstanley to communal property as a solution and his

---

[68] Gerrard Winstanley, *An Appeale to All Englishmen* (1650), in *The Works of Gerrard Winstanley*, ed. by George H. Sabine (Cornell: Cornell University Press, 1941), p. 409.

[69] See *The (first) Agreement of the People* (1647), reproduced in G.E. Aylmer, ed., *The Levellers in the English Revolution* (London: Thames and Hudson, 1975), pp. 88–96 (p. 92). For the aims of the Leveller movement, see *The Levellers in the English Revolution*, pp. 9–55; Hill, *The World Turned Upside Down*, Chapter 7; and David Wootton, 'Leveller democracy and the Puritan Revolution', in *The Cambridge History of Political Thought, 1450–1700* (Cambridge: Cambridge University Press, 1991), pp. 412–42.

[70] *The (third and final) Agreement of the People* (1649), reproduced in Aylmer, ed., *The Levellers in the English Revolution*, pp. 159–68 (p. 168).

[71] Kenyon, *Utopian Communism and Political Thought*, p. 190.

[72] Kenyon, *Utopian Communism and Political Thought*, p. 158.

[73] Davis, *Utopia and the Ideal Society*, p. 183.

ideal of 'Commonwealth's government', which 'governs the earth without buying and selling' and 'seeks to restore the lost peace and freedom of the people'.[74] Although, as Davis points out, Winstanley only advocates a 'partial communism' here, his 'Commonwealth's government' nonetheless reflects a sincere interest in the community of property which suggests a Hythlodean belief in the capacity for social reforms to reform individuals. *The New Law of Righteousness*, which was printed in January 1649, had argued that there was a direct link between private property and the corruption of humanity; in establishing communities of Diggers in Surrey, Winstanley attempted to live according to his ideals with like-minded individuals who were prepared to work communally and live off the land. As with Gott's presentation of the crime-free Nova Solymans, the Diggers' interest in the community of property demonstrates a sincere belief in the capacity of one of the methods shown in More's *Utopia* to achieve genuine change. Although Winstanley's *Law of Freedom* has been called his utopia, this final pamphlet, like so many of the utopian texts considered in this chapter and the previous one, eschews the conventional utopian form in favour of a less ambiguous and more direct approach, in this instance in the form of a direct address to Oliver Cromwell.[75] For Winstanley and the Diggers, as for many others, the utopian form was no longer appropriate to their social and political aims.

Conclusions: Beyond the Utopian Moment

All of these utopian institutions and manifestos involved the bringing together of like-minded people who might work together to effect the necessary changes. Not only did such texts call for dialogue between reformers – whether it be in Petty's Nosecomium Academicum or Winstanley's Commonwealth's government – but they developed an ongoing dialogue between themselves. The idea of utopian dialogue can, by this period, be taken to mean the conversations that were initiated between texts, rather than those represented within individual texts themselves. Writers of utopian literature in this period conceived of a public audience for their texts which was itself comprised in part of writers of utopian literature and like-minded reformers who might be motivated to social and political action through reading. Hence the dialogues between utopias, which we have seen developing in the last two chapters and throughout this book, sought to engage as many readers as possible in the important debates surrounding the questions of how best to live and how to construct the ideal society.

There are two reasons why these utopian dialogues developed between texts in the seventeenth century. The first of these is related to the emerging atmosphere

---

[74] Gerrard Winstanley, *The Law of Freedom*, in *The Law of Freedom and Other Writings*, ed. by Christopher Hill (Harmondsworth: Penguin, 1973), p. 311.

[75] Both Davis and Kenyon refer to *The Law of Freedom* as Winstanley's 'utopia'. See Davis, *Utopia and the Ideal Society*, p. 194, and Kenyon, *Utopian Communism and Political Thought*, p. 192.

of political opportunity described in Chapter 5. As utopian writers saw that it was both possible and, to their minds, desirable to make a difference to society through the writing and dissemination of utopian literature, they sought to contribute to growing networks of utopian texts in order to do so. That is, writing utopias seemed worthwhile in the seventeenth century, and particularly from the middle years of the century, in a manner that it had not done in the previous century. The second reason is related specifically to the dissemination of such texts. By the 1600s there existed a capacity for the wide distribution of printed texts, which utopian writers sought to exploit in order to reach the wider reading public created by this capacity. In this sense, the utopia is one of the many cultural phenomena bound up with the development of print culture in Renaissance England, and has its part to play in the 'new forms of association' which were cultivated by the printed text's potential for widespread dissemination.[76] The utopian dialogues that developed between texts in the seventeenth century represent their understanding of a different imagined audience for utopian literature from that of More, Nicholls and Lupton; these utopias speak to a new sort of public readership and as wide and diverse an audience as possible. In doing so they simultaneously moved away from the closed form of the dialogue towards multiple forms which spoke more clearly to a wide audience.

Utopian literature changed during the middle years of the seventeenth century due to the atmosphere provided by this utopian moment in history. Despite the widespread ridicule of utopia and its own avoidance of conventional utopian forms, utopian writing proliferated in many genres and was to continue to be an influential mode of discourse in political philosophy and in European literature far beyond the Renaissance period. It is impossible to assign an 'endpoint' to English utopian fiction: *Renaissance Utopia* stops here, when the prospect of utopia still seemed truly achieveable. Eventually, the idealism of the Hartlib circle and other millenarian reformers would fade, as 'society resumed its old hierarchical structure: social revolution was to go no further'.[77] In Moses Wall's letter to Hartlib of 1652 is encapsulated the early realization of the disappointment which was to face millenarians and reformers alike. Wall reminds Hartlib that they had anticipated that the conversion of the Jews and 'the worlds great restorac*i*on' would take place in 1650. It is already the middle of 1652, and the reformers are still waiting, as Wall hesitantly points out: 'herupon I am somwhat bold in my addresses to the faithfull, & mercifull God, <to say> *that* the year 1652 is passing, and yet no tidings of their return'.[78] Wall is quick to add that he is sure God needs no reminding, but will instigate the coming millennium in his own time. But behind

---

[76] Yael Margalit, 'Publics: A Bibliographic Afterword', in *Making Publics in Early Modern Europe: People, Things, Forms of Knowledge*, ed. by Bronwen Wilson and Paul Yachnin (New York and London: Routledge, 2010), p. 234. See also Bronwen Wilson and Paul Yachnin's Introduction to *Making Publics*.

[77] Hopton, *Abiezer Coppe*, p. 4.

[78] Moses Wall to Hartlib, 18 June 1652, HP 34/4/1A.

his faithful optimism can be heard the first hints of the disappointment which was to be felt by those who were not only having to wait longer than they expected for the fulfilment of their millenarian hopes, but were also obliged to recognize that Cromwell's Protectorate was not going to live up to their political expectations.

In 1640, Samuel Hartlib noted in his *Ephemerides* that utopias such as More's and Campanella's needed to be remedied if they were to be of use to real people; they tended too much to ignore human defects, and focused on theory rather than practice. Nonetheless, he saw them as 'counsels', advice to help society improve itself.[79] At the end of the decade, he maintained even more strongly that More's *Utopia*, 'a most excell*ent* Booke', could offer 'a true patterne of a rightly constituted Common*wealth* and *whi*ch might easily bee put in practise'.[80] In the 1640s, *Utopia* was read by some not as an ironic jest but as a realistic model for the ideal society, albeit one that needed improvement, and utopian plans seemed timely and appropriate. *Utopia* spoke to Hartlib. But politics underwent a material change in the years that followed. Subsequently, utopia no longer seemed within reach for England. The utopian moment, encapsulated in the optimistic idealism of the mid-seventeenth century, had passed, and in its passing, the unqualified belief in the truth and imminent reality of the ideal society was also left behind. Henceforth, utopianism would be tinctured with the connotations of comedy, impracticality and uselessness with which it had long been associated. This mode of writing, which had seemed so useful and so apposite to the reformers of the 1640s, would once again become the realm of fiction and, eventually, of satire. The utopia would continue to be used beyond the middle years of the seventeenth century, and later utopias would show the influences of the earlier tradition of utopian literature, but the sincere optimism and belief in the imminence of the ideal society which characterized utopian writings of the mid-1600s would eventually fade. Nonetheless, the future of the utopian mode of discourse, whether satirical or idealistic, would have been manifestly different without the proliferation of utopian thought and literature that took place in the mid-seventeenth century.

---

[79] *Ephemerides* (1640, Part 3), HP 30/4/57A, 30/4/57B.
[80] *Ephemerides* (1649, Part 2), HP 28/1/19B, 28/1/20A.

Selected Bibliography

Primary Sources

[n.a.], *A Copie of two writings sent to the Parliament. The one intituled Motions for reforming the Church of England in the present Parliament* (Amsterdam, 1641)

[n.a.], *The Teacher of the English School Soliciting For the Common-Wealth of Learning. Written by one that wisheth verie heartily well towards a more easie and profitable education of English Youth* (London, 1649)

[n.a.], *One More Blow at Babylon* (London, 1650)

Alcock, John, *Mons Perfectionis: otherwyse in englysshe the hyl of perfeccon* (London, 1497)

Andreae, Johann Valentin, *Christianopolis: An Ideal State of the Seventeenth Century*, trans. and intro. by F.E. Held (New York: Oxford University Press, 1916)

———, *Christianopolis*, ed. by Edward H. Thompson (Dordrecht: Kluwer, 1999)

———, *Gesammelte Schriften, Band 3: Rosenkreuzerschriften*, ed. and trans. by Roland Edighoffer (Stuttgart-Bad Cannstatt: Frommann-Holzboog, 2010)

Archer, John, *The Personall Reigne of Christ Upon Earth* (London, 1641 and 1642)

Augustine, *St Augustine: The Lord's Sermon on the Mount*, trans. by John J. Jepson (London: Longmans, Green, 1948)

———, *Augustine: Later Works*, ed. by John Burnaby (London: S.C.M. Press, 1955)

———, *Saint Augustine: Confessions*, trans. by R.S. Pine-Coffin (London: Penguin, 1961)

———, *Saint Augustine: The Trinity*, trans. by Stephen McKenna (Washington: Catholic University of America, 1963; repr. 1970)

———, *Augustinus, Contra academicos. De beata vita. De ordine. De magistro. De libero arbitrio.*, ed. by W. M. Green and K.-D. Daur, Corpus Christianorum Series Latina 29 (Turnhout: Brepols, 1970)

———, *Concerning the City of God against the Pagans*, trans. by Henry Bettenson (London: Penguin, 1984)

———, *Augustine: Political Writings*, ed. by E.M. Atkins and R.J. Dodaro (Cambridge: Cambridge University Press, 2001)

———, *The Works of Saint Augustine: Letters 100–150 (Epistulae)*, Volume 2, Part 2, trans. by Roland Teske (New York: New City Press, 2003)

Bacon, Francis, *New Atlantis. A Worke unfinished*, in *Sylva Sylvarum: Or a Naturall Historie*, ed. by William Rawley (London: John Haviland for William Lee, 1627)

———, *The Aduancement of Learning*, ed. by Michael Kiernan (Oxford: Clarendon Press, 2000)

———, *The Essayes or Counsels, Civill and Morall*, ed. by Michael Kiernan (Oxford: Clarendon Press, 2000)

———, *Francis Bacon: The Major Works*, ed. by Brian Vickers (Oxford: Oxford University Press, 1996; revised 2002)

———, *The* Instauratio magna *Part II: Novum organum and Associated Texts*, ed. and trans. by Graham Rees with Maria Wakely (Oxford: Clarendon Press, 2004)

Birch, Thomas, *The History of the Royal Society of London*, 4 vols (London, 1756–57)

Boyle, Robert, *Works*, ed. by Thomas Birch, 6 vols, 3rd edn (Hildesheim: Georg Olms Verlagsbuchhandlung, 1965

Brahe, Tycho, *Tychonis Brahe Dani Opera Omnia*, ed. by I.L.E. Dreyer, 15 vols (Hanuiae, 1913–29)

Brathwait, Richard, *A Survey of History: Or, A Nursery for Gentry* (London, 1638)

———, *Astraea's Teares. An Elegie Vpon the death of that Reverend, Learned and Honest Judge, Sir Richard Hutton Knight* (London, 1641)

Brightman, Thomas, *The Revelation of St Iohn Illustrated*, 4th edn (London, 1644)

Burton, Robert, *The Anatomy of Melancholy*, ed. by Thomas C .Faulkner, Nicolas K. Kiessling and Rhonda L. Blair, intro. by J.B. Bamborough, 6 vols (Oxford: Clarendon Press, 1989)

Bushell, Thomas, *Mr Bushell's Abridgement of the Lord Chancellor Verulam's philosophical theory in Mineral Prosecutions, etc* (London, 1659)

Campanella, Tommaso, *La Città del Sole: Dialogo Poetico/The City of the Sun: A Poetical Dialogue*, trans. by Daniel J. Donno (Berkeley: University of California Press, 1981)

Cartwright, John, *The Preacher's Travels* (London, 1611)

Comenius, John Amos, *The Great Didactic of John Amos Comenius*, trans. by M. W. Keatinge, 2 vols (London: Adam and Charles Black, 1910)

Coppe, Abiezer, *Abiezer Coppe: Selected Writings*, ed. by Andrew Hopton (London: Aporia, 1987)

Crofton, Zachary, *Bethshemesh Clouded* (London, 1653)

Digby, Kenelm, *A Late Discourse Made in a Solemne Assembly of Nobles and Learned Men at Montpellier in France [...] Touching the Cure of Wounds by the Powder of Sympathy*, trans. by R. White (London, 1658)

Dudley, Edmund, *The Tree of Commonwealth*, ed. by D.M. Brodie (Cambridge: Cambridge University Press, 1948)

Dury, John, *The Purpose and Platform of my Journey into Germany* (1631), BL MS Sloane 654

———, *Israels Call Ovt of Babylon Unto Jerusalem* (London, 1646)

———, *The Reformed School* (1650), ed. by H.M. Knox (Liverpool: Liverpool University Press, 1958)

Eachard, John, *Good Newes for all Christian Soldiers* (London, 1645)

Erasmus, Desiderius, *Convivium Religiosum*, in *Collected Works of Eramsus: Colloquies: Volume 39*, trans. by Craig R. Thompson (Toronto: University of Toronto Press, 1997)

Gorges, Arthur, *The Wisedome of the Ancients, written in Latine by the Right Honourable Sir Francis Bacon Knight, Baron of Verulam, and Lord Chancelor of England. Done into English by Sir Arthur Gorges Knight* (London, 1619)
Gott, Samuel, *Novae Solymae Libri Sex* (London, 1648)
———, *Nova Solyma The Ideal City; or Jerusalem Regained*, ed. and trans. by Walter Begley, 2 vols (London: Murray, 1902)
Gouge, William, *The Progresse of Divine Providence* (London, 1645)
H., R., *New Atlantis Begun by the Lord Verulam, Viscount St. Albans: and Continued by R.H. Esquire. Wherein is set forth A Platform of Monarchical Government with A Pleasant intermixture of divers rare Inventions, And wholsom Customs, fit to be introduced Into all kingdoms, states, and commonwealths* (London, 1660)
Hall, Joseph, *Another World and Yet the Same: Bishop Joseph Hall's Mundus Alter et Idem* (1605), ed. by John Millar Wands (New Haven: Yale University Press, 1981)
Harrington, James, *The Commonwealth of Oceana and A System of Politics*, ed. by J.G.A. Pocock (Cambridge: Cambridge University Press, 1992)
The Hartlib Papers (2 CD-ROMs, Ann Arbor, 1995; enlarged edn, Sheffield, 2002)
Hartlib, Samuel, *Ephemerides* (1635–59), in The Hartlib Papers (2 CD-ROMs, Ann Arbor, 1995; enlarged edn, Sheffield, 2002)
———, *Englands Thankfulnesse, or, An Humble Remembrance presented to the Committee for Religion in the High Court of Parliament* (London, 1642)
———, *Considerations Tending To the Happy Accomplishment of Englands Reformation in Church and State* (London, 1647)
Hume, David, *Political Discourses*, 3rd edn (Edinburgh: Sands, Murray and Cochran, 1754)
[Godwin, Francis], *The Man in the Moone, or a Discourse of a Voyage Thither, by Domingo Gonsales the Speedy Messenger* (London, 1638)
Goodwin, Thomas, *A Glimpse of Sions Glory* (London, 1641)
Lodwick, Francis, *A Country Not Named*, ed. by William Poole (Tempe,: The Arizona Center for Medieval and Renaissance Studies, 2007)
Lucian, *The True History*, in *Lucian: Satirical Sketches*, trans. by Paul Turner (London: Penguin, 1961; repr. Bloomington: Indiana University Press, 1990), pp. 249–94
Lupton, Thomas, *Sivqila, Too Good to be True* (London, 1580)
Maton, Robert, *Israels Redemption* (London, 1642)
Mede, Joseph, *Remaines On some Passages in The Revelation* (London, 1650)
———, *Clavis Apocalyptica: Or, A Prophetical Key* (London, 1651)
———, Epistle XVII, in *The Works of The Pious and Profoundly-Learned Joseph Mede, B.D.* (London, 1677)
Melanchthon, Philip, *A Melanchthon Reader*, trans. by Ralph Keen (New York: Lang, 1988)
———, 'On the order of learning' (1531), in *Philip Melanchthon: Orations on Philosophy and Education*, trans. by Christine F. Salazar, ed. by Sachiko Kusukawa (Cambridge: Cambridge University Press, 1999), pp. 3–8

Milton, John, *Of Education* (1644) in *Complete English Poems; Of Education; Areopagitica*, ed. by Gordon Campbell (London: Dent, 1990)
More, Thomas, *The Complete Works of St. Thomas More, Volume 4: Utopia*, ed. by Edward Surtz, S.J., and J.H. Hexter (New Haven: Yale University Press, 1965)
———, *The Complete Works of St. Thomas More, Volume 9: The Apology*, ed. by J.B. Trapp (New Haven: Yale University Press, 1979)
———, *Utopia by Sir Thomas More, translated by Ralph Robynson, 1556*, ed. by David Harris Sacks (New York: Bedford/St. Martin's, 1999)
More, Thomas de Eschallers de la, *The English Catholike Christian, or The Saints Utopia* (London, 1649)
Nicholls, Thomas, *A pleasant Dialogue between a Lady called Listra, and a Pilgrim. Concerning the gouernement and common weale of the great prouince of Crangalor* (London, 1579)
———, *A Pleasant Description of the Fortunate Ilandes, called the Ilands of Canaria* (1583)
Petty, William, *The Advice of W.P. to Mr. Samuel Hartlib* (London, 1647)
Plattes, Gabriel, *A Description of the Famous Kingdome of Macaria; Shewing its Excellent Government* (London, 1641)
Roper, William, *The Lyfe of Sir Thomas More*, ed. by E.V. Hitchcock (London: printed for the Early English Text Society by H. Milford, Oxford University Press, 1935)
Sedgwick, William, *Zions Deliverance And Her Friends Duty: Or the Grounds of Expecting, and Meanes of Procuring Jerusalems Restauration* (London, 1642)
Smith, Thomas, *De Republica Anglorum*, ed. by Mary Dewar (Cambridge: Cambridge University Press, 1982)
Starkey, Thomas, *A Dialogue between Pole and Lupset*, ed. by T.F. Mayer (London: Royal Historical Society, 1989)
Taylor, John, *All the workes of Iohn Taylor the Water-Poet* (London, 1630)
[Ward, Seth], *Vindiciae Academiarum* (Oxford, 1654)
Webster, John, *Academiarum Examen, or the Examination of Academies* (London, 1653)
Wilkinson, Henry, *Babylons Ruine, Jerusalems Rising* (London, 1643)
Winstanley, Gerrard, *An Appeale to All Englishmen* (1650), in *The Works of Gerrard Winstanley*, ed. by George H. Sabine (Cornell: Cornell University Press, 1941)
———, *The Law of Freedom and Other Writings*, ed. by Christopher Hill (Harmondsworth: Penguin, 1973)

Secondary Sources

Abbeele, Georges van den, *Travel as Metaphor: From Montaigne to Rousseau* (Minneapolis: University of Minnesota Press, 1992)
Ackroyd, Peter, *The Life of Sir Thomas More* (London: Chatto & Windus, 1998)
Acosta, Ana M., *Reading Genesis in the Long Eighteenth Century: From Milton to Mary Shelley* (Farnham: Ashgate, 2006)

Albanese, Denise, *New Science, New World* (Durham: Duke University Press, 1996)
Altman, Joel B., *The Tudor Play of Mind: Rhetorical Enquiry and the Development of Elizabethan Drama* (Berkeley: University of California Press, 1978)
Ames, Russell A., *Citizen Thomas More and His Utopia* (Princeton: Princeton University Press, 1949)
Andrade, E.N. da C., 'Science in the Seventeenth Century', *Proceedings of the Royal Institution of Great Britain*, 30 (1938), 209–40
Appelbaum, Robert, *Literature and Utopian Politics in Seventeenth-Century England* (Cambridge: Cambridge University Press, 2002)
Aylmer, G.E. ed., *English Revolution* (London: Thames and Hudson, 1975)
Baker, David Weil, *Divulging Utopia: Radical Humanism in Sixteenth-Century England* (Amherst: University of Massachusetts Press, 1999)
Baker-Smith, Dominic, More's Utopia (London: HarperCollins, 1991)
———, 'Reading *Utopia*', in *The Cambridge Companion to Thomas More*, ed. by George M. Logan (Cambridge: Cambridge University Press, 2011), pp. 141–67
Baldwin, R.C.D., 'Nicholls, Thomas (1532–1601)', *Oxford Dictionary of National Biography*, Oxford University Press, 2004; online edn January 2008 [http://www.oxforddnb.com/view/article/20124, accessed 11.1.2012]
Baldwin, T.W., *William Shakespeare's Small Latine and Lesse Greeke*, 2 vols (Urbana: University of Illinois Press, 1944)
Bejczy, István, 'More's Utopia: The City of God on Earth?', *Saeculum*, 46 (1995), 17–30
Benedict, Philip, 'The second wave of Protestant expansion', in *The Cambridge History of Christianity, Volume 6: Reform and Expansion 1500–1660*, ed. by R. Po-Chia Hsia (Cambridge: Cambridge University Press, 2007), pp. 125–42
Berneri, Marie Louise, *Journey Through Utopia* (London: Routledge & Kegan Paul, 1950)
Betteridge, Tom, *Literature and Politics in the English Reformation* (Manchester: Manchester University Press, 2004)
Bevington, David M., 'The Dialogue in Utopia: Two Sides to the Question', *Studies in Philology*, 58:3 (1961), 496–509
Biagoli, Mario, *Galileo, Courtier: The Practice of Science in the Culture of Absolutism* (Chicago: University of Chicago Press, 1993)
Bishop, Jennifer, '*Utopia* and Civic Politics in Mid-Sixteenth Century London', *Historical Journal*, 54:4 (2011), 933–53
Blair, Ann, 'Natural Philosophy', in *The Cambridge History of Science, Volume 3: Early Modern Science*, ed. by Katharine Park and Lorraine Daston (Cambridge: Cambridge University Press, 2006), pp. 365–405
Bloch, Ernst, *The Spirit of Utopia*, trans. by Anthony A. Nassar (Cambridge: Cambridge University Press, 2000)
Boesky, Amy, *Founding Fictions: Utopias in Early Modern England* (Athens: University of Georgia Press, 1996)
———, 'Bacon's *New Atlantis* and the laboratory of prose', in *The Project of Prose in Early Modern Europe and the New World*, ed. by Elizabeth Fowler and Roland Greene (Cambridge: Cambridge University Press, 1997), pp. 138–53

Bouwsma, William J., 'The Two Faces of Humanism. Stoicism and Augustinianism in Renaissance Thought', in *Itinerarium Italicum: The Profile of the Italian Renaissance in the Mirror of its European Transformations*, ed. by Heiko A. Oberman with Thomas A. Brady, Jr. (Leiden: Brill, 1975), pp. 3–60

Braaten, Carl E. and Robert W. Jenson, eds, *The Catholicity of the Reformation* (Grand Rapids: William B. Eerdmans, 1996)

Bradshaw, Brendan, 'More on *Utopia*', *Historical Journal*, 24:1 (1981), 1–27

Briggs, John Channing, 'Bacon's Science and Religion', in *The Cambridge Companion to Bacon*, ed. by Markku Peltonen (Cambridge: Cambridge University Press, 1996), pp. 172–99

Brown, Alison, 'Introduction', in *Selected Writings of Girolamo Savonarola: Religion and Politics, 1490–1498*, trans. and ed. by Anne Borelli and Maria Pastore Passaro (New Haven: Yale University Press, 2006), pp. xv–xxxv

Bruce, Susan, 'Virgins of the World and Feasts of the Family: Sex and the Social Order in Two Renaissance Utopias', in *English Renaissance Prose: History, Language and Politics*, ed. by Neil Rhodes (Tempe: Medieval and Renaissance Texts and Studies, 1997), pp. 125–46

Bruckmann, Denis, Laurent Portes and Lyman Tower Sargent for the New York Public Library's 2000 exhibition 'Utopia: The Search for the Ideal Society in the Western World' [http://utopia.nypl.org/primarysources.html]

Buzogany, Deszo, 'Melanchthon as a Humanist and a Reformer', in *Melanchthon in Europe: His Work and Influence beyond Wittenberg*, ed. by Karin Maag (Grand Rapids: Baker Books, 1999), pp. 87–101

Cagnolati, Antonella, *Il Circolo di Hartlib: riforme educative e diffusion del sapere (Inghilterra 1630–1660)* (Bologna: CLUEB, 2001)

Čapková, Dagmar, 'Comenius and His Ideals: Escape from the Labyrinth', in *Samuel Hartlib and Universal Reformation*, ed. by Mark Greengrass, Michael Leslie and Timothy Raylor (Cambridge: Cambridge University Press, 1994), pp. 75–91

Capp, B.S., *The Fifth Monarchy Men: A Study in Seventeenth-Century English Millenarianism* (Oxford: Oxford University Press, 1972)

Castillo, Francisco Javier, 'The English Renaissance and the Canary Islands: Thomas Nichols and Edmund Scory', *SEDERI*, 2 (1992), 57–70

Charlton, Kenneth, *Education in Renaissance England* (London: Routledge & Kegan Paul, 1965)

Chordas, Nina, *Forms in Early Modern Utopia: The Ethnography of Perfection* (Farnham: Ashgate, 2010)

Christianson, Paul, *Reformers and Babylon: English Apocalyptic Visions from the Reformation to the Eve of the Civil War* (Toronto: University of Toronto Press, 1978)

Cioranescu, Alejandro, *Thomas Nichols, mercader de azúcar, hispanista y hereje. Con la edición y traducción de su Descripción de las Islas Afortunadas* (La Laguna: Instituto de Estudios Canarios, 1963)

Clouse, Robert Gordon, 'The Influence of John Henry Alsted on English Millenarian Thought in the Seventeenth Century', unpublished PhD thesis, State University of Iowa, 1963

Clucas, Stephen, 'Samuel Hartlib's Ephemerides, 1635–59, and the Pursuit of Scientific and Philosophical Manuscripts: The Religious Ethos of an Intelligencer', *The Seventeenth Century*, 6:1 (1991), 33–55

———, 'In Search of "The True Logick": Methodological Eclecticism among the "Baconian Reformers"', in *Samuel Hartlib and Universal Reformation*, ed. by Mark Greengrass, Michael Leslie and Timothy Raylor (Cambridge: Cambridge University Press, 1994), pp. 51–74

Cochrane, Eric, *Italy 1530–1630*, ed. by Julius Kirshner (London: Longman, 1988)

Cohen, Walter, 'The Literature of Empire in the Renaissance', *Modern Philology*, 102:1 (2004), 1–34

Colclough, David, 'Ethics and politics in the New Atlantis', in *Francis Bacon's NEW ATLANTIS: New interdisciplinary essays*, ed. by Bronwen Price (Manchester: Manchester University Press, 2002), pp. 60–81

———, '"The Materialls for the Building": Reuniting Francis Bacon's Sylva Sylvarum and New Atlantis', *Intellectual History Review*, 20:2 2010, 181–200

Colie, Rosalie L., 'Some paradoxes in the language of things', in *Reason and the Imagination: Studies in the History of Ideas 1600–1800*, ed. by J.A. Mazzeo (New York: Columbia University Press, 1962), pp. 93–128

Collinson, Patrick, *The Birthpangs of Protestant England: Religious and Cultural Change in the Sixteenth and Seventeenth Centuries* (London: Macmillan, 1988)

———, *The Reformation* (London: Weidenfeld and Nicolson, 2003)

———, *Richard Bancroft and Elizabethan Anti-Puritanism* (Cambridge: Cambridge University Press, 2013)

Coward, Barry, *The Stuart Age: England, 1605–1714*, 2nd edn (London: Longman, 1994)

Cox, Virginia, *The Renaissance Dialogue: Literary Dialogue in Its Social and Political Contexts, Castiglione to Galileo* (Cambridge: Cambridge University Press, 1992)

Crane, Mary Thomas, 'Early Tudor Humanism', in *A Companion to English Renaissance Literature and Culture*, ed. by Michael Hattaway (Oxford: Blackwell, 2000), pp. 13–26

Cummins, Juliet and David Burchell, eds, *Science, Literature and Rhetoric in Early Modern England* (Farnham: Ashgate, 2007)

Davis, J.C., *Utopia and the Ideal Society: A Study of English Utopian Writing 1516–1700* (Cambridge: Cambridge University Press, 1981; repr. 1983)

———, 'Formal Utopia/Informal Millennium: The Struggle between Form and Substance as a Context for Seventeenth-Century Utopianism', in *Utopias and the Millennium*, ed. by Krishan Kumar and Stephen Bann (London: Reaktion, 1993), pp. 17–32

Deakins, Roger L., 'Tudor Prose Dialogue: Genre and Anti-Genre', *Studies in English Literature*, 20 (1980), 5–23

DeCook, Travis, 'The Ark and Immediate Revelation in Francis Bacon's *New Atlantis*', *Studies in Philology*, 105 (2008), 103–22

Deitch, Judith, '"Dialoguewise": Discovering Alterity in Elizabethan Dialogues', in *Other Voices, Other Views: Expanding the Canon in English Renaissance Studies*, ed. by Helen Ostovich, Mary V. Silcox and Graham Roebuck (Newark: University of Delaware Press, 1999), pp. 46–73

Dickson, Donald R., 'Johann Valentin Andreae's Utopian Brotherhoods', *Renaissance Quarterly*, 49:4 (1996), 760–802

———, *The Tessera of Antilia: Utopian Brotherhoods & Secret Societies in the Early Seventeenth Century* (Leiden: Brill, 1998)

Dobbs, Betty Jo Teeter, *The Foundations of Newton's Alchemy, or "The Hunting of the Greene Lyon"* (Cambridge: Cambridge University Press, 1975)

Dolven, Jeffrey Andrew, *Scenes of Instruction in Renaissance Romance* (Chicago: University of Chicago Press, 2007)

Donnelly, Dorothy F., *Patterns of Order and Utopia* (Basingstoke: Macmillan, 1998)

Dudok, Gerard, *Sir Thomas More and His Utopia* (Amsterdam: H.J. Paris v.h. Firma A.H. Kruyt, 1923)

Duke, Alastair, 'Perspectives on International Calvinism', in *Calvinism in Europe, 1540–1620*, ed. by Andrew Pettegree, Alastair Duke and Gillian Lewis (Cambridge: Cambridge University Press, 1994), pp. 1–20

Dunn, Kevin, 'Milton among the monopolists: *Areopagitica*, intellectual property and the Hartlib circle', in *Samuel Hartlib and Universal Reformation*, ed. by Mark Greengrass, Michael Leslie and Timothy Raylor (Cambridge: Cambridge University Press, 1994), pp. 177–92

Dupont, Victor, *L'utopie et le Roman Utopique dans la Littérature Anglaise* (Toulouse: Didier, 1941)

Eamon, William, 'Natural Magic and Utopia in the Cinquecento: Campanella, the Della Porta Circle, and the Revolt of Calabria', *Memorie Domenicane*, n.s. 26 (1995), 369–402

———, *Science and the Secrets of Nature: Books of Secrets in Medieval and Early Modern Culture* (Princeton: Princeton University Press, 1996)

Ebner, Dean, '*The Tempest*: Rebellion and the Ideal State', *Shakespeare Quarterly*, 16:2 (1965), 161–73

Eby, Frederick, *Early Protestant Educators: The Educational Writings of Martin Luther, John Calvin, and Other Leaders of Protestant Thought* (New York: McGraw-Hill, 1931)

Eliav-Feldon, Miriam, *Realistic Utopias: The Ideal Imaginary Societies of the Renaissance, 1516–1630* (Oxford: Clarendon Press, 1982)

Elton, G.R., *Reform and Reformation: England 1509–1558* (London: Arnold, 1977)

———, *Studies in Tudor and Stuart Politics and Government, Volume IV* (Cambridge: Cambridge University Press, 1992)

Engelland, Hans, 'Introduction', in *Melanchthon on Christian Doctrine: Loci Communes 1555*, trans. and ed. by Clyde L. Manschreck (New York: Oxford University Press, 1965)

Eurich, Nell, *Science in Utopia: A Mighty Design* (Cambridge, MA: Harvard University Press, 1967)

Fenlon, Dermot, 'England and Europe: *Utopia* and its Aftermath', *Transactions of the Royal Historical Society*, 5th series, 25 (1975), 115–35
Findlen, Paula, 'The Limits of Civility and the Ends of Science', unpublished paper
Firpo, Luigi, 'Renaissance Utopianism', in *The Late Italian Renaissance, 1525–1630*, ed. by Eric Cochrane (London: Macmillan, 1970), pp. 149–67
———, *L'utopia nell'eta' della controriforma* (Turin: Giappichelli, 1977)
Firth, Katharine R., *The Apocalyptic Tradition in Reformation Britain 1530–1645* (Oxford: Oxford University Press, 1979)
Forshaw, Peter J., 'Astrology, Ritual and Revolution in the Works of Tommaso Campanella (1568–1639)', in *The Uses of the Future in Early Modern Europe*, ed. by Andrea Brady and Emily Butterworth (London: Routledge, 2010), pp. 181–97
Fox, Alistair, *Thomas More: History and Providence* (Oxford: Blackwell, 1982)
Foxley, Rachel, *The Levellers: Radical Political Thought in the English Revolution* (Manchester: Manchester University Press, 2013)
Freeman, Edmund, 'A Proposal for an English Academy in 1660', *Modern Language Review*, 19 (1924), 291–300
Frye, Northrop, *Northrop Frye on Literature and Society, 1936–1989: Unpublished Papers*, ed. by Robert R. Denham (Toronto: University of Toronto Press, 2002)
Gaukroger, Stephen, *Francis Bacon and the Transformation of Early-Modern Philosophy* (Cambridge: Cambridge University Press, 2001)
Gilson, Etienne, *Reason and Revelation in the Middle Ages* (New York: Charles Scribner's Sons, 1950)
Ginzburg, Carlo, 'The Old World and the New Seen from Nowhere', in *No Island Is an Island* (New York: Columbia University Press, 2000), pp. 1–23
Glaser, Eliane, *Judaism without Jews: Philosemitism and Christian Polemic in Early Modern England* (London: Palgrave Macmillan, 2007)
Gorski, Philip S., *The Disciplinary Revolution: Calvinism and the Rise of the State in Early Modern Europe* (Chicago: University of Chicago Press, 2003)
Grace, Damian, '*Utopia*: A Dialectical Interpretation', in *Miscellanea Moreana: Essays for Germain Marc'hadour*, ed. by Clare M. Murphy, Henri Gibaud and Mario A. Di Cesare (Binghamton: State University of New York at Binghamton, 1989), pp. 273–302
Grady, Hugh, 'Reification and *Utopia* in *As You Like It*: Desire and Textuality in the Green World', *Shakespearean Criticism*, 37 (1998), 43–58
Grafton, Anthony and Lisa Jardine, *From Humanism to the Humanities: Education and the Liberal Arts in Fifteenth- and Sixteenth-Century Europe* (London: Duckworth, 1986)
Green, I.M., 'The Persecution of "Scandalous" and "Malignant" Parish Clergy during the English Civil War', *The English Historical Review*, 94 (1979), 507–31
———, *Humanism and Protestantism in Early Modern English Education* (Farnham: Ashgate, 2009)

Greengrass, Mark, Michael Leslie and Timothy Raylor, eds, *Samuel Hartlib and the Universal Reformation: Studies in Intellectual Communication* (Cambridge: Cambridge University Press, 1994)

Hadfield, Andrew, *Literature, Travel, and Colonial Writing in the English Renaissance, 1545–1625* (Oxford: Oxford University Press, 2001)

Hall, A. Rupert and Marie Boas Hall, 'The Intellectual Origins of the Royal Society, London and Oxford', *Notes and Records of the Royal Society of London*, 23:2 (1968), 157–68

Hall, Marie Boas, *Robert Boyle and Seventeenth-Century Chemistry* (Cambridge: Cambridge University Press, 1958)

——, *Promoting Experimental Learning: Experiment and the Royal Society 1660–1727* (Cambridge: Cambridge University Press, 1991)

Hampton, Timothy, *Literature and Nation in the Sixteenth Century: Inventing Renaissance France* (Ithaca: Cornell University Press, 2001)

Hankins, James, *Plato in the Italian Renaissance*, 2 vols (Leiden: Brill, 1990)

Harkness, Deborah E., *John Dee's Conversations with Angels: Cabala, Alchemy, and the End of Nature* (Cambridge: Cambridge University Press, 1999)

Harrison, Carol, *Augustine: Christian Truth and Fractured Humanity* (Oxford: Oxford University Press, 2000)

Harrison, Richard L., Jr., 'Melanchthon's Role in the Reformation of the University of Tübingen', *Church History*, 47:3 (1978), 270–78

Headley, John M., 'Campanella, America, and World Evangelization', in *America in European Consciousness, 1499–1750*, ed. by Karen Ordahl Kupperman (Chapel Hill: University of North Carolina Press, 1995), pp. 243–71

Heitsch, Dorothea and Jean-François Vallée, eds, *Printed Voices: The Renaissance Culture of Dialogue* (Toronto: University of Toronto Press, 2004)

Hexter, J.H., '*Utopia* and Its Historical Milieu', in Thomas More, *The Complete Works of St. Thomas More, Volume 4: Utopia*, ed. by Edward Surtz, S.J., and J.H. Hexter (New Haven: Yale University Press, 1965), pp. xxiii–cxxiv

Hill, Christopher, *The World Turned Upside Down: Radical Ideas During the English Revolution* (Harmondsworth: Penguin, 1978)

——, '"Till the Conversion of the Jews"', in *Millenarianism and Messianism in English Literature and Thought, 1650–1800*, ed. by Richard H. Popkin (Leiden: Brill, 1988), pp. 12–36

——, *The Antichrist in Seventeenth-Century England*, revised edn (London: Verso, 1990)

Hirzel, Rudolf, *Der Dialog: ein literarhistorischer Versuch*, 2 vols (Leipzig: S. Hirzel, 1895)

Hoopes, Robert, *Right Reason in the English Renaissance* (Cambridge, MA: Harvard University Press, 1962)

Hotson, Howard, 'Philosophical Pedagogy in Reformed Central Europe between Ramus and Comenius: A Survey of the Continental Background of the "Three Foreigners"', in *Samuel Hartlib and Universal Reformation*, ed. by Mark Greengrass, Michael Leslie and Timothy Raylor (Cambridge: Cambridge University Press, 1994), pp. 29–50

Houston, Chloë, 'Travelling Nowhere: Global Utopias in the Early Modern Period', in *A Companion to the Global Renaissance 1550–1660: English Culture and Literature in the Era of Expansion*, ed. by J. Singh (Oxford: Blackwell, 2009), pp. 82–98

———, ed., *New Worlds Reflected: Travel and Utopia in the Early Modern Period* (Farnham: Ashgate, 2010)

Hsia, R. Po-Chia, *Social Discipline in the Reformation: Central Europe 1550–1750* (London and New York: Routledge, 1989)

Hunt, John Dixon, 'Gardens in Utopia: Utopia in the Garden', in *Between Dream and Nature: Essays on Utopia and Dystopia*, ed. by Dominic Baker-Smith and C.C. Barfoot (Amsterdam: Rodopi, 1987), pp. 114–38

Hunt, Maurice, '"Stir" and Work in Shakespeare's Last Plays', *Studies in English Literature 1500–1900* 22:2 (1982), 285–304

Hunter, G.K., 'Lupton, Thomas (fl. 1572–1584)', *Oxford Dictionary of National Biography*, Oxford University Press, 2004 [http://www.oxforddnb.com/view/article/17204, accessed 30.1.2012]

Hunter, Michael, *Science and Society in Restoration England* (Cambridge: Cambridge University Press, 1981)

———, *Establishing the New Science: The Experience of the Early Royal Society* (Woodbridge: Boydell, 1989)

Hutton, Sarah, 'The Appropriation of Joseph Mede: Millenarianism in the 1640s', in *Millenarianism and Messianism in Early Modern European Culture: Volume III: The Millenarian Turn: Millenarian Contexts of Science, Politics, and Everyday Anglo-American Life in the Seventeenth and Eighteenth Centuries*, ed. by James E. Force and Richard H. Popkin (Dordrecht: Kluwer, 2001), pp. 1–13

———, 'Persuasions to Science: Baconian Rhetoric and the *New Atlantis*', in *Francis Bacon's NEW ATLANTIS: New interdisciplinary essays*, ed. by Bronwen Price (Manchester: Manchester University Press, 2002), pp. 48–59

———, 'The Man in the Moone and the New Astonomy: Godwin, Gilbert, Kepler', *Études Épistémè*, 6 (2004), 3–13

Innes, David C., 'Bacon's New Atlantis: The Christian Hope and The Modern Hope', *Interpretation*, 22:1 (1994), 3–37

Jardine, Lisa, 'The Place of Dialectic Teaching in Sixteenth-Century Cambridge', *Studies in the Renaissance*, 21 (1974), 31–62

Jones, Stephen K., 'The Authorship of *Nova Solyma*', *Library*, ser. 3:1 (1907), 225–38

Jowitt, Claire, '"Books will speak plain"? Colonialism, politics and Jewishness in Francis Bacon's New Atlantis', in *Francis Bacon's NEW ATLANTIS: New interdisciplinary essays*, ed. by Bronwen Price (Manchester: Manchester University Press, 2002), pp. 129–55

Kallendorf, Craig W., trans. and ed., *Humanist Educational Treatises* (Cambridge, MA: Harvard University Press, 2002)

Katz, David S., *Philosemitism and the Readmission of the Jews to England, 1603–1655* (Oxford: Clarendon Press, 1982)

Kendrick, Christopher, 'The Imperial Laboratory: Discovering Forms in *The New Atlantis*', *English Literary History*, 70:4 (2003), 1021–42

——, *Utopia, Carnival, and Commonwealth in Renaissance England* (Toronto: University of Toronto Press, 2004)

Kenyon, Timothy, *Utopian Communism and Political Thought in Early Modern England* (London: Pinter, 1989)

Keynes, Geoffrey, *A Bibliography of Dr. Robert Hooke* (Oxford: Clarendon Press, 1960)

Kingdon, Robert M., 'The Geneva Consistory in the time of Calvin', in *Calvinism in Europe, 1540–1620*, ed. by Andrew Pettegree, Alastair Duke and Gillian Lewis (Cambridge: Cambridge University Press, 1994), pp. 21–34

Kinney, Arthur F., *Humanist Poetics: Thought, Rhetoric, and Fiction in Sixteenth-Century England* (Amherst: University of Massachusetts Press, 1986)

Kott, Jan, '*The Tempest*, or Repetition', *Shakespearean Criticism*, 29 (1996), 368–73

Kristeller, Paul Oskar, 'Humanism', in *The Cambridge History of Renaissance Philosophy*, ed. by Quentin Skinner and Eckhard Kessler, assoc. ed. by Jill Kraye (Cambridge: Cambridge University Press, 1988), pp. 113–37

Kushner, Eva, *Le dialogue à la Renaissance: Histoire et poétique* (Paris: Librairie Droz, 2004)

Kusukawa, Sachiko, *The Transformation of Natural Philosophy: The Case of Philip Melanchthon* (Cambridge: Cambridge University Press, 1995)

Lach, Donald F., *Asia in the Making of Europe: Volume I: The Century of Discovery* (Chicago: University of Chicago Press, 1994)

Lamont, William, *Godly Rule: Politics and Religion, 1603–1660* (London: Macmillan, 1969)

Langman, Andrew Peter, '"Beyond, both the Old World, and the New": Authority and Knowledge in the works of Francis Bacon, with special reference to the *New Atlantis*', unpublished PhD thesis, University of Sussex, 2007

——, 'The Future Now: Chance, Time and Natural Divination in the Thought of Francis Bacon', in *The Uses of the Future in Early Modern Europe*, ed. by Andrea Brady and Emily Butterworth (London: Routledge, 2010), pp. 142–55

Larmour, David H.J., 'Sex with Moonmen and Vinewomen: The Reader as Explorer in Lucian's *Vera Historia*', *Intertexts*, 1:2 (1997), 131–46

Leary, John E., Jr., *Francis Bacon and the Politics of Science* (Ames: Iowa State University Press, 1994)

Le Guern, Michel, 'Sur le genre du dialogue', in *L'automne de la Renaissance*, ed. by J. Lafond and A. Stegmann (Paris: J. Vrin, 1981)

Leslie, Marina, *Renaissance Utopias and the Problem of History* (Ithaca: Cornell University Press, 1998)

Levine, Joseph, 'Thomas More and the English Renaissance', in *The Historical Imagination in Early Modern Britain: History, Rhetoric, and Fiction, 1500–1800*, ed. by Donald R. Kelley and David Harris Sacks (Cambridge: Cambridge University Press, 1997)

Lewis, Arthur O., *Utopian Literature in The Pennsylvania State University Libraries: A Selected Bibliography* (University Park: Pennsylvania State University Libraries, 1984)

Loewenstein, David, *Representing Revolution in Milton and His Contemporaries: Religion, Politics, and Polemics in Radical Puritanism* (Cambridge: Cambridge University Press, 2001)

Logan, George M., *The Meaning of More's 'Utopia'* (Princeton: Princeton University Press, 1983)

Lynch, William T., 'A Society of Baconians?: The Collective Development of Bacon's Method in the Royal Society of London', in *Francis Bacon and the Refiguring of Early Modern Thought: Essays to Commemorate The Advancement of Learning (1605–2005)* (Farnham: Ashgate, 2005), pp. 173–202

MacCaffrey, Wallace T., 'Cecil, William, first Baron Burghley (1520/21–1598)', Oxford Dictionary of National Biography, Oxford University Press, 2004 [http://www.oxforddnb.com/view/article/4983, accessed 30.1.2012]

———, 'Hatton, Sir Christopher (c.1540–1591)', *Oxford Dictionary of National Biography*, Oxford University Press, 2004 [http://www.oxforddnb.com/view/article/12605, accessed 30.1.2012]

Mack, Peter, 'The dialogue in English education of the sixteenth century', in *Le dialogue au temps de la Renaissance*, ed. by M.T. Jones-Davies (Paris: Centre de Recherches sur la renaissance, 1984), pp. 189–212

Manuel, Frank E. and Fritzie P. Manuel, *Utopian Thought in the Western World* (Oxford: Blackwell, 1979)

Margalit, Yael, 'Publics: A Bibliographic Afterword', in *Making Publics in Early Modern Europe: People, Things, Forms of Knowledge*, ed. by Bronwen Wilson and Paul Yachnin (New York and London: Routledge, 2010)

Marius, Richard C., 'Thomas More and the Early Church Fathers', *Traditio*, 24 (1968), 379–407

———, *Thomas More: A Biography* (New York: Knopf, 1984)

———, 'Augustinianism and Carnival in More's *Utopia*', *Moreana*, 35 (1998), 129–50

Marsh, David, *Lucian and the Latins: Humor and Humanism in the Early Renaissance* (Ann Arbor: University of Michigan Press, 1998)

———, 'Dialogue and Discussion in the Renaissance', in *The Cambridge History of Literary Criticism, Volume 3: The Renaissance*, ed. by Glyn Norton (Cambridge: Cambridge University Press, 1999), pp. 265–70

Martines, Lauro, *Scourge and Fire: Savonarola and Renaissance Florence* (London: Jonathan Cape, 2006)

McCullough, Peter, *Sermons at Court: Politics and Religion in Elizabethan and Jacobean Preaching* (Cambridge: Cambridge University Press, 1998)

McCutcheon, Elizabeth, 'Denying the Contrary: More's Use of Litotes in the *Utopia*', *Moreana*, 31–2 (1971), 107–22

McKie, Douglas, 'The Origins and Foundation of the Royal Society', *Notes and Records of the Royal Society of London*, 15 (1960), 1–37

McKnight, Stephen A., ed., *Science, Pseudo-Science, and Utopianism in Early Modern Thought* (Columbia,: University of Missouri Press, 1992)
McLean, Antonia, *Humanism and the Rise of Science in Tudor England* (London: Heinemann, 1972)
Merchant, Carolyn, *The Death of Nature: Women, Ecology, and the Scientific Revolution* (London: Wildwood House, 1982)
Monfasani, John, *George of Trebizond: A Biography and a Study of his Rhetoric and Logic* (Leiden: Brill, 1976)
Monsuez, R., 'Le Latin de Thomas More dans *Utopia*', *Caliban*, 3 (1966), 35–78
Montgomery, John Warwick, *Cross and Crucible Johann Valentin Andreae (1586–1654), Phoenix of the Theologians*, 2 vols (The Hague: Nijhoff, 1973)
Morrish, Jennifer, 'Virtue and Genre in Samuel Gott's *Nova Solyma*', *Humanistica Lovaniensia*, 52 (2003), 237–317
Moylan, Tom, *Demand the Impossible: Science Fiction and the Utopian Imagination* (New York and London: Methuen, 1986)
Mullett, Michael A., *The Catholic Reformation* (London: Routledge, 1999)
Negley, Glenn, *Utopian Literature: A Bibliography with a Supplementary Listing of Works Influential in Utopian Thought* (Lawrence: Regents Press of Kansas, 1978)
Nielsen, William Allen, 'Nova Solyma: A Romance Attributed to John Milton', *Modern Philology*, 1:4 (1904), 525–46
Norbrook, David, *Poetry and Politics in the English Renaissance* (London: Routledge & Kegan Paul, 1984; rev. edn 2002)
———, *Writing the English Republic: Poetry, Rhetoric and Politics, 1627–1660* (Cambridge: Cambridge University Press, 1999)
Olin, John C., *Catholic Reform: From Cardinal Ximenes to the Council of Trent, 1495–1563* (New York: Fordham University Press, 1990)
Pal, Carol, *Republic of Women: Rethinking the Republic of Letters in the Seventeenth Century* (Cambridge: Cambridge University Press, 2012)
Parry, Graham, 'A troubled Arcadia', in *Literature and the English Civil War*, ed. by Thomas Healy and Jonathan Sawday (Cambridge: Cambridge University Press, 1990), pp. 38–55
Patrick, J. Max, 'Puritanism and Poetry: Samuel Gott', *University of Toronto Quarterly*, 8 (1938–39), 211–16
———, 'Robert Burton's Utopianism', *Philological Quarterly*, 27 (1948), 345–58
———, '*Nova Solyma*: Samuel Gott's Puritan Utopia', *Studies in the Literary Imagination*, 10:2 (1977), 43–55
Poole, William, 'Kepler's *Somnium* and Francis Godwin's *The Man in the Moone*', in *New Worlds Reflected: Travel and Utopia in the Early Modern Period*, ed. by Chloë Houston (Farnham: Ashgate: 2010), pp. 57–69
———, 'Who Wrote the 1660 Continuation of *The New Atlantis*?', unpublished article
Popkin, Richard H., 'Hartlib, Dury and the Jews', in *Samuel Hartlib and Universal Reformation*, ed. by Mark Greengrass, Michael Leslie and Timothy Raylor (Cambridge: Cambridge University Press, 1994), pp. 118–36

Prescott, Anne Lake, 'Introduction', in Jackson Campbell Boswell, *Sir Thomas More in the English Renaissance: An Annotated Catalogue* (Binghamton, New York: Center for Medieval and Renaissance Studies, 1994)

———, *Imagining Rabelais in Renaissance England* (New Haven: Yale University Press, 1998)

Price, Bronwen, ed., *Francis Bacon's NEW ATLANTIS: New interdisciplinary essays* (Manchester: Manchester University Press, 2002)

Prior, Moody E., 'Bacon's Man of Science', in *Essential Articles for the Study of Francis Bacon*, ed. by Brian Vickers (London: Sidgwick & Jackson, 1972), pp. 140–63

Pumfrey, Stephen, '"These 2 hundred years not the like published as Gellibrand has done de Magnete": The Hartlib circle and magnetic philosophy', in *Samuel Hartlib and Universal Reformation*, ed. by Mark Greengrass, Michael Leslie and Timothy Raylor (Cambridge: Cambridge University Press, 1994), pp. 247–67

Raitière, Martin N., 'More's *Utopia* and *The City of God*', *Studies in the Renaissance*, 20 (1973), 144–68, repr. in *The City of God: A Collection of Critical Essays*, ed. by Dorothy F. Donnelly (New York: Lang, 1995), pp. 253–76

Richards, Jennifer, *Rhetoric and Courtliness in Early Modern Literature* (Cambridge: Cambridge University Press, 2003)

Rockett, William, 'Labor and Virtue in *The Tempest*', *Shakespeare Quarterly*, 24:1 (1973), 77–84

Roggen, Vibeke, 'A Protean text: *Utopia* in Latin, 1516–1631', in *Thomas More's Utopia in Early Modern Europe: Paratexts and Contexts*, ed. by Terence Cave (Manchester: Manchester University Press), pp. 14–31

Rose, Elliot, 'Too Good to Be True: Thomas Lupton's Golden Rule', in *Tudor Rule and Revolution: Essays for G.R. Elton from His American Friends*, ed. by Dellroyd J. Guth and John W. McKenna (Cambridge: Cambridge University Press, 1982), pp. 183–200

Rossi, Paolo, *Francis Bacon: From Magic to Science*, trans. by Sacha Rabinovitch (London: Routledge & Kegan Paul, 1968)

Roush, Sherry, *Hermes' Lyre: Italian Poetic Self-Commentary from Dante to Tommaso Campanella* (Toronto: University of Toronto Press, 2002)

Sacks, David Harris, 'Rebuilding Solomon's Temple: Richard Hakluyt's Great Instauration', in *New Worlds Reflected: Travel and Utopia in the Early Modern Period*, ed. by Chloë Houston (Farnham: Ashgate, 2010)

Salyer, Sanford M., 'Renaissance Influences in Hall's Mundus Alter Et Idem', *Philological Quarterly*, 6 (1927), 320–34

Salzman, Paul, 'Narrative contexts for Bacon's New Atlantis', in *Francis Bacon's NEW ATLANTIS: New interdisciplinary essays*, ed. by Bronwen Price (Manchester: Manchester University Press, 2002), pp. 28–47

Sargent, Lyman Tower, *British and American Utopian Literature, 1516–1985: An Annotated, Chronological Bibliography* (New York: Garland, 1988)

Sargent, Rose-Mary, 'Bacon as an advocate for cooperative scientific research', in *The Cambridge Companion to Bacon*, ed. by Markku Peltonen (Cambridge: Cambridge University Press, 1996), pp. 146–71

Schaeffer, John D., 'Socratic Method in More's Utopia', *Moreana*, 69 (1981), 5–20
Schoeck, Richard J., 'Correct and Useful Institutions: On Reading More's Utopia as Dialogue', in *Essential Articles for the Study of Thomas More*, ed. by Richard S. Sylvester and G.P. Marc'hadour (Hamden: Archon Books, 1977)
Sell, Jonathan P.A., *Rhetoric and Wonder in English Travel Writing, 1560–1613* (Farnham: Ashgate, 2006)
Sellevold, Kirsti, 'The French Versions of Utopia: Christian and Cosmopolitan Models', in T*homas More's Utopia in Early Modern Europe: Paratexts and Contexts*, ed. by Terence Cave (Manchester: Manchester University Press, 2008), pp. 67–86
Serjeantson, R.W., 'Proof and Persuasion', in *The Cambridge History of Science, Volume 3: Early Modern Science*, ed. by Katherine Park and Lorraine Daston (Cambridge: Cambridge University Press, 2006)
Shapin, Steven, *A Social History of Truth: Civility and Science in Seventeenth-Century England* (Chicago: University of Chicago Press, 1994)
Shapin, Steven and Simon Schaffer, *Leviathan and the Air-Pump: Hobbes, Boyle, and the Experimental Life* (Princeton: Princeton University Press, 1985)
Shapiro, James, *Shakespeare and the Jews* (New York: Columbia University Press, 1996)
Sherman, William H., 'Anatomizing the Commonwealth: Language, politics and the Elizabethan social order', in *The Project of Prose in Early Modern Europe and the New World*, ed. by Elizabeth Fowler (Cambridge: Cambridge University Press, 1997)
———, 'Stirrings and Searchings (1500–1720)', in *The Cambridge Companion to Travel Writing*, ed. by Peter Hulme and Tim Youngs (Cambridge: Cambridge University Press, 2002), pp. 17–36
Shrank, Cathy, *Writing the Nation in Reformation England 1530–1580* (Oxford: Oxford University Press, 2006)
———, Entry on *A Pleasant Dialogue between Listra and a Pilgrim*, 16 January 2007, The Origins of Early Modern Literature, Humanities Research Online [http://www.hrionline.ac.uk/origins/frame.html, accessed 11.1.2012]
———, 'Stammering, Snoring and Other Problems in the Early Modern English Dialogue', in *Writing and Reform in Sixteenth-Century England: Interdisciplinary Essays*, ed. by John Blakeley and Mike Pincombe (Lewiston: Edwin Mellen Press, 2008), pp. 99–120
Skinner, Quentin, *The Foundations of Modern Political Thought*, 2 vols (Cambridge: Cambridge University Press, 1978)
———, 'Sir Thomas More's *Utopia* and the language of Renaissance humanism', in *The Languages of Political Theory in Early Modern Europe*, ed. by A. Pagden (Cambridge: Cambridge University Press, 1987), pp. 123–57
Slack, Paul, *From Reformation to Improvement: Public Welfare in Early Modern England* (Oxford: Clarendon Press, 1999)
Sloane, Thomas O., 'Rhetorical Education and Two-Sided Argument', in *Renaissance-Rhetorik*, ed. by Heinrich F. Plett (Berlin: Walter de Gruyter, 1993), pp. 163–78

Smarr, Janet Levarie, *Joining the Conversation: Dialogues by Renaissance Women* (Ann Arbor: University of Michigan Press, 2005)
Snyder, Jon R., '*The City of the Sun* and the Poetics of the Utopian Dialogue', *Stanford Italian Review*, 5 (1985), 175–87
———, *Writing the Scene of Speaking: Theories of Dialogue in the Late Italian Renaissance* (Stanford: Stanford University Press, 1989)
Spedding, James, 'Preface to *The New Atlantis*', in *The Collected Works of Francis Bacon*, ed. by James Spedding, Robert Leslie Ellis and Douglas Denon Heath, 7 vols (London: Longmans, 1857–59)
Spitz, Lewis W., *The Renaissance and Reformation Movements, Volume II: The Reformation* (Chicago: Rand McNally College, 1971)
Spitz, Lewis W. and Barbara Sher Tinsley, *Johann Sturm on Education* (St. Louis, MO: Concordia, 1995)
Srigley, Michael, 'Thomas Vaughan, the Hartlib Circle and the Rosicrucians', *Scintilla*, 6 (2002), 31–54
Steadman, John M., '"Beyond Hercules": Bacon and the Scientist as Hero', *Studies in the Literary Imagination*, 4:1 (1971), 3–47
Strauss, Leo, 'What is Political Philosophy?', in *What Is Political Philosophy? And Other Studies* (New York: Free Press, 1959)
Surtz, Edward, 'Aspects of More's Latin Style in *Utopia*', *Studies in the Renaissance*, 14 (1967), 93–109
Suvin, Darko, 'Defining the Literary Genre of Utopia: Some Historical Semantics, Some Genealogy, A Proposal and A Plea', *Studies in the Literary Imagination*, 6:2 (1973), 121–45, repr. in Darko Suvin, *Metamorphoses of Science Fiction: On the Poetics and History of a Literary Genre* (New Haven: Yale University Press, 1979), pp. 37–62
Thomas, Keith, 'The Utopian Impulse in Seventeenth-Century England', in *Between Dream and Nature: Essays on Utopia and Dystopia*, ed. by Dominic Baker-Smith and C.C. Barfoot (Amsterdam: Rodopi, 1987), pp. 20–46
Toon, Peter, *Puritans, the Millennium and the Future of Israel: Puritan Eschatology 1600 to 1660* (Cambridge: Clarke, 1970)
Trevor-Roper, Hugh, 'Three Foreigners: the Philosophers of the Puritan Revolution', in *Religion, the Reformation and Social Change*, 3rd edn (London: Secker & Warburg, 1984), pp. 237–93
Tribby, Jay, 'Cooking (with) Clio and Cleo: Eloquence and Experiment in Seventeenth-Century Florence', *Journal of the History of Ideas*, 52 (1991), 417–39
Trousson, Raymond, *Voyage au pays de nulle part: histoire littéraire de la pensée utopique* (Brussels: Université de Bruxelles, 1975)
Turnbull, G.H., *Hartlib, Dury and Comenius: Gleanings from Hartlib's Papers* (London: Hodder & Stoughton, 1947)
———, 'Johann Valentin Andreae's Societas Christiana', *Zeitschrift für Deutsche Philologie*, 74 (1955), 151–85
Twigg, J.D., 'The Parliamentary Visitation of the University of Cambridge, 1644–1645', *The English Historical Review*, 98 (1983), 51328

Vallée, Jean-François, 'The Fellowship of the Book: Printed Voices and Written Friendships in More's Utopia', in *Printed Voices: The Renaissance Culture of Dialogue*, ed. by Dorothea Heitsch and Jean-François Vallée (Toronto: University of Toronto Press, 2004)

Versins, Pierre, *Encyclopédie de l'utopie des voyages extraordinaires et de la science fiction* (Lausanne: L'Age d'Homme, 1972)

Vickers, Brian, *Francis Bacon and Renaissance Prose* (Cambridge: Cambridge University Press, 1968)

Vieira, Fátima, 'The Concept of Utopia', in *The Cambridge Companion to Utopia*, ed. by Gregory Claeys (Cambridge: Cambridge University Press, 2010), pp. 3–27

Vincent, William Alfred Leslie, *The State and School Education, 1640–1660, in England and Wales* (London: SPCK, 1950)

Walker, John, *The Sufferings of the Clergy during the Great Rebellion* (Oxford: Henry and Parker, 1862)

Wall, Ernestine G.E. van der, 'A Philo-Semitic Millenarian on the Reconciliation of Jews and Christians: Henry Jessey and his "The Glory and Salvation of Jehudah and Israel" (1650)', in *Sceptics, Millenarians and Jews*, ed. by David S. Katz and Jonathan I. Israel (Leiden: Brill, 1990), pp. 161–84

Walzer, Michael, *The Revolution of the Saints: A Study in the Origins of Radical Politics* (London: Weidenfeld and Nicolson, 1966)

Warner, Christopher J., 'Thomas More's Utopia and the Problem of Writing a Literary History of English Renaissance Dialogue', in *Printed Voices: The Renaissance Culture of Dialogue*, ed. by Dorothea Heitsch and Jean-François Vallée (Toronto: University of Toronto Press, 2004)

Watson, Foster, *The English Grammar Schools to 1660: Their Curriculum and Practice* (Cambridge: Cambridge University Press, 1908; repr. London: Frank Cass, 1968)

Webster, Charles, ed., *Samuel Hartlib and the Advancement of Learning* (Cambridge: Cambridge University Press, 1970)

———, *The Great Instauration: Science, Medicine, and Reform, 1626–1660* (London: Duckworth, 1975)

———, *Utopian Planning and the Puritan Revolution: Gabriel Plattes, Samuel Hartlib, and* Macaria (Oxford: Wellcome Unit for the History of Medicine, 1979)

Wegemer, Gerard, '*The City of God* in Thomas More's *Utopia*', *Renascence*, 44 (1992), 115–35

Weinberger, Jerry, 'On the miracles in Bacon's *New Atlantis*', in *Francis Bacon's NEW ATLANTIS: New interdisciplinary essays*, ed. by Bronwen Price (Manchester: Manchester University Press, 2002), pp. 106–28

———, 'Francis Bacon and the Unity of Knowledge: Reason and Revelation', in *Francis Bacon and the Refiguring of Early Modern Thought*, ed. by Julie Robin Solomon and Catherine Gimelli Martin (Farnham: Ashgate, 2005), pp. 109–27

Wheeler, Harvey, 'Francis Bacon's *New Atlantis*: The "Mould" of a Lawfinding Commonwealth', in *Francis Bacon's Legacy of Texts*, ed. by William A. Sessions (New York: AMS Press, 1990), pp. 291–310

Willard, Thomas, 'Andreae's *ludibrium*: Menippean Satire in the *Chymische Hochzeit*', in *Laughter in the Middle Ages and Early Modern Times: Epistemology of a Fundamental Human Behavior, its Meaning, and Consequences*, ed. by Albrecht Classen (Berlin/New York: De Gruyter, 2010), pp. 767–89

Wilson, John F., *Pulpit in Parliament: Puritanism during the English Civil Wars, 1640–1648* (Princeton,: Princeton University Press, 1969)

Wilson, K.J., *Incomplete Fictions: The Formation of English Renaissance Dialogue* (Washington: The Catholic University of America Press, 1985)

Withington, Philip, *The Politics of Commonwealth: Citizens and Freemen in Early Modern England* (Cambridge: Cambridge University Press, 2005)

——, *Society in Early Modern England: The Vernacular Origins of Some Powerful Ideas* (Cambridge: Polity Press, 2010)

Womack, Peter, 'The Writing of Travel', in *A New Companion to English Renaissance Literature and Culture: Volume 1*, ed. by Michael Hattaway (Oxford: Wiley-Blackwell, 2010), pp. 527–42

Wootton, David, 'Leveller democracy and the Puritan Revolution', in *The Cambridge History of Political Thought, 1450–1700* (Cambridge: Cambridge University Press, 1991), pp. 412–42

Yates, Frances, *The Art of Memory* (London: Routledge & Kegan Paul, 1966; repr. London: Penguin, 1978)

——, *The Rosicrucian Enlightenment* (London: Routledge and Kegan Paul, 1972; repr. London: Ark, 1986)

Yoran, Hanan, *Between Utopia and Dystopia: Erasmus, Thomas More, and the Humanist Republic of Letters* (Lanham: Lexington Books, 2010)

Zakai, Avihu, 'Thomas Brightman and English Apocalyptic Tradition', in *Menasseh Ben Israel and His World*, ed. by Yosef Kaplan, Henry Méchoulan and Richard H. Popkin (Leiden: Brill, 1989), pp. 31–44

Zetterberg, J. Peter, 'Echoes of Nature in Salomon's House', *Journal of the History of Ideas*, 43:2 (1982), 179–93

Zlatar, Antoinina Bevan, *Reformation Fictions: Polemical Protestant Dialogues in Elizabethan England* (Oxford: Oxford University Press, 2011)

Index

academy 158–9
Age of Plato/Age of Aristotle 26
age of Saturn 21
Agricola, Rudolph 63
agriculture 33, 71
Alcock, Bishop John 35–6
   Mons Perfectionis 35–6
Alsted, John Henry 128, 147, 152
ambivalence (in utopia) 24–5
Andreae, Johann Valentin 11, 62–3, 64, 68, 71–86, 87–8, 97, 100, 128, 129, 152, 159
   Amicorum singularium clarissimorum Funera, condecorata 74
   Christianae societatis imago 75
   Christiani amoris dextra porrecta 75
   Christianopolis [or *Reipublicae christianopolitanae descriptio*] 11, 62–3, 66, 71–86, 87, 92, 152
   Menippus sive dialogorum satyricorum centuria 77, 78
   The Right Hand of Christian Love Offered 79
   Societas Christiana [or *Civitas Solis*, trans. as *A Modell of Christian Society*] 73, 75, 79
   Unio Christiana 73
   Verae unionis in Christo Jesu Specimen 75
angels 33
apocalypse (*see also* millenarianism) 119, 121, 122–6
army 25, 71, 153
astrology 68, 69, 80
Augustine 5, 11, 16, 26, 30, 31–40, 45, 135, 155
   De beata vita 33, 37–8
   Of the City of God against the Pagans [or *De civitate dei contra paganos*] 31–3, 34, 36, 37
   Commentary on the Gospel of St John 37
   Confessions 36, 39

   De Genesi ad litteram 33
authority (in travel writing) 47–8
authorship 48

Bacon, Francis 3, 12, 58, 61, 89–117, 119, 126, 129, 131, 137–8, 143, 158, 159
   Advancement of Learning 96, 109, 110–11
   Cogitata et Visa 100
   New Atlantis 3, 12, 58, 61, 89–117, 129, 138, 143
   Sylva Sylvarum 92, 116
   Valerius Terminus 96–97
Baker, David Weil 24–5, 43–4
Baker-Smith, Dominic 15, 29, 30
baptism 82
Basel 42
Begley, Walter 146
Bellarmine, Robert 26
The Bible/Scripture 25, 32, 35–6, 82, 85, 102
   exegesis of 52, 58
Boesky, Amy 23, 93, 107
Boyle, Robert 113, 138
Brahe, Tycho, *De nova stella* 70
Brightman, Thomas 147, 149
Bruni, Leonardo 26
Budé, Guillaume 21–2
Burchell, David 106–7
Burton, Robert 89, 141–2
   The Anatomy of Melancholy 89, 141–2
Bushell, Thomas 138

Calvin 84–5
   Ecclesiastical Ordinances 84
Cambridge 135, 137, 145, 146, 149
Campanella, Tommaso 3, 11, 62, 63, 66–71, 86, 87–8, 97, 163
   The City of the Sun [or *La Città del Sole*] 3, 11, 62–3, 66–71, 72, 81, 86, 88
cannibals 54
Catholicism 5, 44, 54, 66, 102–3, 122

Cavendish, Margaret
    The Blazing-World 119
Cecil, William 42, 55
Chordas, Nina 17, 62, 71–2, 107
The Church, management of 100, 112–13
Cicero 17, 19, 45
    Tusculan Disputations 17
City of God 13, 31–3, 129, 134–5, 156
clothing 48–9, 56, 68, 81
Colclough, David 95, 116
Colet, John 21
Comenius, Jan Amos 126, 128, 152–3, 159
common good 28, 131
Commonwealth 1, 5, 6, 24, 26, 29, 31, 33, 39, 50, 55, 89–91, 116, 144–5, 160–61
community of property 21, 28, 31–2, 34, 161
Confessio fraternitatis 74
conversation 3, 4, 9, 11, 12–13, 16–17, 19, 20, 23–5, 38, 46, 47–9, 54, 59, 63, 66–7, 72, 81–3, 85–6, 87–8, 92–5, 98–100, 104–8, 115–17, 119–20, 131–2, 134, 151, 156, 161
Coppe, Abiezer
    A Fiery Flying Roll 157
counsel 17, 23, 106, 123–4, 127, 129, 163
countryside 24–5
court service 19–20
Cox, Virginia 4, 9, 49, 59
crime – playing with dice 34, 57, 58
Crofton, Zachary 147
Cupiditas/sin of desire 34

Davis, J. C. 2, 2 fn. 4, 7, 55, 160–61
Decembrio, Uberto 26–7
dialogue
    archaism of 10
    closed 4, 109, 111, 116, 162
    decline of 10, 11, 61–2, 88, 107
    dramatic nature/qualities of 9, 45–6, 53, 59
    educational function/didacticism of 4, 11, 16, 20, 45–6, 59, 66, 67, 70–72, 81, 87–8, 132, 151, 156
    efficacy of 4, 22–3, 25, 58
    form of 4, 10–13, 15–23, 35, 37, 40–41, 44–6, 48, 49, 53, 59, 61–3, 66–7, 70–72, 77–8, 86, 88, 92, 117, 120, 132, 145, 151, 156
    incomplete nature of 93

multiple voices in 10–11, 15, 17, 25, 48, 59
    open 4, 67, 115–16
    playfulness of 16, 20, 25, 30, 72, 120
    polemical dialogues 11, 41–2, 45–6, 53
    popularity of 9 fn. 26, 17, 44–5
    self-criticism in 11, 16, 22–3
Dolven, Jeffrey 19
Dudley, Edmund
    The Tree of Commonwealth 6
Dury, John 3, 12, 13, 123, 125–9, 130–31, 133–5, 137, 152, 153, 159
    The Purpose and Platform of my Journey into Germany 127
    The Reformed Librarie-Keeper 135
    The Reformed School 3, 130, 135, 153
    A Supplement to the Reformed School 135
Dyer, Edward 46, 48, 53
dystopia (link to utopia) 61–2

Eamon, William 108–11
early science fiction 13, 144
education 63–6, 69–71, 74–6, 80–87
    gymnasia 65
    reform of 63–6, 75–6
    schools 64–6, 69–70
    social function of 63–6, 69–70, 80–81
    spiritual purpose of 65–6, 81–3
    utility of 63–6, 69–70, 74–5
Elizabeth I 51
Elton, G.R. 40
Elysian Fields 21
encyclopaedia 82
Erasmus 21, 24–5, 63, 77, 78
    Convivium religiosum 24–5
eugenics 69

fable 89, 92, 111, 116
Fairfax, Nathaniel 113
faith 33, 35–6, 38–9, 84, 101, 155
Fama fraternitatis 74
family 145, 151
Ficino, Marsilio 26
Florence 5, 42
food 16–17, 58, 80, 101
Foxe, John 43–4, 149
friends, friendship 74, 76–7, 78–9

Galileo 106–7
garden 1, 16, 20, 25, 80–81, 158

Gaukroger, Stephen 110–11
Geneva 84–5
George of Trebizond 27–8
godly reform 44, 121, 149
Godwin, Francis
  The Man in the Moone 144
gold 21, 50
golden age 21
the good life 4, 16, 17–18, 35–6, 37, 40, 45, 74, 122, 156, 159
Goodwin, Thomas
  Sions Glory 125, 133
Gorges, Arthur 89
Gott, Samuel 13, 119, 141, 145–56, 161
  Nova Solyma 13, 119, 141, 145–56

Hall, Joseph 61–2, 77–8, 144
  Mundus Alter et Idem 61–2, 77
Hankins, James 26
Harrington, James 144–5
  The Commonwealth of Oceana 144–5
Hartlib, Samuel 12–13, 119–20, 121, 123, 124–31, 134, 135, 137–8, 147, 152–3, 157–9, 162–3
  Ephemerides 152, 163
  A Further Discoverie of the Office of Address 124–5
Hatton, Christopher 53–54, 55
Heaven, afterlife 13, 25, 28, 33, 58, 72–3, 80–83, 95, 102, 156, 159–60
honesty 22, 50, 52–3, 76, 91
'H., R.' 111–6
  New Atlantis Begun by the Lord Verulam, Viscount St. Albans: and Continued by R. H. Esquire. Wherein is set forth A Platform of Monarchical Government with A Pleasant intermixture of divers rare Inventions, And wholsom Customs, fit to be introduced Into all kingdoms, states, and commonwealths 111–16
human perfectibility 119–20, 124–5, 128
humanism, humanist 6–7, 9, 10, 17–18, 21, 22, 26–7, 28, 31, 44–5, 63–6, 80, 82, 87–8, 89–90
Hume, David 33–4
humility 35, 81

individuality 51–2, 56, 58, 59

irony 10, 16, 59, 120, 155–6
island 15–16, 21, 38, 46–7, 66–7, 90

Jerusalem, as alternative to England 147, 149–51
Jessey, Henry
  The Glory and Salvation of Jehudah and Israel 148
Jews 124, 147–50, 162
  the conversion of 147–50, 162
  scattered nation 149–50
jokes 76–7
journey 3, 8–9, 10, 38, 61–2, 71–3, 76, 77, 116, 120, 129, 131, 133–4, 144–5

Keckermann, Bartholomäus 128, 152
Kenyon, Timothy 161

Langman, Pete 105
Larmour, David H. 91
legislation, the law 21, 50, 56–7, 115
liberty 2, 28
library 158–9
Lilburne, John 159
London 6, 42, 46, 51, 110, 131, 132, 134, 138, 147, 152
The 'Long Parliament' 121, 126–7, 130, 147
Louvain 42
Lucian 11, 16, 17, 25, 29–30, 31, 45, 77, 78, 91
  True History [or *Vera Historia*] 29–30, 91
Lupset, Thomas 21
Lupton, Thomas 4, 11, 41, 45, 53–8, 59, 62, 162
  All for Money 54
  The Christian against the Jesuit 54
  A Persuasion from Papistry 53–4
  The second part and knitting vp of the Boke entitled Too good to be true 55
  Sivqila, Too Good to be True 11, 41, 53–8, 59
Luther, Martin 5, 64, 73, 75, 84
lying/falsehood 22, 47, 91, 132

maps 8, 158
Maton, Robert
  Israels Redemption 148
Mede, Joseph 123, 124, 150
  Clavis Apocalyptica 123

medieval 5, 26, 35, 39, 45, 108–9
Melanchthon, Philip 64–6
memory, forgetting 24, 72
millenarianism 4, 12, 119, 122–3, 126, 127, 129, 144, 147–50, 159, 162–3
Milton, John 1, 146, 153
   Of Education 153
miracles 93, 102, 103–5, 114
monarchy 122, 126, 136
monastery 61, 63–4
monologue 15, 17, 59, 71, 107, 116
Montgomery, John Warwick 73–4
the moon 91, 144
More, Thomas 3, 4, 7, 8, 10–11, 13, 15–40, 41, 43–4, 48–9, 62, 69, 76, 77, 78, 86, 87, 89, 95, 155–6
   A Dialogue of Comfort Against Tribulation 16
   Dialogue Concerning Heresies 16
   Utopia 15–40, and *passim*
      bishop of 24
      bridge in 25
      dialogue of counsel 17, 19–20
      prefatory letters of 21–4, 30
More, Thomas de Eschallers de la 126
   The English Catholicke Christian, or, the Saints Utopia 126
museum 158–9

narrative/narrator 48
nationalism 53
natural Christianity 69
natural philosophy 12, 69, 79, 92, 95–7, 99–101, 103–4, 106–7, 108–13, 116–17, 119
   dissemination of public knowledge 12, 79, 92, 106–7, 109–12
   experimentation in 103, 113–14
   institutionalization of 12, 96–7, 110–11
   political functions of 111–12, 113
   secretive nature of (see secrets)
Nicholls, Thomas 4, 11, 41, 46–53, 54, 55, 58, 59, 62, 162
   A pleasant Dialogue between a Lady called Listra, and a pilgrim. Concerning the gouernement and common weale of the great prouince of Crangalor 11, 41, 46–53, 54, 55, 56, 57, 58, 59
Norbrook, David 120

the novel 119, 141, 143, 145–6

oligarchy 28
One More Blow at Babylon 136
optimism 12, 13, 28, 76, 83–4, 86, 125, 139, 142, 162–3
original sin 40
otium 19
ou-topos 1, 13, 156
Oxford 135–6

pagan/paganism 26, 34, 36, 155
pansophia 126, 152
paradise 50–51, 132, 142, 144
paratext 20–21, 49
parerga 20–21
Paris 42
patronage 11, 42, 50, 54, 55, 56
peace 6, 21, 127, 132, 134, 160–61
pessimism 40, 44
Petty, William 157–9, 161
   The Advice of W.P. to Mr. Samuel Hartlib 157–8
Philosemitism 147–8
philosophy 4, 7, 10–11, 17–18, 20, 23–4, 25–9, 36, 38, 40, 41, 43, 63, 69, 83, 88, 154, 162
picaresque 13, 144
pilgrim/ pilgrimage 47–53
plain speech 22
Plato 11, 16, 17, 25–9, 30, 31, 33, 36, 45, 71, 143
   Republic 25–9, 33, 77, 143
   Symposium 17
Platonism, Platonic dialogue 25–6, 36
Plattes, Gabriel 1, 12, 120, 130–32, 159
   Macaria 1, 12, 120, 129–32, 138–9, 144
Pocock, J.G.A. 144
political utopia 143–5, 159–61
prayer 82, 85–6, 95
pride 31, 35, 36, 86
private property 27, 161
prostitution 94
Protestantism 5, 11, 41–4, 46, 51–4, 59, 64, 66, 79, 102, 128, 130, 132
   consolidation of 11, 41–2, 46, 59
   Protestant brotherhoods 73, 76, 129
public/readership 10, 13, 33, 43–4, 49, 51–2, 58, 72, 76, 89, 141, 154, 159, 161–2

Rabelais, François 61–2, 71
    Gargantua and Pantagruel 61
radical 4, 157, 159
Rawley, William 92, 93 fn. 13, 99–100, 111
reason versus faith 33, 35, 38–9
reception of *Utopia* 42–4
reformation 5, 11, 41–2, 51, 54, 59, 64, 73, 85, 121, 127
    Further Reformation 64, 73, 76, 82, 86, 128, 152
    Protestant Reformation 46, 63, 73
'Reformation fictions' 11, 41–2, 59
Renaissance 1–3, 17–19, 26, 35, 63, 107, 108–9, 130, 162
revelation 35, 69, 93, 98, 99, 102–5
rhetoric 80, 82–3
Robynson, Ralph 42–3, 55
Roggen, Vibeke 43
romance (the genre) 141–2
Rome 1, 34, 54, 65
Rose, Elliot 54, 55
The Royal Society 96, 107, 110–14, 138

Sacks, David Harris 43
salvation 5, 13, 36, 102, 104, 148, 151
satire 10, 11, 13, 23, 29, 30, 40, 41, 43, 51, 59, 61, 62, 75, 77, 78, 88, 142–3, 163
Savonarola, Girolamo 5
scepticism 23, 29
sea, sea travel 10, 38, 77, 82
secrets 108–11
Sedgwick, William 121
serio ludere 78
sermons 37, 51–3, 56, 121, 126–7, 133–5, 159–60
servitude 19–20
sexual activity 57–8, 94
Sherman, William 55
shipwreck 67, 80, 82
Shrank, Cathy 22, 23, 41, 45, 46, 51–2, 58
silver 21
sin 31, 34, 36–7, 40, 51–2, 56, 76, 94
Skinner, Quentin 15, 19
Slack, Paul 44, 51
Smarr, Janet Levarie 54
Smith, Sir Thomas 44–5
social discipline 84–6
social reform 4, 6–7, 10, 13, 40–43, 45, 53, 55–6, 63, 68, 73, 83, 87, 97, 112, 119, 123, 138, 141–4, 146, 155, 157–8, 161

Societas Reformatorum et Correspondency 126, 127
Starkey, Thomas 28–9
    A Dialogue between Pole and Lupset 28–9
Stoughton, John 126
Sturm, Johann 64
Supreme Good/*summum bonum* 36

Tadlowe, George 42
The Teacher of the English School 133
Thompson, Edward 77
time 16–7
transmigration of souls 26
travel literature 8, 30, 91
travel narrative 2, 4, 7–10, 12, 40, 47, 62, 72, 77, 79, 82, 86, 88, 91–3, 117, 119, 139, 144
Tübingen 65, 73, 78

the university 134–7, 138
utopia
    the arrival of 4, 156–61
    as a genre 1–3, 38, 90, 155–6
    as a mode 1–4, 7, 10, 13, 41, 59, 78, 86, 92, 95, 97, 116, 130, 141–2, 144–5, 146, 156–7, 162–3
    comic associations of 10–11, 16, 20–21, 22, 25, 30, 48, 72, 141, 163
    definition of 1–3, 2 fn. 3
    diffusion of 12, 120
    forms of 1–3, 4, 12, 119, 162
    inaccessibility of 24, 58
    journey to 3, 8–9, 38, 61–2, 71–3, 76, 120, 129, 131, 144–5
    proliferations of 1–3, 4, 7, 12, 119–20, 143, 157, 162–3
    rejection of traditional utopian form 10, 12–13, 63, 78, 119–20, 138–9
    unachievable nature of 13, 31, 33, 36, 39, 95–6
utopian moment 7, 162–3
utopian tradition 3, 4, 13, 61, 78, 117, 129, 139, 158–9

Vaihingen 75
Venice 1, 27
Vergerio, Pier Paolo 63
violence 19, 155

vita activa/active life 19–20, 28, 40
da Viterbo, Egidio 5
Vives 63

Wall, Moses 124, 162–3
Wands, John Millar 77
Ward, Seth 135–6
   Vindiciae Academiarum 136
Warner, J. Christopher 18
wealth 27

Webster, John 13, 135–6, 143
   Academiarum Examen 13, 135–6, 143
Wilson, K.J. 9
Wilson, Thomas, *A discourse upon Usurye* 23
Winchelsea 146
Winstanley, Gerrard 1, 159–61
   The Law of Freedom 160, 161
   The New Law of Righteousness 161

Zlatar, Antoinina Bevan 45–6, 51, 53